Natural New York

Natural

Bill and Phyllis Thomas

Holt, Rinehart and Winston • *New York*

New York

Overleaf: *Frederick C. Schmid*

Published by Holt, Rinehart and Winston,
383 Madison Avenue, New York, New York 10017.
Published simultaneously in Canada by Holt, Rinehart and
Winston of Canada, Limited.

Library of Congress Cataloging in Publication Data
Thomas, Bill, 1934–
    Natural New York. / __ and __ . · · First ed. · ·
    Includes index.
    1. Natural areas—New York (State)—Guide-books.
2. Natural areas—New Jersey—Guide-books. 3. Natural
areas—Connecticut—Guide-books. 4. Parks—New York
(State)—Guide-books. 5. Parks—New Jersey—Guide-books.
6. Parks—Connecticut—Guide-books. 7. New York (State)
—Description and travel—1960— —Guide-books.
8. New Jersey—Description and travel—1960— —Guide-
books. 9. Connecticut—Description and travel—1960—
—Guide-books. I. Thomas, Phyllis, 1935–.
II. Title.
QH76.5.N7T48   917.470443   81-13218   AACR2

ISBN Hardbound: 0-03-057554-0
ISBN Paperback: 0-03-057553-2

First Edition
Designer: Jacqueline Schuman
Maps by David Lindroth
Printed in the United States of America
10 9 8 7 6 5 4 3 2 1

ISBN 0-03-057554-0   HARDBOUND

ISBN 0-03-057553-2   PAPERBACK

For Bonnie
Who Blessed Us with Many Happy Memories

Contents

1. Natural Attractions Interstate

2. Natural Attractions in Connecticut

3. Natural Attractions in New Jersey

4. Natural Attractions in New York City

5. Natural Attractions in Long Island

6. Natural Attractions in New York State

Acknowledgments

A list of all the people who so generously shared their time and knowledge with us when we were preparing this book would include hundreds of names. Space does not permit us to thank them individually as they deserve to be thanked, but we are grateful to every one of them. This book would not exist without them.

A Note to the Reader

Public Transportation

Since public transportation is such an important part of getting around in New York City and its environs, we have listed several sources of information to help you in your travels.

New York City Bus Service

New York City buses serve all five boroughs (the Bronx, Brooklyn, Manhattan, Queens, and Staten Island). For information, phone 212-330-1234. A map of Manhattan bus routes appears in the Yellow Pages of the Manhattan phone directory. For free maps of the bus routes in each borough, send a self-addressed stamped envelope along with your request to: MAPS, Box NYBT, New York City Transit Authority, 370 Jay Street, Brooklyn, NY 11201. Be sure to specify the names of the boroughs in which you are interested. Free maps are also available at Grand Central Station or Penn Station, or at the New York Convention and Visitors Bureau in Manhattan (2 Columbus Circle, New York, NY 10019; phone 212-397-8222). Some of the borough maps will list other transit systems within that borough.

Suburban Bus Service

Nassau County bus information may be obtained from the Metropolitan Suburban Bus Authority; phone 516-222-1000.

Suffolk County bus information may be obtained from the Suffolk County Department of Transportation; phone 516-582-6363.

The Short Line Bus System serves Hudson and Bergen Counties in New Jersey, and Orange and Rockland Counties in New York; phone 212-736-4700.

Westchester County bus information may be obtained from the Westchester County Department of Transportation, County Office Building, White Plains, NY 10601; phone 914-682-2020.

New York City Subway Service

Subways operate twenty-four hours a day. They serve Manhattan, the Bronx, Queens, and Brooklyn. For information, phone 212-330-1234. Route maps are posted in every station and in most subway cars. Individual copies may be picked up at most token booths. A map also appears in the Yellow Pages of the phone directory for each borough. To obtain a map through the mail, send a self-addressed stamped envelope to: MAPS,

Box NYBT, New York City Transit Authority, 370 Jay Street, Brooklyn, NY 11201.

Greater New York Railroad Service

Amtrak serves the entire New York City region from both Grand Central Station and Penn Station. Phone 212-736-4545 for information.

The Harlem, Hudson, and New Haven Lines of Conrail provide service from Grand Central Station. The Harlem Line serves the Bronx and towns in central Westchester and Putnam Counties. The Hudson Line serves the Bronx and towns in Westchester and Putnam Counties along the east bank of the Hudson River. The New Haven Line serves towns in lower Westchester along Long Island Sound and in southwestern Connecticut. Phone 212-532-4900 for information.

Conrail's Erie-Lackawanna line provides service in Bergen, Essex, Morris, Passaic, Somerset, and Union Counties in New Jersey, and in Orange and Rockland Counties in New York from Hoboken, New Jersey (take PATH train from Manhattan to Hoboken—see below). Phone 212-736-6000, 212-227-6500, or 201-622-5686 for information.

The Long Island Railroad (LIRR) provides service from Penn Station to Long Island towns. Phone 212-739-4200 for information.

PATH (Port Authority Trans-Hudson) train operates from the 33rd Street station and the World Trade Center in Manhattan to Hoboken and Newark in New Jersey. It connects with other rail and bus services in New Jersey. For recorded information about schedules, phone 212-732-8920 or 201-434-6100. For travel assistance, phone 212-466-7649 or 201-622-6600 (ext. 7649) from 9:00 A.M. to 5:00 P.M. Monday through Friday, or 201-963-2558 at other times.

Staten Island Rapid Transit Operating Authority (SIRTOA) serves Staten Island twenty-four hours a day between St. George and Tottenville. For information, phone 212-447-8601 or 212-447-8602. The Staten Island Ferry carries passengers and cars between Manhattan and St. George on Staten Island (see description under Battery Park). Stops along the SIRT route and ferry information appear on the Staten Island bus map (free if you send a self-addressed stamped envelope along with your request to: MAPS, Box NYBT, New York City Transit Authority, 370 Jay Street, Brooklyn, NY 11201).

Personal Safety

Personal safety is something you should always be concerned about when visiting the natural areas and parks. Of course, some areas—particularly those in New York City—pose greater threats than others. And some areas are safe during the day but not at dusk or after dark. It's difficult to say just when an area will be safe for you to visit and when it will not, for it all depends upon who else is visiting the area at the same time and what his or her intentions might be. So, it's a good rule of thumb to plan your visits with a friend, first of all, for the greatest security is in numbers. Second, do your visiting during the daylight hours and be gone before dark. Third, be aware of the prevailing atmosphere of the place. If you are alert, you can usually sense danger and avoid it by quickly departing. The best deterrent against an assailant is your own common sense.

Introduction

New York is a wonderful town. We've been told that countless times in drama, song, and literature. Actually, it's more amazing than wonderful. For New York has a bit of everything, even pockets of wildness. Not the vast expanses of primeval wilderness we would expect to find in remote parts of Alaska or western Canada, but small, serene oases that offer many of the elements—and even some of the solitude—of a place apart from the pressures of everyday living.

Before there was New York City, there were overwhelming stretches of natural beauty throughout this area. There were great swamps, glacial fields with outcroppings of striated rock and kettle ponds, thousands of acres of marshes, and sprawling meadowlands laced with meandering streams. The Hudson River flowed clear and pure. Many of those elements are still present, even if in declining quality and quantity.

Three natural forces have had greater impact upon the area than any other: the mighty Wisconsin glacier, which slid southward from Hudson Bay 70,000 to 10,000 years ago to form a deep grinding sheath of ice over the area and reshape the land; the Hudson River, with its rich estuary and remarkable geological features; and the Atlantic Ocean, whose awesome hurricanes and storms periodically and continually alter the New York coastline.

Of these three, the Hudson has the greatest natural impact upon the greater New York City area today. Born at Lake Tear of the Clouds on Mount Marcy in the Adirondacks, it flows past Manhattan to mingle with the sea at Lower New York Bay. Once it flowed onward across the Continental Shelf another 120 miles before meeting the Atlantic and, en route, carved a canyon 120 feet deep and sometimes 2 miles wide. That was during the early stages of the Great Ice Age of Pleistocene times, but when the ice melted and raised the ocean's water level, the canyon drowned. Today, it is a major habitat for a multitude of fish and marine life.

Extending now only 315 miles, the Hudson is often considered not as a single river but as a series of interconnecting streams, each continuing where the other ends. Near the headwaters, the Hudson is a fine trout stream, and you can drink the water directly from the stream; in turns, it becomes a bass and pike river, a canal, a septic tank at Albany, and ultimately, at New York City, an estuary and seaport. The lower portion is actually not a river at all, but an arm of the sea fluctuating with the tides. At times, the ebb and flow of salt water and fresh water interact with one another all the way to Poughkeepsie. The river is saltier at the bottom, since the fresh mountain water, being lighter, overrides the salt water.

This fluctuating mix of salt and fresh water in the lower Hudson creates some interesting marine situations, permitting both freshwater fish and ocean species to share the same stream. Harbor seals and even porpoises have been spotted as far upstream as Troy, some 150 miles from the mouth. America's national bird—the bald eagle—once was frequently seen diving into the river just upstream from New York City along the Jersey Palisades, but no more. Occasionally, one is spotted today during the fall migration of waterfowl down the Hudson flyway, following the ducks and geese and preying upon them.

At New York City, the river seems undecided at times about which way to go. It does flow out to sea, but only minimally. A stick pitched into midstream at Manhattan might drift 10 miles downriver and 9 back up during a single twenty-four hour period. This is quite a contrast to the era when the last great glacier was melting. Then the Hudson was the feeder stream from the Great Lakes, which poured an unbelievable volume of water down the valley with tremendous force. Gradually, it carved away the embankments and created the sharp cliffs we see in places today, as well as the great subterranean canyon.

Many southern species of birds and animals have moved into the Hudson Valley during the past two centuries. The Carolina wren, for instance, which normally requires a warm climate, now lives in the cliffs of the Hudson Palisades in New Jersey, which tower 525 feet above the river. The fence lizard, the opossum and raccoon, the Canada warbler, the white-tailed deer, the river otter, mink, and even beaver are still inhabitants of the lower Hudson Valley within 50 miles of Manhattan's skyline.

While man has achieved remarkable engineering and architectural feats in building one of the world's great cities, the natural qualities of the area are what make it bearable, even habitable, for mankind. In the concrete jungles of Manhattan still lives an amazing population of wild creatures—squirrel, cottontail rabbit, raccoon, skunk, rock dove, vole, mole, snake, lizard, salamander, snail, and numerous birds. Great blue herons sometimes wander along the shoreline at Battery Park, just yards from the financial center of the world on Wall Street. During the autumn, rafts of pintails and canvasback ducks swim just off the shipping docks on Manhattan's West Side, while across the river in New Jersey are salt marshes filled with wildlife of all kinds.

Staten Island, one of the five boroughs of New York City, proudly boasts a greenbelt sprawling through the center of the island, preserved against the intrusions of development and the inroads of humanity. And at Pelham Bay Park, also within New York City limits, some 2,000 acres of marsh and woodland and water and estuaries form a veritable urban wilderness, a natural microcosm providing refuge for all kinds of birds, mammals, and marine creatures. On any spring or summer day, you can go canoeing there and, with the use of earplugs to block out the noises of air and street traffic, find yourself surrounded by an environment eons removed from the metropolis. Green herons stoically fish from the spartina marsh, common and snowy egrets feed in the shallows, marsh hawks glide just above the vegetation, owls call from the dark woodlands, muskrat swim to and fro, and raccoons meticulously fish along the water's edge for crustaceans to breakfast upon. Oyster beds are found there, and shrimp breed among the salt marshes before making their way back out to sea.

Udalls Cove, shared by the borough of Queens and Nassau County, is another pristine marsh area; and on the south side of Long Island is that pencil-thin sand barrier, Fire Island, with its extraordinary virgin marine forest. Even in the city itself, an impressive virgin forest grows at the New York Botanical Garden.

Within a 50-mile radius of the city are great stretches of wild sand beach, dunes, vast woodlands, stunted pine barrens, great meadowlands, unpolluted streams ranging through primeval territory. The Mianus River Gorge in Westchester County, with its stately old-growth hemlocks, is as unspoiled as anything one might find at virtually any locale in the nation.

Great trees, many of them predating the founding of this nation, still stand like old soldiers heavily burdened with centuries of memories. And there are islands—river islands and ocean islands and bay islands, many of which are preserved either in total or in part and thereby provide habitat for considerable numbers of wildlife. In New Jersey, osprey nest at Sandy Hook; and the Great Swamp National Wildlife Refuge, less than an hour's drive from Times Square, offers one of the nation's most extensive botanical wetlands. In the 1960s it came close to being another of the metropolitan area's international airports, but an intensive public outcry saved it.

On the Passaic River, within the city limits of Paterson, New Jersey, is one of the most spectacular waterfalls of the entire eastern United States. Here the river drops hundreds of feet through a rocky chasm, and during extremely cold winters, such as those experienced in the mid-1970s, it is transformed into a stupendous ice sculpture.

Of course, these wild and natural places are susceptible to, and certainly greatly affected by, all kinds of intrusions—acid rain, air pollutants, litter. It is difficult to find a breath of fresh air in greater New York City at any time of year. And since plants, trees, and shrubs, as well as wildlife, depend upon the quality of air and water as much as we humans do, all this has to have detrimental effects on the natural environment.

While there are increasing numbers of people with increasing needs for creature comforts and services, all of which will diminish the quality of the environment, there is still some hope for the future. More and more people are becoming aware of the need to preserve green space, to protect wildlife, to clean up rivers and streams, to pick up the litter and leave only footsteps as they visit parks and preserves and nature centers. Greater efforts are being made, too, to set aside more such places within the city and in close proximity to it.

The primary purpose of this book is to provide a convenient guide to some of the so-called natural and wild places within a 50-mile radius of Manhattan. But more than that, we want to call public attention to the existence of such places and to the need for protecting them, preserving them, and adding to their character instead of diminishing it. As Thoreau put it more than a century ago: "In wildness is the preservation of the world. . . ." It is truer today than ever, and unless those who have the power to do so take progressive steps toward that goal, there will be no tomorrow.

Within this volume is a collection of more than 200 locations where natural experiences of varying degrees and kinds can be sampled. There are many other sites within the 50-mile radius of the city that could well be added, but we were limited by the physical size of this book.

It is our sincere hope that you will search out the places described herein, and by so doing will enrich your lives and gain a greater respect for the land and all living things.

Above all, as you visit the places contained in this volume, be concerned. Enjoy them, but leave as little evidence of your passing as possible, so that your children and those of subsequent generations will find life on this planet an enriching experience for all the years to come.

Part 1

Natural Attractions
Interstate

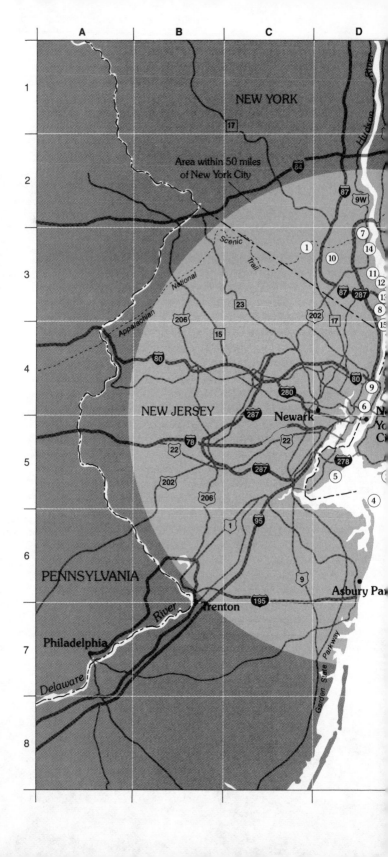

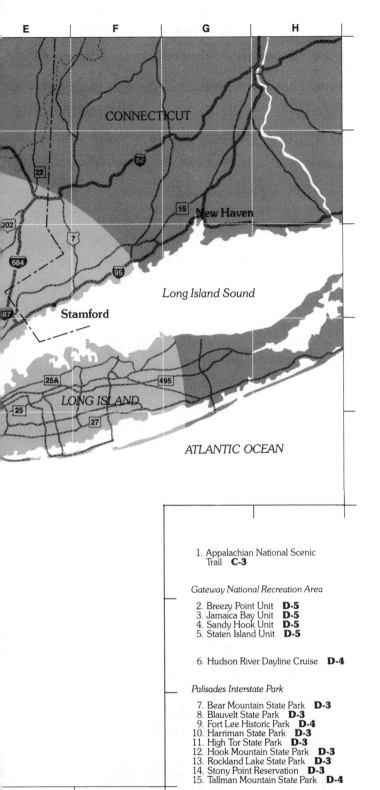

1. Appalachian National Scenic
   Trail **C-3**

Gateway National Recreation Area

2. Breezy Point Unit **D-5**
3. Jamaica Bay Unit **D-5**
4. Sandy Hook Unit **D-5**
5. Staten Island Unit **D-5**

6. Hudson River Dayline Cruise **D-4**

Palisades Interstate Park

7. Bear Mountain State Park **D-3**
8. Blauvelt State Park **D-3**
9. Fort Lee Historic Park **D-4**
10. Harriman State Park **D-3**
11. High Tor State Park **D-3**
12. Hook Mountain State Park **D-3**
13. Rockland Lake State Park **D-3**
14. Stony Point Reservation **D-3**
15. Tallman Mountain State Park **D-4**

Appalachian National Scenic Trail

Some 60 miles of the most famous hiking trail in the east, the Appalachian National Scenic Trail, cross portions of New York and New Jersey within the 50-mile radius covered by this book. The trail, running from Springer Mountain, Georgia, to Mount Katahdin in northern Maine, wends its way up the eastern backbone of America for some 2,000 miles and is considered the most challenging hike east of the Rockies.

The New Jersey segment extends northeast from the I-80 toll bridge across the Delaware River along the crest of the scenic, rugged Kittatinny Mountains, then weaves back and forth across the New York–New Jersey border, seemingly always upgrade. Then comes what is popularly known as Agony Grind, a descent over boulders and down cliffs to I-87.

The trail enters Harriman and Bear Mountain State Parks, and within a few miles, the hiker is on the original section of the Appalachian Trail, a well-traveled, deeply worn path that winds through oak and hickory, mountain laurel and trillium, to the top of Bear Mountain. Far below, the Hudson River flows serenely. Then the trail plunges down the mountainside to Bear Mountain Inn and turns into a sidewalk through the Trailside Zoo.

Nearby, the trail passes the only toll station on its 2,000-mile route—it costs ten cents at this writing for hikers to walk across the Bear Mountain Bridge over the Hudson. This is also the lowest point on the trail, 115.4 feet above sea level. The once-clear water is now a polluted brown, but it's less contaminated than it was before efforts began in earnest several years ago to get it cleaned up.

Off US 9D, at the eastern end of Bear Mountain Bridge, the trail climbs up Anthony's Nose, then jogs off to Lake Alice near Graymoor Monastery. From there, it enters the twilight of the ancient hemlock forest at Fahnestock State Park, near the perimeter of the 50-mile radius prescribed for this book. After leaving Fahnestock, the trail continues north and east into New England.

How to Get There: Portion of trail within radius of book lies between Stokes State Forest (described in Part 3) in New Jersey's Sussex County and Fahnestock State Park (described in Part 6) in New York's Putnam County. Pick up trail in either park.

Open at all times, year-round. Free. Excellent maps and a guide to the Appalachian Trail in New York and New Jersey, which includes campsites along the way, are sold by the New York–New Jersey Trail Conference or the Appalachian Trail Conference.

For Additional Information:

New York-New Jersey Trail
Conference
20 W. 40th St.
New York, NY 10018
212-679-8017

The Appalachian Trail
Conference
P.O. Box 236
Harpers Ferry, WV 25425
304-535-6331

Gateway National Recreation Area

In the 1960s, when serious thoughts were first given to the concept of bringing parks to the people, an urban national park for New York City was one of the first projects considered. Located on the doorstep of the metropolitan area, Gateway National Recreation Area guarantees some open space in a critically crowded area. Consisting of four units called Jamaica Bay, Sandy Hook, Staten Island, and Breezy Point, Gateway now encompasses nearly 27,000 acres, and new areas are still being added. The National Park Service has been administering these parklands since 1974.

A variety of attractions within the recreation area includes marshland, ocean beaches, dunes, wooded uplands, bays, a unique holly forest, a wildlife refuge (which, incredibly, exists and thrives virtually in the shadow of Kennedy International Airport), three old forts, two historic airfields, and the nation's oldest operating lighthouse. Besides its natural and historic features, Gateway provides opportunities for all kinds of outdoor recreation—hiking, bicycling, swimming, boating, canoeing, fishing, jogging, organized sports, and, of course, many nature-oriented activities.

The main headquarters for Gateway are located at Floyd Bennett Airfield in Brooklyn, adjacent to the Jamaica Bay Wildlife Refuge; there are four unit headquarters as well.

Various sections of the national recreation area are discussed separately in the following listings.

For Additional Information:

Superintendent
Gateway National Recreation Area
Floyd Bennett Field, Building 69
Brooklyn, NY 11234
212-252-9150

Breezy Point Unit

Breezy Point is a spit of land lying south of the Rockaway Inlet in Queens. Its major component is Jacob Riis Park, which has perhaps the highest density of public use of any part of the national recreation area. Before it was transferred to the National Park Service, Breezy Point was administered by the City of New York as a public beach, heavily used during warm weather months—and basically, that's what it remains today.

The swimming beach is one of the finest in the metropolitan region, and surf fishing is permitted in designated areas.

There are, however, some small tracts, including windswept sand dunes and a stretch of bay beach where you can explore life in a salt marsh and tidal stream, which have been set aside as natural areas. Hawks streak westward over the park in the fall, and a long rock jetty at the westernmost end of the spit provides a good lookout for seabirds in the winter.

How to Get There: From Exit 11S on Belt Pkwy. (also known as Shore Pkwy.) in Brooklyn, turn south and go across Gil Hodges Bridge to Beach Channel Dr., which lies within park. *By subway:* #3 or #4 to Flatbush Ave., Q35 bus to park. *By bus:* B6, B41, or B44 to Flatbush and Nostrand Aves., Q35 bus to park.

Open daily, year-round, during daylight hours. Some fee areas.

For Additional Information:
Breezy Point Unit
Gateway National Recreation Area
Fort Tilden, NY 11695
212-474-4600

Jamaica Bay Unit

Beneath the vast air traffic sky lanes of Kennedy International Airport is Jamaica Bay Wildlife Refuge, one of the most unexpected natural places in greater New York. Common egrets, great blue herons, rafts of ducks, V-formations of Canada and snow geese . . . all share the skies with jetliners over this expanse of salt marsh, islands, and water. It is one of the prime natural areas of the metropolitan region.

Acclaimed as the largest city-owned wildlife refuge anywhere on earth when it was owned and administered by New York City, this 6,000-acre sanctuary is a major haven for migratory birds on the Atlantic and Hudson River flyways. Many varieties of waterfowl, land birds, and shorebirds find the conditions of this habitat suitable for nesting. Others merely stop in for periods of rest, and some winter in the area.

Among the birds using the area are Canada and snow geese, blue geese, coot, gallinule, ruddy duck, grebe, black duck, green- and blue-winged teal, shoveler, gadwall, redhead, and baldpate. Most of these nest here, too. A heron roost is occupied by black-crowned, yellow-crowned, great and little blue, and green heron, as well as an occasional Louisiana heron. Snowy and common egrets are also found here in considerable numbers, along with the glossy ibis. Brant come in increasing numbers. A total of 257 species of birds have been sighted, including the osprey and bald eagle, although both are quite rare. Clapper rail and cottontail rabbits also live here.

Among the plants of Jamaica Bay, many of which make this a more attractive place for wildlife, are autumn olive, Japanese black pine (the predominant evergreen of the refuge), red cedar, rugosa rose, red and black chokeberry, bayberry, and holly trees. Two types of grasses are predominant: tall marsh grass (or phragmites) and beach grass. Many species of trees and grass have been labeled for visitors.

Two principal parts of the sanctuary, both on Broad Channel Island, are West Pond, a 20-acre pond with some landscaped plantings, and 100-acre East Pond, where the vegetation is all natural. Best times of year to visit are during the spring nesting seasons and the fall migration, when bird life is most abundant.

Hiking is limited, but there are some nature walks. A 2-mile loop trail, with a few secondary trails leading off of it, encircles West Pond. Several lesser trails provide limited access to East Pond and to the landscaped open spaces along the east side of the boulevard.

Picnicking boaters and fishermen use some of the larger islands, including Canarsie Pol, Ruffle Bar, and Little Egg Marsh. A marina is located at Dead Horse Bay. Fishing is popular at the south end of North Channel Bridge. The remainder of the wildlife refuge is closed, except by permit, for special nature study activities.

Jamaica Bay Wildlife Refuge straddles the Queens-Brooklyn boundary and consists of bay islands and marshes. Several easily accessible recreation areas, also part of the Jamaica Bay unit, lie along the western edge of the bay. Directly west of Jamaica Bay is a large, city-owned tract known as Marine Park; it offers more waterside recreation opportunities for human visitors—picnic spots, game fields, tennis courts, rental rowboats, a golf course—and additional marshlands for the birds. Jogging is popular along the flat, scenic trails.

How to Get There: There are three entrances off Belt Pkwy. (also known as Shore Pkwy.) in Brooklyn and Queens. Flatbush Ave. south from Exit 11 leads to Floyd Bennett Field and unit headquarters. The Canarsie Pier area is immediately south of Exit 13. Jamaica Bay Wildlife Refuge is south from Exit 17 on Cross Bay Blvd.; take North Channel Bridge to Broad Channel Island and proceed to Visitor's Center on right in island's midsection. *By subway:* #2 to New Lots Ave., Q21A bus to wildlife refuge; A or E to Broad Channel, walk to refuge; #3 or #4 to Flatbush Ave., Q35 bus to Floyd Bennett Field entrance; LL to Rockaway Pkwy., B42 bus to Canarsie Pier entrance. Open daily, year-round, during daylight hours. Some fee areas.

For Additional Information:

Jamaica Bay Unit
Gateway National Recreation Area
Floyd Bennett Field
Brooklyn, NY 11234
212-252-9286

Sandy Hook Unit

In New Jersey is a great hook of sand that juts into the entranceway to New York Harbor. It's called, appropriately enough, Sandy Hook, and although it is now connected to the mainland, in recent geological history (since 1778) it was twice an island, severed from the mainland by ocean storm currents.

Along the inner curve, protected from the open sea by dunes, is the largest stand of holly forest on the Atlantic coast. A number of trees, reaching upward more than 50 feet, are estimated to be more than 300 years old. Visitors are permitted into the forest only on naturalist-guided walks, which are scheduled regularly during the summer.

Several distinctly different ecological communities exist on the bay side of Sandy Hook, including dunes, salt marsh, mud flats, upland thickets, freshwater ponds, and beaches. In early May there are clouds of white beach plum flowers, and by June, the roselike yellow blossoms of the prickly pear cactus can be seen. Hosts of water birds, such as plovers, gulls, rails, several species of herons, common and snowy egrets, and skimmers, use the bay area. Ospreys nest here, and occasionally bald eagles are seen passing through as they migrate to the south. Numerous hawks come this way during the fall migrations, too, as do extensive rafts of ducks and Canada and snow geese.

Mammals include the cottontail rabbit, opossum, raccoon, and squirrel. Muskrat are found in marsh areas, and fox in the upland thickets.

Among the man-made features on Sandy Hook is the U.S. Coast Guard lighthouse, off limits to the public, but close enough to the beach for photographers and artists to include in their settings. Constructed in 1762, it towers to a height of 103 feet and is still in use. It is the oldest lighthouse in continuous service in the entire western hemisphere.

Sandy Hook is also famed in legend. One legend contends that a huge pine tree, known as Captain Kidd's tree, marks the spot where the famous pirate buried a sizable treasure. Neither tree nor treasure has ever been discovered, but if it were, it would belong to the National Park Service, which now owns the land.

The beaches and dunes of Sandy Hook are excellent for hiking and watching seabirds and other wildlife along the marshes, inlets, and coves.

If you enjoy ocean swimming, there are two beaches along the Atlantic shoreline. They're crowded on summer weekends, less so other times.

Canoeing can be rewarding on the bay side of Sandy Hook, particularly early in the morning and on weekdays. Skeleton Hill and South Islands offer interesting habitats you can see by paddling close to their shorelines. You must bring your own canoe, however.

Several shoreline fishing areas exist along the thin neck that leads to the main portion of Sandy Hook, or you may want to bring a small boat for fishing in the back bay area.

How to Get There: At Highlands Beach in New Jersey's Monmouth County, look for signs leading you north into park. *By rail:* NY and Long Branch RR to Red Bank; boro bus 4 to Highlands. *By bus:* NY–Keansburg–Long Branch Bus Co. from Port Authority Terminal in Manhattan to Highlands.

Open daily, year-round, during daylight hours. Some fee areas.

For Additional Information:
Sandy Hook Unit
Gateway National Recreation Area
P.O. Box 437
Highlands, NJ 07732
201-872-0115

Staten Island Unit

The Staten Island unit of Gateway contains three public-access areas at present—Great Kills Park; Miller Field, a site of historical and recreational interest; and Fort Wadsworth, a former military facility recently acquired by the National Park Service, for which plans are still being formulated. All three border the waterfront along Staten Island's eastern shore. Just offshore, in Lower New York Bay, are tiny Hoffman and Swinburne Islands, both a part of this Gateway unit but not accessible to the public.

Great Kills Park, which encompasses the major portion of the Staten Island unit, is some 1,200 acres of woodland, dunes, marsh, and beach. At one point, a peat bog reaches into the bay. Fishing for flounder, fluke, striped bass, and bluefish is a year-round activity in Raritan Bay. From the bulkhead inlet adjacent to the marina, crabbing is a popular pastime during hot weather months. There is a small but clean sandy beach for swimming in the bay, and hiking trails and nature trails run for several miles.

Shorebirds and migrating birds abound here; the best bird-watching is from late September to early December. Rabbit, squirrel, fox, raccoon, and opossum share the park with pheasant, muskrat, and turtle.

Environmental education is a major function of this park, and many guided nature walks are scheduled regularly. Part of the park is being allowed to return to a natural state and will be preserved as a habitat for plants and wildlife. One of the most popular offerings is the butterfly walk, conducted when the monarch butterflies stop by on their migration to and from Mexico, usually in October and April.

How to Get There: Park lies east of Hylan Blvd. on eastern shore of Staten Island. Emmet Ave. leads east off Hylan into park. *By rail*: SIRT to R111 bus at Oakwood Heights Station; R111 bus to Great Kills. *By bus*: Domenico bus to Great Kills from Port Authority terminal in Manhattan.

Open daily, year-round, during daylight hours. Some fee areas.

For Additional Information:
Staten Island Unit
Gateway National Recreation Area
P.O. Box 37
Staten Island, NY 10306
212-351-8700

Hudson River Dayline Cruise

A refreshing way to see the natural sights of the Hudson River Valley is from the Hudson River Dayliner, which plies the river between Manhattan and Poughkeepsie. On its 150-mile round trip, the boat passes many unusual and interesting points, including historical sites whose significance reaches back in time to the very beginning of our nation's history.

The boat ride gives you an opportunity to spot marshes from the river side, see great wading birds feeding in the shallows, marvel at the beauty of the Palisades where a wall of dark red rock rises some 540 feet above the river mile after mile along its western shoreline.

A cafeteria, bar, and restaurant are located on board, and there are comfortable seats for viewing the scenery.

How to Get There: Departs from Pier 81 at the foot of W. 41st St. in Manhattan. *By bus*: Crosstown M16, M27, M106.

Leaves 10:00 A.M. each sailing day between late May and mid-September. Schedule varies; check for exact days. Entire trip takes nine hours and returns the same day. Cheaper on weekdays. If you prefer not to travel the full distance, you may buy one-way or round-trip tickets to Bear Mountain State Park or West Point Military Academy, where the dayliner stops en route.

For Additional Information:
Hudson River Day Line
Day Line Pier 81
Foot of W. 41st St.
New York, NY 10036
212-279-5151

Palisades Interstate Park

Along the west bank of the Hudson River lies a remarkable fault escarpment known as the Palisades, one of the geological miracles of the greater New York City area. The igneous-rock cliffs, which parallel the river for some 45 miles, actually rise out of the ground at Staten Island, but are most prominent along the area just north of the George Washington Bridge in New Jersey. They finally swing inland after a final curtsy at High Tor near Haverstraw, New York.

Native Americans called them *we-awken*, meaning "rocks that look like trees," as indeed the columnar formations do. Towering at some points as much as 540 feet above the river, the Palisades are a geologist's dream. At the foot of the traprock are horizontal layers of red sandstone into which molten material was intruded as a "sill" eons ago. The zones of baked rock where the heat of the intrusion changed the sandstone can readily be seen to this day.

There also are the scars left by mining operations around 1860 when it appeared the Palisades would be converted to concrete for Manhattan skyscrapers. The sound of dynamite blasts along the Hudson was once as commonplace as the sound of the passing subway in downtown Manhattan is today. By the late 1800s, several prominent citizens of New York, including then-governor Theodore Roosevelt, began lobbying against the possible demise of the Palisades. In the spring of 1900, New York and New Jersey passed bills creating the Palisades Interstate Park. Today, it encompasses some twenty parks and historic sites, sprawled over 75,000 acres in both states. Several of those within the 50-mile radius prescribed for this book—Bear Mountain, Harriman, High Tor, Tallman Mountain, Rockland Lake, Blauvelt, Hook Mountain, Fort Lee, and Stony Point—are discussed individually at the end of this section.

Stretching for roughly 40 miles along the Hudson's west bank, the Palisades Interstate Park now includes a scenic parkway that laces together many of the park units. All along this drive, which is open to passenger cars only, there are picnic areas and striking overlooks.

A 12-mile stretch of the Palisades, with picnic areas, motorboat basins, hiking trails, and sweeping views, forms a long, narrow greenbelt adjacent to the Hudson River in New Jersey. The remainder lies in Rockland and Orange Counties in New York and offers an even greater variety of scenic beauty and recreation opportunities. Bear Mountain and Harriman State Parks are the only contiguous units in the New York section of Palisades Park; some parks edge the shoreline of the Hudson, while others are located inland.

Two major hiking trails, both designated National Recreation Trails by the U.S. Department of the Interior, pass through Palisades Interstate Park. In New Jersey, the Shore Trail runs along the bank of the Hudson River from the southern end of the parkland strip to the New Jersey–New York state line, a

The Palisades along the west bank of the Hudson River

total of 11 miles. The Long Path follows the top of the Palisades cliff 11¼ miles from the George Washington Bridge to the state line, then continues another 16 miles through Rockland County into Harriman State Park. Part of the Appalachian National Scenic Trail passes through Harriman and Bear Mountain, and numerous other trails are contained within the separate parks.

Bear Mountain State Park

Rising dramatically above the west bank of the Hudson, just south of Bear Mountain Bridge, is Bear Mountain State Park, one of the most beautiful of all parks in the greater New York City area. Its 5,066 acres encompass a mountain environment of forest, lakes, rushing streams, and boulder-strewn glacial terrain. For many years, it has been a popular place of escape for New Yorkers.

Just 45 miles away from Manhattan, the park features Bear Mountain Inn, which serves as the area's information center; Hessian Lake, where one can fish, boat, or canoe; nature trails; a huge swimming pool; and areas for roller skating, skiing, ski jumping, and ice skating. There are also picnic areas, a scenic drive with overlooks above the Hudson, and a variety of hilly trails to hike.

New York State Department of Environmental Conservation Photo by J. Goerg

One of the region's most fascinating trailside museums and nature centers, visited by more than 600,000 persons each year, is also located in the park. Several nature trails, each devoted to a specific aspect of natural resources in the area, lie within the center's complex. More than sixty different species of trees and shrubs grow here, as well as numerous wildflowers, mosses, and ferns. Exhibits in the museum buildings complement what has been seen on the trails. Local animals are displayed in several enclosures.

A wide variety of birds and wildlife are found in the wild here, including black bear, white-tailed deer, bobcat, otter, mink, opossum, rabbit, squirrel, woodchuck, and porcupine. More than 100 species of birds have been sighted, and during the fall, rafts of wild ducks, migrating down the Hudson flyway, alight on Hessian Lake. Sometimes they are joined by Canada geese.

Bear Mountain is nearly as popular in winter as in summer—and winter is also a good time to spot wildlife. The system of trails is kept open for cross-country skiing and snowshoeing, and there are slopes for sledding and downhill skiing. Ice skating is permitted on the lake.

In the spring, dogwood trees blossom and mushrooms sprout, while early October brings splashes of exquisite fall

A bird's-eye view of Bear Mountain Bridge

color among the many oaks, maples, and tulip trees.

In the Hudson River opposite the entrance to Bear Mountain is Iona Island, a recent acquisition of the Palisades Park system. The island and the brackish marshes between it and the mainland will be maintained as a wildlife sanctuary.

How to Get There: Exit 15 on Palisades Interstate Pkwy. is within Park; many signs to follow. *By bus*: Mohawk Bus Line runs frequent daily buses from Port Authority Bus Terminal in Manhattan to Bear Mountain. Phone 212-563-3488 for schedule. *By boat*: Hudson River Dayline Cruise (described elsewhere) stops at park between late May and mid-September.

Open daily, year-round, during daylight hours. A nominal parking fee is charged, except on off-season weekdays.

Blauvelt State Park

Blauvelt State Park is worth a visit at all seasons of the year. It includes 590 acres of wooded ridges and hollows, as well as an old parade ground with fine brushlands and neglected pine

plantations where northern finches gather during winter. Once a Balanced Rock attracted visitors, but vandals destroyed it in 1966.

Currently undeveloped, the park has some excellent trails for hiking, and mixed woodlands where animals roam. Raccoon, white-tailed deer, rabbit, opossum, skunk, and woodchuck are found here, and more than 150 species of birds have been sighted.

How to Get There: From Exit 5 on Palisades Interstate Pkwy., go north on NY 303 to park on right side of highway.

Open daily, year-round, during daylight hours. Free.

Fort Lee Historic Park

Acclaimed as one of the most pleasant green spaces in the metropolitan area is tiny Fort Lee Historic Park, stretching along the Hudson River just south of the George Washington Bridge. It features striking rock formations along the Palisades, a lush mixed hardwood forest and marvelous views of the Palisades, the Hudson River, and, on clear days, Manhattan.

The fort played an important role in the 1776 Revolutionary War campaign for the control of New York City and the Hudson River.

More than 100 species of birds have been sighted here. During autumn migrations, waterfowl use the Hudson backwaters immediately adjacent to the park.

How to Get There: In Fort Lee, go east on Main St. to Hudson Terrace; turn left. Park entrance road is on right.

Open daily, year-round, 9:30 A.M.–5:00 P.M. Nominal parking fee daily, Memorial Day through Labor Day, and all weekends. Groups by advance reservation only.

Harriman State Park

A vast mountainous tract of forestland just southwest of Bear Mountain, Harriman State Park contains some 46,500 acres of wild territory dotted with spring-fed lakes, streams, rhododendron bogs, and huge glacial boulders. The second largest park in New York State, it was largely the gift of Edward H. Harriman, the developer of railroads, and his wife.

In May each year, it's worth a trip to Harriman just to see the splash of dogwood in bloom across the land. You'll also want to return to view the fall foliage. A network of trails laces the entire area and links up with trails in adjacent Bear Mountain State Park, and the best cross-country skiing in the New York area is in Harriman.

Several lakes adorn the landscape, with swimming permitted at three of them. Bird-watching is a major activity, too. Among the species to be seen here are the pileated woodpecker, broad-winged hawk, common or yellow-shafted flicker, house wren, Canada warbler, black-throated blue warbler, rose-breasted grosbeak, and tufted titmouse. Ninety-six species nest here, and a great number of owls are in residence year-round. During autumn, ducks gather on the lakes. Porcupine, black bear, squirrel, rabbit, white-tailed deer, bobcat, skunk, raccoon, and opossum dwell in the woodlands, sharing the park with otter, mink, and woodchuck.

Beaver Pond Campground has sites for tents and trailers up to 30 feet in length. No hookups are available. A nominal fee is charged, and reservations are accepted. It's open mid-May through mid-October. The Sebago Family Campsite cabins are available at very reasonable fees from April 15 through October 15. Each will accommodate four to six people; reservations are required.

How to Get There: From Exit 13 on Palisades Interstate Pkwy., go west on NY 210 (Gate Hill Rd.) into park.

Park open daily, year-round, during daylight hours. Free; several fee areas.

High Tor State Park

One of the most eye-catching landmarks on the west bank of the Hudson is High Tor, rising upward some 830 feet behind the village of Haverstraw in Rockland County. It is the highest headland on the Palisades; a mile west is Little Tor, with an elevation of 710 feet.

Most of the 492-acre park has been left in its natural state—a vast woodland sanctuary for birds and mammals, where only hiking trails permit man to enter. There is a swimming pool on the south side of Little Tor.

How to Get There: From Exit 12 on Palisades Interstate Pkwy., take US 202 east to NY 45 at Mt. Ivy. Turn right. Continue to South Mountain Rd. and turn left; proceed to Little Tor Rd. and turn left again. Park is on right.

Open daily, late June to early September, during daylight hours. Nominal parking fee.

Hook Mountain State Park

Hook Mountain, containing some 661 acres, climbs to an apex of 720 feet. From its summit, you have a 360-degree view of the surrounding area; at its base, the Hudson River flows serenely by. Extending some 6 miles along the river, the park contains woodland and marsh areas, and also offers many high overlooks. It is one of the prime places in the New York City region from which to watch the annual hawk migration. Ducks and geese, too, migrate down the Hudson flyway each fall, and occasionally eagles are spotted.

Largely undeveloped, the park offers some of the ruggedest hiking trails and most scenic views in the Palisades Park system.

How to Get There: From Exit 11 on NY Thruway (I-87), go north on US 9W past Rockland Lake State Park to Hook Mountain on right side of highway.

Open daily, year-round, during daylight hours. Free.

Rockland Lake State Park

At the center of this 1,078-acre park is spring-fed Rockland Lake, a haven for flocks of ducks, swans, and geese in the summer, and for ice skaters in the winter. It's surrounded by upland meadows and woodlands bordering the Hudson River that offer fine habitat for a variety of birds and mammals, but it is also extensively developed, with pools, golf courses, and parking lots.

In the northwest corner of the park is a nature center. Its trails include a boardwalk into a swampy area where plants of the region are identified.

How to Get There: From Exit 11 on NY Thruway (I-87), go north on US 9W to park on right side of highway.

Open daily, year-round, during daylight hours. Nominal parking fee daily, late June through early September, and on weekends and holidays, May through mid-October.

Stony Point Reservation

About 3 miles north of the village of Haverstraw is Stony Point Reservation, a rugged promontory jutting some 2,000 feet into the Hudson River. At its widest point, it is 1,500 feet across. The park offers 80 acres of outstanding scenic beauty in a wonderfully isolated spot.

Stony Point is mostly upland grassland and forest, criss-crossed by shady paths that make for pleasant walking. In spring, a canopy of dogwood blossoms blankets the park. A picturesque lighthouse at the tip of the park stands about 150 feet above the river, affording the visitor beautiful views both upstream and downstream.

Of historical interest, Stony Point was the site of several Revolutionary War encounters.

How to Get There: From Exit 12 on Palisades Interstate Pkwy., go east and then north on US 202. Look for park entrance road on right side of highway.

Open daily, 9:00 A.M.–5:00 P.M., mid-April through October. Free.

Tallman Mountain State Park

Just north of the New York–New Jersey line is Tallman Mountain State Park. Located along the west bank of the Hudson, Tallman Mountain contains some 680 acres of lush woodland, marsh, and glacial till.

Tallman is primarily a broad, wooded plateau with two higher peaks from which there's a good view of the Hudson, particularly when the trees shed their leaves.

Besides the upland forest, the park includes cliffs, rock outcroppings, striated glacial boulders, and a salt marsh vibrant with life. Shellfish thrive in the tidal creeks, and bird life is profuse. It is the only place known in New York State where the seaside sparrow nests away from the coast, and in the winter, it's a lookout point for grebes, waterfowl, gulls, and possibly bald eagles. Periodically, naturalist-guided tours are offered into the marsh areas, which are particularly worth seeing during the spring and fall months as birds migrate through the area.

A swimming pool is located at the foot of the mountain overlooking the marsh.

How to Get There: From Exit 4 on Palisades Interstate Pkwy., go north on US 9W to park on right side of road.

Open daily, year-round, during daylight hours. Nominal parking fee daily, late June through Labor Day.

For Additional Information

Palisades Interstate Park
Commission
Bear Mountain State Park
Bear Mountain, NY 10911
914-786-2701

Palisades Interstate Park
Commission
New Jersey Office
Box 155
Alpine, NJ 07620
201-768-1360

Part 2

Natural Attractions in
Connecticut

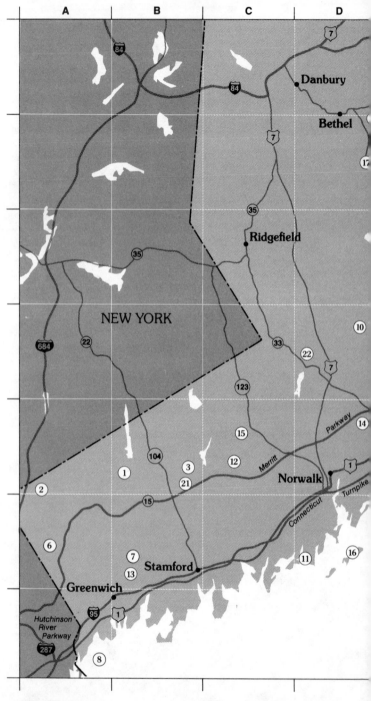

CONNECTICUT

1. Altschul Preserve **B-5**
2. Audubon Center in Greenwich and Fairchild Wildflower Garden **A-5**
3. Bartlett Arboretum **B-5**
4. Beardsley Park Zoo **G-4**

5. Birdcraft Sanctuary and Museum **F-5**
6. Byram River Gorge **A-6**
7. Caldwell Wildlife Sanctuary **B-6**
8. Calf Island **A-7**
9. Connecticut Audubon Center **E-4**
10. Devil's Den Preserve **D-4**
11. Farm Creek Marsh **D-6**

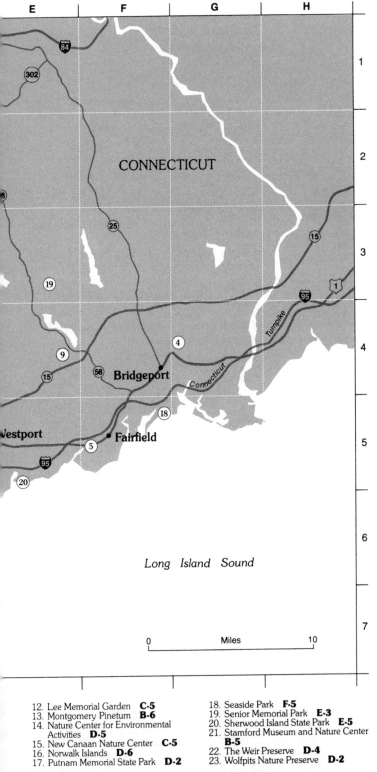

Altschul Preserve

In Stamford, some 160 acres owned by The Nature Conservancy make up the Altschul Preserve. It consists of gently rolling hills, forests, and open meadows, and some interesting geological formations. The east branch of the Mianus River flows through the preserve into an artificial pond with a dam just off the property. In the middle of the 3-acre pond is an island where waterfowl often stop to rest and occasionally nest. The land surrounding the pond is rugged with some large rock outcrops.

The preserve's forest is largely made up of chestnut oaks and huckleberry, with red maple and buttonbush swamps in some of the lowlands. White-tailed deer, raccoon, fox, opossum, cottontail rabbit, and squirrel are among the residents.

Hiking

Hiking and nature study are the principal activities offered by the preserve. A trail system leads through the tract and, if you observe carefully what you see along the way, takes several hours to do adequately.

How to Get There: From Exit 31 on Merritt Pkwy. (CT 15), take North St. north to N. Stanwich Rd., and turn right; at Taconic Rd. turn left and go to Farms Rd.; turn right. Head to Riverbank Rd. and turn right again. At Riverbank Dr. turn left and continue to preserve.

Open daily, year-round, during daylight hours. Check with The Nature Conservancy or the Altschul Preserve Committee before entering preserve. Free.

For Additional Information:

Mrs. Edward Hughes
Altschul Preserve Committee
Carrington Drive
Greenwich, CT 06830
203-622-1700 or 203-629-2916

The Nature Conservancy
Connecticut Chapter
Science Tower
P.O. Box MMM
Wesleyan Station
Middletown, CT 06457
203-344-0716

Audubon Center in Greenwich and Fairchild Wildflower Garden

In Greenwich is a quiet nature sanctuary covering nearly 500 acres. Divided into two major sections, the Audubon Center in Greenwich and the Fairchild Wildflower Garden, as well as several lesser tracts, it's maintained and operated by the National Audubon Society.

The center consists of 288 acres of streams, ponds, marsh, and woodlands, while the 135-acre Fairchild Garden is a combination of woods and meadows enhanced by a small lily pond. More than 800 species of plants, 35 species of animals, and 150 species of birds have been documented at the two sections. Canada geese, green heron, and several varieties of woodpeckers nest here, and the eastern bluebird has been sighted in recent years. A vernal pond at the center has remained virtually untouched since the last ice age, and Mead Lake has several bird blinds.

Fairchild Garden was a gift in 1945 from Benjamin T. Fairchild, who began the garden in the early 1900s. At that time, he owned a large pharmaceutical company and was particularly interested in the many varieties of medicinal plants. Most of them still grow here today, along with the wild ferns and flowering plants native to Connecticut that Fairchild also introduced into his garden. Rare pink and yellow lady's slippers and red and white trilliums grow along woodland trails.

The sanctuary offers a variety of educational programs, including the annual Audubon Ecology Workshop for adults 18 and older. Week-long workshops are scheduled continually from late June through late August.

Although the center and garden are not contiguous, they are within two blocks of each other.

Hiking

Eight miles of trails lace the grounds of the center, with some boardwalks over wet or marsh areas. Most trails are short, but may be combined for longer walks. Many short walks lead through the garden. Trail guides, as well as maps, plant and bird lists, and a history of the area, are available from the Environmental Book and Gift Shop at the center's Interpretive Building.

How to Get There: From Exit 28 on Merritt Pkwy. (CT 15), go north on Round Hill Rd. to John St. and turn left. Center is on northeast corner of John St. and Riversville Rd. To reach garden from center, go south one block on Riversville Rd. to N. Porchuck Rd. and turn left. Garden is about half a block down on right side of road. Free parking both areas.

Both center and garden are open 9:00 A.M.–5:00 P.M., Tuesday through Saturday, year-round; closed Sundays, Mondays, New Year's, July 4, Thanksgiving, and December 25. Nominal charge for non-National Audubon Society members. A special exhibit area in the center's Interpretive Building is open 2:00–5:00 P.M., Tuesday through Friday; and 9:00 A.M.–5:00 P.M. on Saturday.

For Additional Information:

Director
Audubon Center in Greenwich
613 Riversville Rd.
Greenwich, CT 06830
203-869-5272

National Audubon Society
Environmental Information &
Education Division
950 Third Ave.
New York, NY 10022
212-832-3200

Bartlett Arboretum

It was here, at the Bartlett Tree Research Laboratory that once occupied these grounds, that the Bartlett pear was developed. Now the area has become strictly an arboretum, with more than 2,000 specimens of exotic and native plants, shrubs, and trees on 63 acres of gently rolling hill country. One particularly interesting collection includes trees and shrubs grown for their purple or golden leaves.

Maintained by the College of Agriculture and Natural Resources of the University of Connecticut in Storrs, the arboretum contains about 10 acres of cultivated grounds that include demonstration gardens helpful to the public in planning home landscaping. The rest of the property is natural woodland; native oak, maple, and hickory are interspersed with some scattered ash, birch, beech, and yellow poplar.

Nature Trails

Nature trails lead through the woodlands, around a swamp, and into open fields. They are all very easily traveled. One trail leads to the Stamford Museum and Nature Center (described elsewhere), about one-quarter mile away.

How to Get There: Located in Stamford. From Exit 35 on Merritt Pkwy. (CT 15), take CT 137 (High Ridge Rd.) north about 1½ miles to Brookdale Rd. and turn left. Entrance is at 151 Brookdale Rd. on right side of road.

Grounds open daily, 8:30 A.M.–sunset, year-round. Free. Headquarters building open Monday–Friday, 8:30 A.M.–4:30 P.M. Group tours by advance reservation.

For Additional Information:

Bartlett Arboretum
University of Connecticut
151 Brookdale Rd.
Stamford, CT 06903
203-322-6971

Beardsley Park Zoo

Situated on nearly 30 acres within a 285-acre municipal park, Beardsley Park Zoo is the largest in the state. Tigers, mountain lions, black bears, and wolves are among the more than 600 animals housed here. Children are allowed to feed the animals in the zoo's farmyard. Two trained elephants perform at 2:00 P.M. every day during the spring and summer. Volunteers are happy to give guided tours, even to individual families, to visitors who make prior arrangements.

The woodlands here are manicured, but there are many acres of them to roam. Two lovely ponds and the Pequonnock

River, which meanders through the park, add to the picturesque setting. Shaded picnic tables dot the park.

During blooming season, the park becomes particularly attractive. There are several well-tended gardens, including a Shakespeare garden that contains the plants mentioned in his plays, and a greenhouse.

How to Get There: Park is located at corner of E. Main St. and Noble Ave., Bridgeport. From I-95, take Exit 28 onto E. Main St. (just after crossing mouth of Pequonnock River) and follow Main St. north into park.

Park open daily, 9:00 A.M.–dusk, year-round; free. Zoo open daily, 9:00 A.M.–5:00 P.M., June through Labor Day; 9:00 A.M.–4:00 P.M., rest of year; closed major holidays. Nominal entrance fee; children under 5, senior citizens, and handicapped admitted free.

For Additional Information:

Director
Beardsley Zoological Gardens
Noble Ave.
Bridgeport, CT 06604
203-576-8082

Superintendent of Parks
Dept. of Parks & Recreation
Administration Bldg.
263 Golden Hill
Bridgeport, CT 06604
203-576-7233

Birdcraft Sanctuary and Museum

Established in 1914 as the first songbird refuge in New England, this 7-acre sanctuary also provides a nesting ground for Canada geese and several species of duck.

Famous for its spring passerine migration, Birdcraft Sanctuary is a permanent bird-banding station. Several public workshops each year demonstrate the methods used in capturing, measuring, recording, and banding wild birds. The sanctuary also maintains a "rare-bird alert" as a public service.

More than 4,000 wildlife specimens, including all species of birds native to Connecticut, are exhibited in the small museum here. Only birds and animals that died from natural causes are mounted. In addition, the world's largest collection of Charles "Shang" Wheeler decoys are on display; Wheeler is considered the best in his field.

The sanctuary and museum are operated by the Connecticut Audubon Society.

Hiking
A self-guided trail encircles the pond near the center of the grounds.

How to Get There: Located at 314 Unquowa Rd., Fairfield. From Exit 19 on I-95, go east on US 1 (Boston Post Rd.) for about one mile to Unquowa Rd. and turn left. Cross railroad tracks and proceed to sanctuary entrance on right side of street. Parking on street.

Open weekends only, year-round; 10:00 A.M.–5:00 P.M. Saturday, noon–5:00 P.M. Sunday; closed Easter, Thanksgiving, Christmas. Free.

For Additional Information:

Birdcraft Museum
314 Unquowa Rd.
Fairfield, CT 06430
203-259-0416

Connecticut Audubon Society
2325 Burr St.
Fairfield, CT 06430
203-259-6305

Byram River Gorge

Lying along both banks of the Byram River, a small coastal stream that originates in Byram Lake in New York, the Byram River Gorge preserve in Greenwich contains some 133 acres in five sections.

Most of the preserve lies in a steep ravine dominated by hemlock and interspersed with such hardwoods as birch, beech, oak, and maple. A large tract of red maple swamp and three dams on the Byram River itself provide diverse habitats for wildlife and plant life. Rock outcrops, ledges, and exposed bedrock in the river make this an area of significant geological interest.

White-tailed deer, red and gray fox, opossum, and raccoon live here, as well as numerous birds.

Hiking

A 3-mile trail along the west bank of the Byram River traverses some of the most scenic areas in Greenwich. It runs in a north-south direction between Sherwood Avenue and Cliffdale Road. Pay careful attention to trail markers.

How to Get There: From Exit 27 on Merritt Pkwy. (CT 15), take King St. north. Access to preserve is from two streets that run east off King St.: Sherwood Ave., about 1⅓ miles north of Merritt Pkwy., and Cliffdale Rd., about 2¼ miles north of Merritt Pkwy. Park on Sherwood Ave. or at Bruce Memorial Golf Course at corner of King St. and Cliffdale Rd. Preserve is more easily accessible on west bank of river.

Open daily, year-round, during daylight hours. Free. Obtain permission before entering preserve. Groups should make advance reservations. The Nature Conservancy or the Byram River Gorge Committee will supply more specific directions when contacted.

For Additional Information:

Mrs. Gerrish Milliken
Byram River Gorge Committee
39 Pierson Dr.
Greenwich, CT 06830
203-869-7969

The Nature Conservancy
Connecticut Chapter
Science Tower
P.O. Box MMM
Wesleyan Station
Middletown, CT 06457
203-344-0716

Caldwell Wildlife Sanctuary

Just fifteen minutes from downtown Greenwich is a beautiful 22-acre woodland known as the Mildred Bedard Caldwell Wildlife Sanctuary. It is a peaceful year-round retreat, penetrated only by foot trails and boardwalks leading through a dense climax forest of beech, maple, and oak. From early spring through fall, the preserve is vibrant with the color of wildflowers—jack-in-the-pulpit, yarrow, white woodland aster, goldenrod. Masses of jewelweed appear in the summer, and the crimson heads of skunk cabbage poke through wet soil in late winter. Arrowhead, lady fern, and sensitive fern can be seen along the banks of a small brook that meanders through the property. At any time of the year, visitors may see lichen-covered rocks, mushrooms, and mosses. Skunks, raccoons, ruffed grouse, red and gray squirrels, and chipmunks live in the shelter of the woods, and the songs of a variety of birds accompany you as you walk.

Nature Trails
You can comfortably walk the 1¼ miles of trails in less than an hour. There are some hilly areas, with the Loop Trail reaching the sanctuary's high point of 152 feet. One trail connects the sanctuary to the nearby Montgomery Pinetum (described elsewhere) for a longer walk.

How to Get There: Located in community of Cos Cob in Greenwich. From Exit 4 on I-95, take Indian Field Rd. north to US 1 (known in this stretch as E. Putnam Ave.) and turn right. Go to Orchard St., turn north (left) and continue for approximately two blocks; Orchard St. veers west while Bible St. continues north. Follow Bible St. past Montgomery Pinetum, to Caldwell Sanctuary on left side of road. Entrance to the sanctuary parking lot is about 100 yards south of intersection of Bible St. and Cat Rock Rd. The loose rock parking area becomes soft following a hard rain, so use caution in parking after a wet spell.

Open daily, year-round, during daylight hours. Free.

For Additional Information:
Mr. Joseph Zeranski
Greenwich Audubon Society
163 Fieldpoint Rd.
Greenwich, CT 06830
203-661-9607

Calf Island

Those who love the sea and who love the special lure of an island will enjoy this 28-acre outdoor recreation center in Long Island Sound off the coast of Greenwich. Intended primarily for use by families and youth groups, Calf Island is owned by the Greenwich YMCA and is open to the public on a daily and seasonal basis.

Much of the interior of the island is occupied by woods and marsh, while the outer edge is rimmed by a large sandy beach. The trees here include many maples and oaks, and there's an abundance of elderberries, blackberries, and red raspberries. Picnic tables and cookout sites are scattered about the island.

A resident manager is available at all times.

Hiking and Bicycling

Several trails, with the longest extending about three-quarters of a mile, wind through the woods; or you may walk along the beach around the entire island.

Camping

Campsites are available for weekend camping only. Six tents on platforms are maintained from mid-May through late September, while other sites, some at the water's edge, are provided for those who want to set up their own tents. Sites are rented by the weekend, and camping fees are charged in addition to day-use fees. All sites must be reserved in advance.

Sailing

Several adult (18 and older) sailing classes are offered in June and July. Calf Island's fleet of Sunfish sailboats is used for this purpose.

Swimming

A wide, sandy beach makes for good swimming and sunbathing. Visitors may pay a daily use fee or purchase a seasonal membership.

How to Get There: From Exit 2 on I-95, turn south on Byram Shore Rd. and look for Byram Dock Rd.; turn left to boat docks. Visitors must provide their own boat transportation to Calf Island (marked Calves Island on some maps), which is nearly one mile from shore; boats may be rented or chartered at several area marinas. Head southwest by water from Byram Shore Docks. On the way, you will pass Shell Island, smaller than Calf Island. There is a dock at the island.

Day-use area open 9:00 A.M.–9:00 P.M. daily, mid-May to late September. Two types of entrance fees—a nominal daily, per-person fee, or a seasonal family membership.

For Additional Information:
Greenwich YMCA
Calf Island Branch
50 E. Putnam Ave.
Greenwich, CT 06830
203-869-1630

Connecticut Audubon Center

Located on 170 acres of wild land, the Connecticut Audubon Center (also known as the Roy and Margot Larsen Sanctuary) serves as headquarters for the Connecticut Audubon Society. The diverse habitat here includes woodlands, meadows, ponds, streams, and wetlands. The preserve is home to nearly 100 different kinds of birds and animals, including deer, muskrat, turtles of all kinds, and many songbirds. Five types of ponds are designed to demonstrate different water habitats, luring a wide variety of waterfowl during major migration periods. Wildflowers and ferns run rampant, and there are many fine tree specimens.

The center also houses a research library, nature exhibits, and a nature store; and there are special demonstrations on solar energy and organic gardening. Injured and orphaned animals are cared for at a compound near the headquarters building. The center can also provide information about other Audubon sanctuaries in the nearby area that are open to the public.

Nature Trails

A network of trails totaling 6½ miles offers walks from one to three hours long; a descriptive booklet is available. A special trail for the handicapped features wide, soft paths, and smooth wooden handrails.

Winter Sports

When weather permits, hiking trails are used by cross-country skiers.

How to Get There: Located at 2325 Burr St., Fairfield. From Exit 21 on I-95, turn north onto Mill Plain Rd., which becomes Burr St. Entrance to center is on left side of Burr St. just north of Merritt Pkwy. (CT 15).

Sanctuary open daily, year-round, during daylight hours; nominal admission charge for those 12 and over. Center open Tuesday–Saturday, 9:00 A.M.–5:00 P.M.; Sunday, noon–5:00 P.M.; closed Monday and major holidays; free.

For Additional Information:

Connecticut Audubon Center
Roy & Margot Larsen Sanctuary
2325 Burr St.
Fairfield, CT 06430
203-259-6305

Connecticut Audubon Society Family Field Trips

Each year, the Connecticut Audubon Society conducts a number of outstanding natural history field trips, especially oriented toward families. Among them are a Norwalk Islands (described elsewhere) tour, the most popular of all; a tidal pools and mud flats trip out of Southport; sailing on Long Island Sound out of New Haven; and a whale-watching trip out of Provincetown, Massachusetts.

The Norwalk Islands tour departs from Norwalk via *The Conservator*, a flat-decked boat operated by the Saugatuck Valley Audubon Society. It features close-up bird-watching and a walking tour of Shea, Chimmons, and Sheffield Islands.

Included in the tidal pools and mud flats tour are an exploration of hidden tide pools and mud flats, views of seldom-seen marine life, and a chance to wade around in the mud when the tide is out.

The Long Island Sound sailing trip, aboard a 52-foot schooner called the *J. N. Carter*, is a good birding and marine life expedition.

During the whale-watching trip, a weekend adventure, humpbacks, finbacks, and minkes are often observed in the Gulf Stream off Provincetown on Cape Cod. The trip begins and ends in Fairfield, Connecticut, with all costs included in one fee. A number of pelagic birds are also observed on this trip.

Some of the more popular trips, such as the Norwalk Islands tour, are offered every year, while others are scheduled irregularly. Rates are very reasonable. Non-Connecticut Audubon Society members pay slightly higher fees than members.

Write for more details and a printed schedule for each season.

For Additional Information:

Director
Natural History Services Dept.
Connecticut Audubon Society
314 Unquowa Rd.
Fairfield, CT 06430
203-259-0416

Connecticut Audubon Society
2325 Burr St.
Fairfield, CT 06430
203-259-6305

Devil's Den Preserve

Devil's Den Preserve near Weston, sometimes referred to as the Lucius Pond Ordway Preserve, is one of the largest wild areas in southwestern Connecticut. Owned by The Nature Conservancy, a national environmental organization, and ad-

Bobcat are occasionally seen in
Devil's Den Preserve. *Bill Thomas*

ministered by the Devil's Den Preserve Committee, it encompasses the four upper tributary watersheds of the West Branch of the Saugatuck River. More than 1,500 acres sprawl across the rolling wooded hills, where there are fascinating rock outcroppings, streams, wetlands, and a pond.

Shagbark hickory, beech, red maple, tulip, and several varieties of oak abound among the great tracts of hardwood forest. More than 500 species of wildflowers, including Dutchman's-breeches, adorn the landscape from spring through fall. A healthy population of wildlife includes white-tailed deer, raccoon, opossum, skunk, cottontail rabbit, squirrel, red fox, bobcat, and the northern copperhead. Some resident birds are the osprey, great blue heron, and great horned owl.

Evidence of man's use of the land goes back some 5,000 years and includes Indian shelters, a mill and pond site dating back to the American Revolution, farms of the 1800s, and more than fifty charcoal production sites. The Weston Historical Society has developed one demonstration charcoal site to give visitors a glimpse of living history.

There is a full-time resident director. A 62-acre tract near Devil's Den known as the Katharine Ordway Preserve, recently willed to The Nature Conservancy, is also administered by the director of Devil's Den and the Devil's Den Preserve Committee.

Hiking and Horseback Riding

More than 20 miles of well-maintained foot trails range in length from 0.3 to 3.1 miles and may be combined any number of ways. Although much of the terrain is rugged, with an elevation of 250 to 600 feet, several of the trails are classified as easy. Three ridge-top vistas of Long Island Sound are accessible by hiking 2 to 3 miles round-trip along Great Ledge, Ambler, and Deer Knoll Trails. Trail maps are available at the parking lot, or you may write in advance for them. The Nature Conservancy also publishes several trail guide study booklets about the area's flora.

Horseback riding is permitted on designated trails; no rentals.

Winter Sports

There are 8 miles of fire trails available for cross-country skiing, but skiers are not permitted on the trails until the snow cover is 6 to 10 inches deep. Skiing is also permitted on certain hiking trails accessible from the Pent Road parking lot; loops from 1 to 7 miles long are possible. Skiers travel here at their own risk; there are no areas in the preserve suitable for beginners.

How to Get There: From Weston, go north on CT 57 to Godfrey Rd. and turn right; continue for about half a mile. Just after crossing a small bridge, turn left on Pent Rd. (follow sign) and proceed to parking lot at end of road.

Open daily, year-round, dawn to dusk, except during high fire-risk season or when ice creates hazardous conditions. Free, but any contributions are gratefully accepted, since the preserve is self-supporting. A permit is required for entry; issued free to individuals on an annual basis and to groups for one-day use.

For Additional Information:

Director
Devil's Den Preserve
P.O. Box 1162
Weston, CT 06880
203-226-4991

The Nature Conservancy
Connecticut Chapter
Science Tower
P.O. Box MMM
Wesleyan Station
Middletown, CT 06457
203-344-0716

Fairchild Wildflower Garden

See listing under Audubon Center in Greenwich and Fairchild Wildflower Garden, page 24.

Farm Creek Marsh

In the middle of Rowayton are two small tracts of land that border a tidal inlet. Known as the Kulze and Langdon Preserves, they are managed together as the Farm Creek Marsh Complex by a local Farm Creek Committee. Although the complex is a little less than 5 acres in size, those 5 acres are extremely significant in the ecology of the area. Containing both shore and tidal wetlands, the marsh is home to large numbers of ribbed mussels, fiddler crabs, and mud snails. More than twenty-five species of water birds and shorebirds have been observed here, and many of the important marsh grasses, such as black grass and several of the spartinas, thrive. The Langdon Preserve provides a complete transition from heavily wooded to marshland environment.

Owned by The Nature Conservancy, a national preservation organization, the Farm Creek complex is easily accessible to the public. The surrounding area is quite open, so that the preserves may also be visually enjoyed by those just driving or walking by.

How to Get There: From Exit 12 on I-95, head southeast on CT 136 (first called Tokenecke Rd., then McKinley Ave.). After crossing Fivemile River, look for intersection of McKinley and Roton Aves. Kulze Preserve extends southeast from this intersection; it's bounded by McKinley Ave. on north, Roton Ave. on west, and Sammis St. on south. To reach the smaller Langdon Preserve, turn right on Roton

Ave. and go to Sammis St.; turn left. Preserve is on right side of street opposite Highland Ave. Parking on street.

Open daily, year-round, during daylight hours. Free.

For Additional Information:

Farm Creek Committee
P.O. Box 117
Rowayton, CT 06853

The Nature Conservancy
Connecticut Chapter
Science Tower
P.O. Box MMM
Wesleyan Station
Middletown, CT 06457
203-344-0716

Greenwich Audubon Center

See listing under Audubon Center in Greenwich and Fairchild Wildflower Garden, page 24.

Huntington State Park

See listing under Putnam Memorial State Park, page 43.

Larsen Sanctuary

See listing under Connecticut Audubon Center, page 31.

Lee Memorial Garden

A small garden with extraordinary collections of rhododendrons and azaleas, the Lee Memorial Garden in New Canaan also maintains a multitude of herbaceous plants, many ferns, daffodils, and a great variety of ground covers.

In early spring, drifts of winter aconite inaugurate a procession of blooms that continues throughout the season. The primroses, abundant in mid-April, are followed quickly by daffodils. Rhododendrons bloom from mid-April to early June, while the azaleas reach their full glory in mid-May.

Some of the 3-acre grounds are wooded and provide a sanctuary for area wildlife. Paths through the garden and woods total three-quarters of a mile in length.

How to Get There: From New Canaan, go west on Elm St. until it ends at Weed St. Turn right and go about ⅓ mile to Wahackme Rd.; then left and head 0.7 mile to Chichester Rd. Turn right onto Chichester and go 0.2 mile to garden on right side of road.

Open daily, year-round, during daylight hours. Free. Groups should call ahead for reservations, since parking space is limited.

For Additional Information:
New Canaan Garden Center
P.O. Box 4
New Canaan, CT 06840
203-966-2120 (Mrs. William Gillerlain)
203-966-1064 (Mrs. Robert Erb)

Montgomery Pinetum

Bequeathed to the community of Greenwich by Colonel Robert H. Montgomery for use as a public park and garden, this 60-acre woodland is noted for its outstanding conifer collection. More than 100 varieties, several of them quite rare, were established here in the 1930s, and many bear identification labels. The shores of Hemlock Pond are adorned with groves of weeping hemlocks. In late May and June, primroses bloom along a brook fed by the waterfall of Rock Garden Pond. Several greenhouses are open to the public, and seasonal displays of tulips, daffodils, azaleas, summer annuals, and chrysanthemums are featured. Amid the cool depths of the conifers, from spring through fall, wildflowers blanket the ground in colorful disarray.

Other attractions include two swampy areas and a rock garden. Picnicking is permitted in designated areas. The pinetum is maintained by the Parks & Recreation Division of the Town of Greenwich.

At the Greenwich Garden Center, located in the old Montgomery residence near the pinetum's entrance, lectures, workshops, and courses are offered to the general public. Consignors from Connecticut, New York, New Jersey, and Massachusetts gather here for an annual May Market sponsored by the center; the public is invited to view exhibits and buy plants.

Nature Trails

A network of trails winds through every corner of the pinetum. Most are one-quarter mile or one-half mile in length. A connecting trail leads from the pinetum to the nearby Caldwell Wildlife Sanctuary of the Greenwich Audubon Society (described elsewhere). Trail maps are available at the garden center.

Winter Sports

An ice skating pond in the northernmost part of the pinetum is open daily when weather permits.

How to Get There: Located in community of Cos Cob in Greenwich. From Exit 4 on I-95, take Indian Field Rd. north to US 1 (known in this stretch as E. Putnam Ave.) and turn right. At Orchard St., turn north (left) and proceed for approximately two blocks; Orchard St. veers west while Bible St. continues north. Follow Bible St. to entrance road on left. Parking on property near Garden Center.

The pinetum is open daily, 8:00 A.M.–sunset, from mid-March through mid-November; closed weekends and holidays rest of year. The garden center is open 9:00 A.M.–4:00 P.M., Monday–Friday, September through June; open 9:00 A.M.–noon daily during July; closed during August for vacation. Free.

For Additional Information:

Montgomery Pinetum
Bible Street
Cos Cob, CT 06807
203-622-7823 (Pinetum
Headquarters)
203-869-9242 (Greenwich
Garden Center)

Superintendent
Parks & Trees Division
Department of Parks &
Recreation
Town Hall, 101 Field Point Rd.
Greenwich, CT 06830
203-622-7814

Nature Center for Environmental Activities

Located in Westport, the Nature Center for Environmental Activities features a native wild animal shelter that houses injured and orphaned creatures. Many of the animals are victims of human carelessness, and it's a good place to demonstrate to a child how dangerous an arrow can be or what a BB gun can do to a bird.

One exhibit very popular with children is an aquarium filled with Long Island Sound fish and shellfish.

During spring and fall migration seasons, bird-banding goes on every day. Visitors who want to see a demonstration may call ahead and find out what time the staff will be banding.

Four distinct animal habitats are found on the 53 acres of grounds occupied by the center. The animal shelter, the aquarium, an exhibit hall, and a wildflower atrium are all housed in a huge museum at the entrance to the sanctuary.

Nature Trails

Observation trails lead throughout the sanctuary. The Swamp Loop Trail passes through a red maple swamp, along Stony Brook, and past a bog. The High Woods Trail follows a high ridge through forest and fields. Twenty varieties of fern may be seen along the Lillian Wadsworth Trail, and a Boy Scouts of America mini-trail displays many native Connecticut trees. A trail map is available at the museum; trails take from five to thirty minutes to walk.

How to Get There: From Exit 17 on I-95, take CT 33 and CT 136 north. Stay on CT 33 north to US 1. At US 1 turn left. At Kings Hwy. North, turn right and continue to Woodside Ave.; turn left. Woodside dead-ends at nature center.

Open daily, year-round; 9:00 A.M.–5:00 P.M., Monday–Saturday, and 1:00–4:00 P.M. Sunday; closed major holidays. Nominal admission charge.

For Additional Information:
The Nature Center for Environmental Activities, Inc.
P.O. Box 165, 10 Woodside Ln.
Westport, CT 06880
_203-227-7253_

The Nature Conservancy, Connecticut Chapter

One of the finest preservation organizations in the world is The Nature Conservancy. Its Connecticut Chapter has been instrumental in obtaining more than 110 tracts of land in the Constitution State, varying in size from ¼-acre to nearly 1,500 acres. New preserves, as well as additions to existing preserves, are being added all the time.

The Altschul Preserve, Byram River Gorge, Devil's Den Preserve, Weir Preserve, and Wolfpits Nature Preserve are described separately elsewhere, but the other preserves within the 50-mile radius prescribed for this book are too numerous to list. Among them are Wood Duck Swamp, a nesting area for woodpeckers and wood ducks; the John Sargent Woodlands, glacially formed land with a spring-fed swamp; and the Delafield Cove, comprised of tidal salt marsh and mud flats on Long Island Sound. Some are accessible only by water, many have no trails, but all are open to the public free of charge for such passive use as hiking and nature study. They represent some of the choicest natural areas in the state.

The Connecticut Chapter will be happy to send you a map of its properties and provide additional information. You must obtain permission to visit some of the preserves; directions will be given at the time you arrange for your visit.

For Additional Information:
The Nature Conservancy
Connecticut Chapter
Science Tower
P.O. Box MMM
Wesleyan Station
Middletown, CT 06457
_203-344-0716_

New Canaan Nature Center

The New Canaan Nature Center actually consists of four separate areas that total about 80 acres. In the main portion, the nature center museum area, are approximately 40 acres of woodlands. Also found here are working greenhouses, a live animal exhibit, and a bookshop. The center offers many special programs throughout the year, as well as several natural history and horticultural field trips available to both members and nonmembers.

A 15-acre bird sanctuary/nature preserve lies nearby. Within this small area are a marshy thicket, hardwood swamp, wooded hillside, a brook, and a natural pool.

Both of the aforementioned units are owned by the Town of New Canaan, while the remaining two are owned by the New Canaan Audubon Society.

The 13-acre Kelly Lowlands Sanctuary is mostly inaccessible at the moment, but it encompasses a splendid overgrown marsh and has the potential for some outstanding bird-watching. Plans for the future include the development of a trail into the preserve.

A reverting field of 12 acres, the Kelly Upland Sanctuary contains a wide variety of hardwoods and thickets.

The four areas are not contiguous, but are quite close to each other. All four have paths or trails.

Nature Trails

At the nature center museum complex, a network of short trails leads through the woods and past a marshy area. The bird sanctuary/nature preserve also contains a system of several short trails, so well planned and laid out that visitors are scarcely aware of the trails' proximity to each other. A single trail leads along the margin of the Kelly Lowlands Sanctuary marsh, while several paths, some poorly maintained, wander through the Kelly Upland Sanctuary. The varying habitats provide a fine opportunity to study a diversity of wildlife and birds at all times of the year.

How to Get There: From New Canaan, go northwest on CT 124 (here called Oenoke Ridge) for about ½ mile. Center is on left side of road opposite St. Mark's Church. Since the other three sections of the center are somewhat difficult to locate, check here for specific directions.

Open daily, year-round, 10:00 A.M.–5:00 P.M., Tuesday–Saturday; 1:00–5:00 P.M., Sunday; closed Mondays and major holidays. Hours are subject to change, however, so it's best to call ahead. Free admission, but donations are accepted.

For Additional Information:

New Canaan Nature Center
144 Oenoke Ridge
New Canaan, CT 06840
203-966-9577

President
New Canaan Audubon Society, Inc.
Box 241
New Canaan, CT 06840
203-966-4995 or *203-966-3987*

Norwalk Islands

In Long Island Sound just off Norwalk is a cluster of islands whose undisturbed state belies their proximity to the outer limits of the New York metropolitan area. This archipelago today represents one of the most important ecological areas in the state of Connecticut. The sixteen islands total nearly 300 acres in area and extend from just east of the Westport-Norwalk town line to the waters off Darien. Dotting the waters around them and providing additional sanctuary for seabirds are numerous hummocks, rocks, and ledges.

Of prime interest to nature lovers is Chimon Island, at 70.2 acres the biggest in the chain. A major heron rookery, the largest of its kind in New England, has been making ornithological news since the birds began to breed here in the early 1960s. Vegetation is so dense that green herons sometimes nest on the ground. Chimon Island also hosts the first breeding pairs of double-crested cormorants in Connecticut, initially observed in 1979. Other birds who make their home here include the black-crowned night heron, yellow-crowned night heron, little blue heron, great blue heron, glossy ibis, common egret, snowy egret, and cattle egret. Herring gulls nest along some sections of the rocky shoreline and in open areas during May and June. A great variety of ducks and pheasants, as well as numerous songbirds, have been observed here. As of this writing, Chimon Island is privately owned, but the City of Norwalk is negotiating to purchase it.

Goose Island, only 3.4 acres in size, is a favorite stopover for many species of migrating birds. It's owned by the Saugatuck Valley Audubon Society.

Canfield Island lies just off the mainland and is connected to Norwalk by a single-lane wooden bridge maintained by the thirteen property owners on the island. Between the privately owned island and the Norwalk shoreline, however, extends a large marsh that is a natural breeding ground for muskrats, rabbits, raccoons, geese, ducks, and many other forms of wildlife. Herons from the Chimon Island rookery come here to feed. One acre of the marsh is owned and managed by the Connecticut Chapter of The Nature Conservancy.

Grassy Island, owned by the City of Norwalk, comprises 23.8 acres. Just 10 feet above mean high water at its highest point, this island is surrounded by tidal flats except on its northwestern edge, where the water is 2 to 7 feet deep. The swampy northern edge is bordered by reefs and large rocks. More large rocks edge the eastern and southern shores. Grassy Island is open to the public, but there is no supervision, and maintenance is limited. Some space is provided for picnicking, but visitors are urged to avoid the island's sea gull nesting grounds.

The prickly pear cactus, uncommon in this area, blooms in late June and early July on 46-acre Shea Island. Sparrow hawks have been observed here, and a great variety of birds come here to nest. Shea Island and Little Ram Island, comprising 6 acres just northwest of Shea, are owned by the City of Norwalk.

Visitors may cruise among the islands aboard the *Lady Joan*, a replica of a Mississippi riverboat, which sails from the Norwalk Cove Marina. During the 1½-hour tour by water, the captain describes points of interest along the way. Bird sanctuaries, Norwalk Indian camping grounds, homes of famous personalities, even the point from which Nathan Hale departed on his last, fatal mission—all are covered in the narration. Shoreline Boating Service, which owns the *Lady Joan*, also offers day-long cruises to Long Island and back aboard the *Long Island Queen*.

The Connecticut Audubon Society sponsors tours to the archipelago each summer that include walks on Shea, Chimon, and Sheffield Islands (described elsewhere under Connecticut Audubon Society Family Field Trips). Tours sponsored by the Saugatuck Audubon Society are run from Norwalk's public boat ramp aboard the society's own boat, *The Conservator*. Since schedules vary and reservations are necessary, check sailing times in advance.

Plans are currently being drawn up for a ferry or cruise boat that will sail from Norwalk to several of the larger islands, including Shea, Sheffield, Chimon, and Grassy. Such a service may be available by the time this book is published.

There also are numerous marinas along the mainland where you may rent boats of all types. Maps of the islands are available at many places throughout the area.

How to Get There: From Exit 16 on I-95, turn south on East Ave. Continue toward waterfront on East Ave. (it will jog to east and become Gregory Blvd.) to Fifth St., turn left, and proceed. Turn right onto Calf Pasture Beach Rd., which ends at a public beach, where visitors are welcome to swim for a fee; the *Lady Joan* docks at Norwalk Cove Marina on right side of road just before you reach beach entrance, and a large sign marks the spot. Although this route is a bit difficult to follow, there will be direction signs for Norwalk Cove Marina and Calf Pasture Beach along the way.

The *Lady Joan* sails daily June to September, departing once a day at 1:30 P.M., Monday–Friday, and twice a day at 1:30 P.M. and 3:15 P.M. Saturday and Sunday. Fees are nominal, with special rates for children and groups. Reservations are advised.

Directions for reaching departure points for Audubon tours will be sent when reservations are made.

For Additional Information:

Shoreline Boating Service
Beach Rd.
East Norwalk, CT 06855
203-838-9003

Director
Natural History Services Dept.
Connecticut Audubon Society
314 Unquowa Rd.
Fairfield, CT 06430
203-259-0416

President
Saugatuck Valley Audubon
Society, Inc.
P.O. Box 684
Westport, CT 06880
203-838-0455

Director
Recreation & Parks Dept.
City of Norwalk
City Hall Annex, Rogers Sq.
East Norwalk, CT 06855
203-838-7531, Ext. 306

The Nature Conservancy
Connecticut Chapter
Science Tower
Box MMM
Wesleyan Station
Middletown, CT 06457
203-344-0716

Ordway Preserve

See listing under Devil's Den Preserve, page 32.

Putnam Memorial State Park

Located on 183 acres of scenic land near Redding, this state park memorializes the site of the 1778–79 winter encampment of the Continental Army's Connecticut and New Hampshire troops. The commander was General Israel Putnam, for whom the park is named.

Although maintained primarily for its historical value, it is a quiet, lovely spot where visitors may walk along shaded paths, wander over wooded hills, and listen to the melodies of numerous songbirds. Along the way, they may visit the Revolutionary War Museum, look at reconstructed blockhouses and log cabins, view the heaps of stones believed to have served as barracks foundations, and explore a cave. A healthy oak tree growing in the park sprouted from an acorn produced by the famous Charter Oak of Hartford.

Picnicking is permitted in two areas along picturesque Lake Putnam in the eastern part of the park. Although Putnam Park may occasionally be crowded on holidays and summer weekends, it generally provides a serene atmosphere with few people around.

Just a few miles east of Putnam Park is 878-acre Collis P. Huntington State Park. Though slightly out of the 50-mile radius prescribed for this book, it is mentioned because of its proximity to Putnam Park and because it is managed as a nature preserve. Totally undeveloped as of this writing, it is used by fishermen, hikers, cross-country skiers, snowshoers, and bird-watchers. The works of Anna Hyatt Huntington, a noted sculptress and the daughter-in-law of the man for whom the park is named, are displayed in the park's lovely setting. From Putnam Park, take CT 58 southeast for about 2 miles. A left turn onto a small back road will lead you east and then north to Huntington Park. However, the area is somewhat difficult to find since Huntington Park does not appear on many Connecticut maps and the only access roads are not well marked. Ask directions locally or at Putnam Park.

Hiking

The only maintained trail leads through the historical area of the park, a loop through dense woods and past the remnants of the encampment. The woods in the westernmost part of the park may be roamed at will. Terrain is quite hilly in places.

Fishing

Fishing is permitted in the park pond.

Winter Sports

This is a fine area for cross-country skiing and snowshoeing; part of the park is quite hilly.

How to Get There: From Redding, go north on CT 107 to park.
    Park open daily, year-round, from 8:00 A.M.–sunset. Museum open daily from Memorial Day to Labor Day, noon–4:00 P.M. Both free.

For Additional Information:

Putnam Memorial State Park
Museum
RFD 1
West Redding, CT 06896
203-938-2285

Public Information Officer
Headquarters, Region II
Dept. of Environmental Protection
Judd Hill Rd.
Middlebury, CT 06762
203-758-1753

Public Information Officer
Parks & Recreation Unit
Dept. of Environmental
Protection
Hartford, CT 06115
203-566-2304

Seaside Park

Virtually undeveloped as of this writing, Seaside Park is a long, narrow strip of sandy beach extending into Long Island Sound just south of Bridgeport. In the summer, this city-owned park is a popular place to swim and picnic; in the winter, it's a quiet place where one may stroll along the beach and observe water birds and waterfowl. There are fine views of Long Island and the sheltered waters of Black Rock Harbor. Motorists may follow Sound View Drive, which traverses the 200-acre park near the water's edge. Seaside Park is one of very few places along the southwestern Connecticut shoreline open to out-of-state residents.

Swimming

Swimming is the primary activity at this park. There's a bath-house in which to change, and lifeguards are on duty.

How to Get There: From Exit 27 on I-95, take Main St. south toward Long Island Sound to park entrance. Main St. will become Sound View Dr.

Open daily, year-round, during daylight hours. During peak visitation season, there's an admission charge. Out-of-state visitors pay more than Connecticut residents; charge is per vehicle rather than per person.

For Additional Information:

Superintendent of Parks
Dept. of Parks & Recreation
Administration Bldg.
263 Golden Hill
Bridgeport, CT 06604
203-576-7233
203-576-7237 (Superintendent of Recreation)
203-576-7717 (Park Bathhouse)

Senior Memorial Park

One of the finest mini-wetlands in the greater New York City area is Samuel T. Senior Memorial Park in Easton. The 10-acre wildlife refuge consists of a variety of land types, including brushy uplands, open grass areas, and wooded uplands, but it's the eerie beauty of the swampy sections that appeals most to visitors.

Great numbers of wildflowers are found here during spring and early summer—jacks-in-the-pulpit, violets, marsh marigolds. Among the wildlife living in the sanctuary are turtles, frogs, snakes, owls, hawks, occasionally great wading birds, raccoons, opossums, skunks, rabbits, and squirrels.

A raised boardwalk allows people to penetrate the damp areas without getting their feet wet or damaging the fragile ecology. The park is administered and maintained by a special board formed for that purpose.

How to Get There: From intersection of CT 59 and Center Rd. in Easton (a firehouse is on one corner), go west on Center Rd. to park, opposite Easton's Town Hall. Parking is on road near entrance.

Park open at all times, but visitors are encouraged to use it only during daylight hours. Free.

For Additional Information:

Senior Memorial Park, Inc.
c/o Donald Waterman
99 Flat Rock Rd.
Easton, CT 06612
203-372-6848

Sherwood Island State Park

This lovely stretch of beach on Long Island Sound lures huge crowds of visitors on hot summer days to Sherwood Island, the only Connecticut state beach that falls within a 50-mile radius of Manhattan. When visitors tire of the sun, they may retreat to the cool shade provided by a woodland of maples and lindens near the shore.

One of the first state parks in the nation, Sherwood Island today includes more than 234 acres near Westport.

In a cove in the western portion of the park is a saltwater marsh. A good area in which to observe shorebirds and herons, the marsh also hosts many types of waterfowl during the winter. Atop a hilly peninsula poking out into the marsh is a picnic grove that makes a good spot for bird-watching.

Hiking

Though there are no trails as such, this is a marvelous place to explore a winter beach, its adjacent marsh, and the nearby woods. In winter, the crowds have vanished, and the marsh is alive with waterfowl.

Swimming and Scuba Diving

Sherwood Island offers saltwater swimming and sunbathing along a 1½-mile stretch of sandy beach; a bathhouse is available, and lifeguards are on duty from 9:00 A.M. to 6:00 P.M.

Scuba diving is permitted in designated areas only; two or more people must dive together, a marker buoy must be used, and no underwater fishing is permitted.

Fishing

A rocky fishing point is located approximately midway along the beach. Surf fishing is permitted at night, and the sport of crabbing is enjoyed in the cove to the west.

Camping

Since there are virtually no campgrounds available in the southwestern corner of Connecticut, Sherwood Island State Park participates in the state's Emergency Stopover Program. Out-of-state travelers with self-contained campers may use certain state parks for an overnight stop when they are unable to find lodging elsewhere. Campers must arrive between sunset and 11:30 P.M.and vacate the area before 8:00 A.M. the next day. If the gate at the park access is closed, remain there with your lights on until a park official arrives. Campers at Sherwood Island stay in the parking lot, and a camping fee is charged.

How to Get There: From Exit 18 on I-95, go south on Sherwood Island Connector to park.

Open daily, 8:00 A.M. to a half hour before sunset, year-round. A nominal parking fee is charged daily from Memorial Day weekend through Labor Day and on weekends from Labor Day through late September. Free rest of year.

For Additional Information:

Public Information Officer
Parks & Recreation Unit
Dept. of Environmental
Protection
Hartford, CT 06115
203-566-2304

Public Information Officer
Headquarters, Region II
Dept. of Environmental
Protection
Judd Hill Rd.
Middlebury, CT 06762
203-758-1753

Stamford Museum and Nature Center

The Stamford Nature Center, located on 100 acres of dense woodlands, fields, and ponds, offers a zoo, a beaver pond, a planetarium, an observatory with a 22-inch telescope, a real dairy farm with milking demonstrations, a weather station, and natural history exhibits.

Young visitors are permitted to pet the farm animals. In the zoo are such indigenous creatures as deer, raccoons, woodchucks, foxes, and a pair of river otters. The main building of the museum includes a Discovery Room featuring a live reptile and amphibian exhibit.

Nature Trails

Six marked trails, totaling about 3 miles in length, begin at the museum's rear door and disappear into the woodlands and fields. Terrain is gentle here. One trail connects to the Bartlett Arboretum (described elsewhere), about ¼ mile away. Trail maps available at the nature center.

How to Get There: From Exit 35 on Merritt Pkwy. (CT 15), go north on CT 137 (High Ridge Rd.). Museum is located at corner of CT 137 and Schofieldtown Rd. (first traffic light north of Merritt Pkwy.).

Open daily, year-round, 9:00 A.M.–5:00 P.M., Monday–Saturday; 1:00–5:00 P.M. Sunday; closed New Year's, Thanksgiving, Christmas. Free admission to museum and nature center, but a nominal parking fee is charged.

For Additional Information:
Stamford Museum and Nature Center
39 Scofieldtown Rd.
Stamford, CT 06903
203-322-1646

The Weir Preserve

On 86 acres of scenic beauty near Wilton is this small Nature
Conservancy preserve, once a typical New England farm. Now
nature is reclaiming the area. Dense growths of mountain
laurel climb steep slopes, and bold rock outcrops overlook the
swamp along Comstock Brook. Glacial boulders are scattered
over the hillsides; there are freshwater springs and a waterfall
(this may dry up during late summer), acres of wildflowers in
the spring, and several species of wild animals and birds. Fox
and deer are often seen; raccoons are abundant. Wood ducks
and mallards nest in the swamp, and pileated woodpeckers
and ruffed grouse are quite common.

Hiking

Hiking is the primary activity here; the only way to see the
preserve is via footpaths. Maps posted at each entrance point
outline the trail system, which is marked by colored blazes. At
your request, The Nature Conservancy will send you a folder
that contains a map of the trail system, a description of the
preserve, and a list of the flora found there.

How to Get There: From Wilton, take CT 33 west to Millstone Rd.;
turn right. Go to Nod Hill Rd., and turn left. Continue straight to
preserve, which extends southwest from intersection of Nod Hill Rd.
and Pelham Ln. (a tract of land immediately southwest of this intersection is privately owned, with the preserve just beyond it). Two
entrance points are available. One is from Nod Hill Rd. about ⅓ mile
south of its intersection with Pelham Ln.; a trail leads west into
sanctuary, and there is limited parking along roadside. A second
entrance trail leads south off Pelham Ln. approximately 450 ft. west
of Pelham's intersection with Nod Hill Rd.; no parking allowed on
Pelham Ln.
  Open daily, year-round, during daylight hours. Free.

For Additional Information:
The Nature Conservancy
Connecticut Chapter
Science Tower
P.O. Box MMM
Wesleyan Station
Middletown, CT 06457
203-344-0716

Wolfpits Nature Preserve

An excellent example of coastal uplands has been preserved at 59-acre Wolfpits Nature Preserve in Bethel. Ranging from 500 to 670 feet in elevation, the preserve is centered around a hillside covered with a mixed beech-oak forest. The western slope is believed to have served as an encampment area for soldiers of the Revolutionary Army, an extension of the camp at Putnam Memorial State Park (described elsewhere), just south of here. Lichen-covered rock circles used as fireplaces by the troops have been found. During Prohibition, several moonshine stills were located here.

Within the preserve are a late successional bog, swamplands, a wet meadow that supports a wide variety of plant and animal species, and a mature beech-oak forest.

How to Get There: From Bethel, go east on CT 302, past CT 58 on right. Turn right onto Wolf Pit Rd. Go past Codfish Hill Rd., to preserve on left. Enter preserve on foot; you'll have to find your own way, since there are no established trails at this entrance as yet. Parking is difficult and limited along Wolf Pit Rd. at present; a parking area is planned for future.

Open daily, year-round, during daylight hours. Free.

For Additional Information:

Dr. Ellen Rosenberg
Wolfpits Preserve Committee
Codfish Hill Rd.
Bethel, CT 06801
203-743-7194

The Nature Conservancy
Connecticut Chapter
Science Tower
P.O. Box MMM
Wesleyan Station
Middletown, CT 06457
203-344-0716

Part 3

Natural Attractions in
New Jersey

NEW JERSEY

1. Abram S. Hewitt State Forest **D-1**
2. Allaire State Park **E-6**
3. Allamuchy Mountain State Park **B-3**
4. Assunpink Wildlife Management Area **C-6**
5. Belmont Hill Park **E-3**
6. Bergen County Wildlife Center **D/E-2**
7. Berkshire Valley Wildlife Management Area **C-2/3**
8. Branch Brook Park **D-3**
9. Brookdale Park **D-3**
10. Campgaw Mountain County Reservation **D-2**
11. Caven Point Cove **E-4**
12. Celery Farm **D/E-2**
13. Cheesequake State Park **D-5**
14. Clinton Wildlife Management Area **B-4**
15. Colliers Mills Wildlife Management Area **D-6**
16. Colonial Park **C-4**
17. Davis Johnson Park and Gardens **E-3**
18. Duke Gardens **C-4**
19. Eagle Rock Reservation **D-3**
20. East Hill Preserve **E-2/3**
21. Flat Rock Brook Environmental Center **E-3**
22. Fort Lee Historic Park **E-3**
23. Franklin Mineral Museum **C-2**
24. The Frelinghuysen Arboretum **C/D-3**
25. Garret Mountain Reservation **D-3**
26. Great Adventure Safari **C/D-6**
27. Great Falls of the Passaic **D-2/3**
28. Great Swamp National Wildlife Refuge **C/D-3**
29. Great Swamp Outdoor Education Center **D-3**
30. Greenbrook Sanctuary **E-3**
31. Hacklebarney State Park **B-3**
32. Harmony Ridge Farm and Campground **B-1**
33. Hartshorn Arboretum **D-3**
34. Herrontown Woods Arboretum **C-5**
35. High Point State Park **C-1**
36. Holmdel Park **D-5**
37. Hutcheson Forest **C-4**
38. Island Beach State Park **E-7**
39. Jenny Jump State Forest **B-3**
40. Lewis Morris Park **C-3**
41. Liberty State Park **E-3/4**
42. Loantaka Brook Reservation **C-3**
43. Lockwood Gorge Wildlife Management Area **B-4**
44. Lord Stirling Park **C-3/4**
45. Lorrimer Nature Center **D-2**
46. Mahlon Dickerson Reservation **C-2**
47. Mills Reservation **D-3**
48. Moggy Hollow Natural Area **C-4**
49. Morristown National Historic Park **C-3**
50. Norvin Green State Forest **D-2**
51. Ocean County Park **D-6**
52. Old Troy Park **D-3**
53. Pinelands National Reserve **C-8**
54. Pleasant Acres Farm Campground **C-1**
55. Princeton University Campus **C-5**
56. Ramapo Mountain State Forest **D-2**
57. Ramapo Valley County Reservation **D-2**
58. Reeves-Reed Arboretum **D-3**
59. Riker Hill Park **D-3**
60. Ringwood State Park **D-1/2**
61. Round Valley State Recreation Area **B-4**
62. Rutgers University Campus **C/D-5**
63. Sandy Hook **E-5**
64. Sawmill Creek Wildlife Management Area **E-3**
65. Scherman-Hoffman Wildlife Sanctuaries **C-3**
66. Shark River Park **E-6**
67. South Mountain Reservation **D-3**
68. Spruce Run State Recreation Area **B-4**
69. Stokes State Forest **B-1**
70. Tourne Park **C/D-3**
71. Troy Meadows **D-3**
72. Turkey Swamp **D-6**
73. Van Saun Park **E-2**
74. Voorhees State Park **B-4**
75. Watchung Reservation **D-4**
76. Wawayanda State Park **D-1**
77. Weis Ecology Center **D-2**
78. West Essex Park **D-3**
79. Whittingham Wildlife Management Area **B-2**
80. Willowwood Arboretum **C-3**

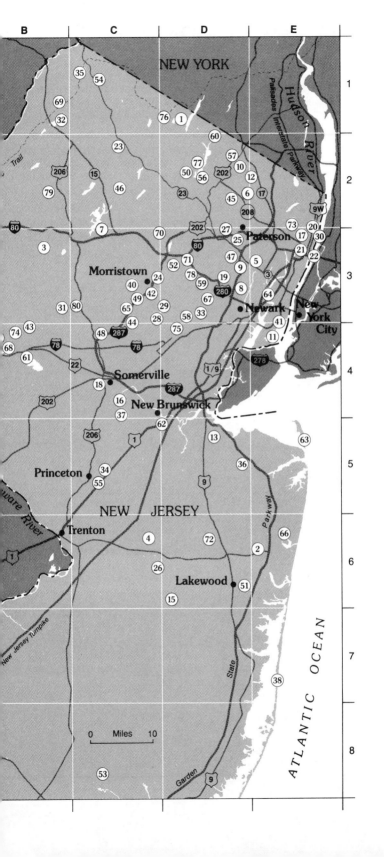

Abram S. Hewitt State Forest

Rough and mountainous, Abram S. Hewitt State Forest extends over the high ridges of the Bearfort Mountains in northwest Passaic County and overlooks 7-mile-long Greenwood Lake. The predominantly oak and maple woodlands that cover the forest's 1,890 acres are home to a considerable population of deer. Within this natural tract are two small lakes, good for fishing and accessible by foot only.

Hiking

Several very rugged trails, including approximately 0.6 mile of the Appalachian Trail, wind through this natural area. The 2.5-mile Bearfort Ridge Trail ascends Bearfort Mountain and runs along picturesque rock ridges.

Winter Sports

When weather permits, trails are used by cross-country skiers and snowshoers.

How to Get There: From West Milford, go north on Co. Rd. 513 (Union Valley Rd.) to Warwick Turnpike, and turn left. Warwick Turnpike skirts the southern boundary of Hewitt Forest. Park alongside roadside; no roads into forest.

Open daily, year-round, during daylight hours. Free.

For Additional Information:

Abram S. Hewitt State Forest
c/o Supt., Wawayanda State Park
P.O. Box 198
Highland Lakes, NJ 07422
201-764-4120

Allaire State Park

The 2,600-acre Allaire State Park in lower Monmouth County features a restored iron village as well as a great natural area (the state-designated Swimming River Natural Area is within the park).

Consisting of pine and oak forest, Allaire encompasses the type of terrain and vegetation one would expect to find in New Jersey's Pine Barrens. Holly forest, swamps, meadows, and pine barrens are its most prominent features. The flood plain of the Manasquan River bisects the park, giving it a diversity capable of supporting more than 200 species of plants, wildflowers, trees, shrubs, and vines.

Because it is located along the Atlantic flyway, great numbers of migrating birds, including a multitude of ducks and geese, come this way during spring and fall migration seasons.

During the summer months, a park naturalist conducts daily nature tours of the area. The remainder of the year, you may make reservations for special guided tours on weekends.

Hiking and Horseback Riding

You can hike through a restored iron village; a self-guided tour booklet is available at the visitor's center. There are also several miles of hiking trails and old woods roads throughout the park. Five special trails in the natural area are marked to guide the hiker. More than 6 miles of bridle trails traverse the park's woodlands; horse rentals in park. Bridle trails are also good for hiking. Terrain throughout park is primarily level.

Winter Sports

Cross-country skiing and snowshoeing are permitted during winter months when snow cover exceeds 6 inches.

Camping

In a wooded area about a mile from the restored village are some fifty campsites for family and group use. Each site has a picnic table, protected space for campfires, and a graded space for tents and trailers of up to 24 feet. Hot showers usually available. No hookups. Open all year.

How to Get There: Located southeast of Farmingdale. From Garden State Pkwy., take southbound Exit 96 or northbound Exit 97A; follow signs to park, which lies west of parkway.

Open daily, year-round, 8:00 A.M.–sunset. Nominal admission charge daily, April through October 31, and on weekends in March.

For Additional Information:

Superintendent
Allaire State Park
P.O. Box 218
Farmingdale, NJ 07727
201-938-2371

Allamuchy Mountain State Park

One of the newest parks in the state system, Allamuchy Mountain Park contains more than 7,000 acres of undeveloped woodland, used primarily by hikers. Within its boundaries lie Allamuchy and Deer Park Ponds, and the Musconetcong River meanders through its heart. Part of the park is preserved as the Deer Lake Park Natural Area.

Adjoining this vast woodland tract on the south is a more developed area of 222 mostly wooded acres, known as the Stephens section (many maps still designate this area by its former name, Stephens–Saxton Falls State Park).

The well-preserved remains of one of the twenty-eight locks of the old Morris Canal, used in the 1800s for transporting freight across the state, are worth a visit. Directly below the lock structure, a section of the old canal is adjoined by a remnant of its original towpath. Near the lock, on the Musconetcong River, you'll find a picturesque waterfall.

Hiking

A trail system is still being developed in this park, but hikers may now take off through the woods at their own risk. Rugged terrain.

Swimming

The remaining section of the old Morris Canal in the Stephens section of the park has been filled with water and is used by swimmers. A lifeguard is on duty.

Winter Sports

All parts of the park include some fine areas for cross-country skiing, snowshoeing, and sledding in the winter.

Camping

A family campground in the Stephens section offers about fifty sites for tents and trailers of up to 24 feet. No hot water. No hookups. Open mid-March through October.

How to Get There: Located in Sussex, Warren, and Morris Counties. From Hackettstown, go north on Willow Grove–Waterloo Rd. about 2 miles to park entrance road on right.

Open daily, year-round, during daylight hours; no entrance fee, but there is a nominal charge for picnic tables.

For Additional Information:

Chief Ranger
Allamuchy Mountain State Park
Hackettstown, NJ 07840
201-852-3790

Assunpink Wildlife Management Area

Most of the 5,400 acres of the Assunpink Wildlife Management Area are woodlands and fields surrounded by hedgerows, all encircling five man-made lakes. Assunpink, the largest, is 225 acres in size.

White-tailed deer, cottontail rabbit, woodcock and grouse, squirrel, raccoon, pheasant, opossum, quail, and red and gray fox inhabit the park. Assunpink WMA has earned a reputation as one of the best bird-watching areas in central New Jersey. Migrating waterfowl, including Canada geese and a multitude of duck species, use the lakes during the autumn months, sometimes even wintering in the area.

Hiking and Horseback Riding

A complex of dirt roads good for hiking leads throughout the area.

Part of the WMA has been turned over to the New Jersey Department of Agriculture for an Equine Activity Center, which plans to make available a variety of activities such as horse shows, trail riding, and programs for the handicapped. Check for up-to-date information.

Fishing and Boating

Largemouth bass, bluegill, pickerel, and catfish are the principal species found. Launching ramps available on all three lakes; any motors used must be electric.

How to Get There: Located in Monmouth County south of Roosevelt. From Roosevelt, take Roosevelt-Clarksburg Rd. (Co. Rd. 571) east towards Clarksburg. WMA access road will be on right; look for signs.
   Open daily, year-round, 5:00 A.M.–9:00 P.M. Free.

For Additional Information:
Assunpink Wildlife Management Area
c/o Nacote Creek Lab
Star Route 9
Absecon, NJ 08201
609-652-9519

Belmont Hill Park

This small hilltop park in Garfield is noted for its rose garden. More than sixty-five varieties of roses lure visitors during the June and early fall blooming seasons. It's a pleasant place to visit at other times of the year, too, and features a scenic lookout, picnic tables, and some playground equipment.

How to Get There: Located in Bergen County. From Exit 61 on I-80, take Co. Rd. 507 (River Rd.) south for about 3 miles to Botany St. and turn left. Park is on left side of Botany St.
   Open daily, year-round, during daylight hours. Free.

For Additional Information:
Bergen County Park Commission
327 Ridgewood Ave.
Paramus, NJ 07648
201-646-2680

Bergen County Wildlife Center

This remarkable center, encompassing about 80 acres, welcomes more than 280,000 people a year and serves as the hub of nature-oriented activities in Bergen County. The natural area includes upland forest, stream, and swamp habitats. Also on the grounds are a deer pen and two octagonal shelters that contain live native animals and birds. In the observatory building, a window wall overlooks a pond that is home to various waterfowl species; binoculars are available for closer scrutiny. You'll also see a console of lighted color photographs; natural science exhibits; a nature library, and a rock collection. In March and April, 25,000 daffodils dot the grassy slopes beside the main park drive; nearby is a shaded terrace garden dominated by rhododendron and azaleas from April through June. Picnickers will find tables nestled in a wooded area.

This park is identified on some maps as Wyckoff County Park.

Nature Trail

A ⅔-mile-long, self-guided trail winds through the natural area. Printed trail guides, including a Braille version, are available.

How to Get There: Located east of Wyckoff. From Wyckoff, take Co. Rd. 502 (first called Franklin Ave., then Wyckoff Ave.) east to W. Crescent Ave. Turn right and continue straight to park entrance on left side of road.

Grounds open daily, year-round, from sunrise to a half hour after sunset; building open 8:30 A.M.–5:00 P.M. Free.

For Additional Information:

Bergen County Wildlife Center
Crescent Ave. West
Wyckoff, NJ 07481
201-891-5571

Bergen County Park
Commission
327 Ridgewood Ave.
Paramus, NJ 07648
201-646-2680

Berkshire Valley Wildlife Management Area

The Berkshire Valley Wildlife Management Area, containing 1,527 acres of woodlands near Dover in Morris County, is managed for upland game, deer, waterfowl, and fish. It is also a favorite area with bird-watchers, photographers, and hikers, although there are no developed trails. Stephens Brook, Rockaway River, and Baker Mill Pond are all located in the WMA.

Pheasant, white-tailed deer, quail, grouse, squirrel, rabbit, Canada geese, wood ducks, mallard, and black ducks are found here. Trout are stocked in the Rockaway River.

Lake Hopatcong and Hopatcong State Park (described elsewhere) are nearby.

How to Get There: From Dover, go north on NJ 15 to Berkshire Valley Rd. and turn west (left) to WMA.

Open daily, year-round, 5:00 A.M.–9:00 P.M. Free.

For Additional Information:

Berkshire Valley Wildlife Management Area
c/o Clinton Wildlife Management Area
Box 409
Hampton, NJ 08827
201-735-8793

Branch Brook Park

This is the place to be in April. Though cherry trees are abundant throughout the New Jersey park system, the most lavish display of all occurs in 350-acre Branch Brook Park in Newark. More than 3,000 Japanese cherry trees burst into bloom, creating a canopy of fragrant pink and white blossoms through the entire month. At night, the trees are lighted to create a special effect.

Visitors will find ten varieties of cherry trees, including one species that also flowers in the fall. And each year in mid-April, in celebration of spring, the Newark Cherry Blossom Festival is held.

Following the profusion of cherry blossoms, and keeping the park in bloom through June, are flowering dogwood, forsythia, rose of Sharon, azalea, mountain laurel, and rhododendron. In the fall, a chrysanthemum show is featured in the park greenhouses.

There are numerous recreation facilities here, too, including tennis courts, a cross-country run, and in winter an indoor ice skating rink.

A very popular park, Branch Brook is crowded on nice weekends, especially on Sundays. As many as 155,000 people have been counted here during one eleven-hour period when the cherry trees were in full bloom.

How to Get There: Located in northern Newark, extends into Belleville. From Newark, take NJ 21 north to Co. Rd. 506 (Belleville Ave.). Turn west and proceed to Union Ave. Turn left onto Union, go to Mill St., and turn right. Continue straight through tiny Belleville Park, another Essex County facility that also contains numerous cherry trees, into adjoining Branch Brook Park. At fork in road, where Mill St. veers right, bear left onto main Branch Brook Park road.

Grounds open daily, year-round, during daylight hours. Night hours when cherry trees are blooming. Free.

For Additional Information:

Essex County Dept. of Parks,
Recreation & Cultural Affairs
115 Clifton Ave.
Newark, NJ 07104
201-482-6400

Center for Environmental Studies
621 Eagle Rock Ave.
Roseland, NJ 07068
201-228-2210

Brookdale Park

Brookdale Park boasts one of the grandest rose gardens in the metropolitan area. It dates to 1959, when the North Jersey Rose Society donated 750 rosebushes to this 121-acre park near Bloomfield.

Many of the trees and shrubs are exotic or rare species, such as crabapple, Japanese cherry, purple and European beech, Katsura trees, Korean rhododendron, and Chinese azalea. Half of the park has been designed for passive recreation; the other half contains tennis courts, a picnic area, and an archery building.

Hiking, Bicycling, and Nature Trails

Six miles of walking and bicycle paths traverse the park, and there's a ¼-mi. running track. One foot trail, the Brookline Interpretive Trail, is described in detail in a pamphlet that may be obtained from the Essex County Parks Department or the Center for Environmental Studies.

How to Get There: From Exit 151 on Garden State Pkwy., head west on Watchung Ave. to park entrance road on right.

Grounds open daily, year-round, during daylight hours. Free.

For Additional Information:

Essex County Dept. of Parks, Recreation & Cultural Affairs 115 Clifton Ave. Newark, NJ 07104 *201-482-6400*

Center for Environmental Studies 621 Eagle Rock Ave. Roseland, NJ 07068 *201-228-2210*

Campgaw Mountain County Reservation

Traditionally regarded by residents as Bergen County's version of Central Park, this reservation offers more than 1,300 wooded acres for bird-watching, hiking, and nature study. A lecture hall at the visitor's center offers live animal exhibits and natural science displays.

While much of Campgaw Reservation is forested and remains in its natural state, there are also developed, year-round recreation areas.

Hiking and Horseback Riding

Several marked foot trails are shown on a sketch map available at the Campgaw Park Office and the Bergen County Wildlife Center (described elsewhere). Though the terrain here is partially mountainous, most trails are only moderately strenuous; they skirt swampy areas and pass through hemlock groves and among old cedars. Some follow traces of old Indian paths. Group walks and hikes are scheduled some weekends.

Saddle Ridge Horseback Riding Area adjoins the reservation on the south; for a set fee, visitors ride on guided tours of the reservation along a wooded bridle trail.

Swimming

Lake swimming is allowed most of the summer at Darlington County Park, a recreational facility located on Darlington

Avenue just northeast of Campgaw; open daily July through Labor Day, on Memorial Day weekend, and on certain June days.

Winter Sports

There are several downhill skiing slopes and a toboggan run in the park. Skiing equipment may be rented or purchased, and instruction is available. The visitor's center doubles as a ski lodge.

Camping

A small campground, open year-round, provides nearly thirty sites for tents and trailers up to 16 feet. No hot showers; no hookups. Advance reservation required.

How to Get There: Located northeast of Oakland. From Oakland, take US 202 (Ramapo Valley Rd.) north to Darlington Ave. and turn right. Go to Campgaw Rd.; turn right and head straight to park entrance on right side of road.

Grounds open daily, year-round, from sunrise to a half hour after sunset. Free admission.

For Additional Information:

Bergen County Wildlife Center
Crescent Ave.
Wyckoff, NJ 07481
201-891-5571

Bergen County Park Commission
327 Ridgewood Ave.
Paramus, NJ 07648
201-646-2680

Caven Point Cove

One of the last undisturbed tidal marshes along the lower Hudson River rests virtually within the shadow of Manhattan's skyscrapers on the New Jersey shore. Called Caven Point Cove, it's just south of Liberty State Park in Jersey City, and it's a bird-watcher's paradise. Up to 10,000 canvasback ducks, the largest concentration north of the Delmarva Peninsula, winter in this area, and thousands of other birds are sighted here each year.

Once a fishing area for Dutch and English settlers, Caven Point is now bound on the south by a 4,300-foot concrete pier and on the north by a small section of Liberty State Park. The cove shares the park's stunning views of the Statue of Liberty, Ellis Island, and the lower Manhattan skyline. In fact, for photographers, it is one of the most alluring spots in the city.

Jersey City bought the cove from the federal government in 1972. It is now home to fishermen, sunbathers, a variety of waterfowl, oyster beds, and wild animals such as raccoons, muskrats, rabbits, reptiles, and amphibians. Some naturalists report that it is the best location in the greater New York City area for spotting black-headed gulls. In winter, there are black ducks, loons, great cormorants, horned and red-necked grebes, mergansers, Canada geese, buffleheads, American widgeons, and gadwalls. Several different species of sandpiper also use the area.

How to Get There: From the toll station at Exit 14B of the NJ Turnpike Extension, go left at Caven Point sign, then right onto Caven Point Rd. Follow Caven Point Rd. out to military base gate house on left side of road. It may be necessary to stop at gate house and request permission to enter area. Just beyond gate house, turn left onto a road leading to Caven Pier. Park at end of pier. Halfway out to pier, on the right, is an old abandoned red brick building with a narrow lagoon behind it. Many birds can usually be spotted here.

Open daily, year-round, during daylight hours. Free.

For Additional Information:
Naturalist
Liberty State Park
Wolf Drive
Jersey City, NJ 07304
201-435-0736

Celery Farm

Astride Allendale Brook in the Bergen County community of Allendale is a 78-acre tract of unspoiled wetland known as Celery Farm. A freshwater marsh studded with cattails and phragmites and bordered by trees, the former working farm is a home or resting place for nearly 200 species of birds. Bald eagles and peregrine falcons come here, as well as herons, swans, geese, ducks, and pheasants. Among the resident mammals are foxes, white-tailed deer, and opossum.

Celery Farm also serves as a giant sponge for the waters of Allendale Brook in an area frequently threatened with floods. The underlying sands and gravels of the marsh absorb the brook's water, then slowly release it downstream.

Visitors may study nature, watch birds, and walk along shaded pathways. A two-mile trail skirts the periphery of the property.

How to Get There: From NJ 17 near Allendale, take Allendale Ave. west. Turn right onto Cottage Place. Go to Franklin Turnpike and turn right again. Entrance is about 700 ft. farther on right side of Franklin Turnpike. Parking area near entrance.

Open daily, year-round, during daylight hours. Free.

For Additional Information:

Mr. Stiles Thomas
P.O. Box 168
Allendale, NJ 07401
201-327-4600

City Hall, Borough of Allendale
500 W. Crescent Avenue
Allendale, NJ 07401
201-825-3700

Cheesequake State Park

Less than 40 miles from Manhattan is Cheesequake State Park, an oasis of woodlands, marsh, and meadows. Established in 1937 near Raritan Bay some 5 miles south of Perth Amboy, the park contains about 1,000 acres, with its southern end preserved as wilderness. Near the center of the park is Hooks Creek Lake; Cheesequake Creek meanders along the western border.

Because of the varying terrain, there's a wide variety of flora and fauna. The salt marshes along Cheesequake Creek attract marsh birds and fiddler crabs. Common and snowy egrets, ducks, geese, great blue and green herons, and glossy ibises inhabit the park. An upland hardwood forest of beech, oak, hickory, and tulip is home to squirrel, southern flying squirrel, deer, raccoon, opossum, and fox. Some laurel-covered slopes, a hardwood swamp, and even a sample of pine barrens are found within this park. It also is a meeting ground where certain plants from southern New Jersey reach their northernmost terminus, and other plants from the northern part of the Garden State reach their southernmost climatic range.

Just one thing detracts from the beauty of this natural park, and that only slightly: the Garden State Parkway cuts through the eastern half of it.

Hiking

Well-planned and well-maintained hiking trails are provided throughout the park; in the wilderness area, set aside for nature study, a trail leads from the marshes through a variety of habitats to upland forests.

Fishing

Fishing is permitted in Hooks Creek Lake and in Cheesequake Creek.

Swimming

A safe bathing beach is situated at Hooks Creek Lake. Bathhouses are nearby, and a lifeguard is on duty. Some beach supplies are sold here.

Camping

An excellent campground offers some fifty wooded sites for tents and trailers up to 24 feet. Open March 1 through November 30. No hookups; central bathhouse with hot showers.

How to Get There: From Exit 120 on Garden State Pkwy., road leads west into park. Follow signs.

Open daily, year-round, 9:00 A.M.–dusk. Nominal entrance fee: daily from Memorial Day through Labor Day; on Saturday and Sunday, May 1 to Memorial Day and Labor Day through October.

For Additional Information:
Superintendent
Cheesequake State Park
Matawan, NJ 07747
201-566-2161

Clinton Wildlife Management Area

On Spruce Run Reservoir near the town of Clinton is the
Clinton Wildlife Management Area, containing 1,082 acres of
woodland, open field, and water. The hardwood forest is
dominated by oak, hickory, and sassafras.

Since the WMA lies along a sprawling reservoir and has an
abundant food supply, the area is an ideal wildlife habitat,
attracting many species of wild creatures. It is also considered
a prime bird-watching site.

White-tailed deer, rabbit, squirrel, grouse, pheasant, Canada
geese; mallard, scaup, ring-necked, black, and canvasback duck
live here.

There is an office that administers both Clinton WMA and
the Angler Access area at Round Valley Reservoir (see description for Round Valley State Recreation Area) and also serves
as regional headquarters for all WMAs in the northern part of
New Jersey. A wildlife biologist is in residence.

The Clinton Tract is one of the most heavily used WMAs in
the Garden State. Most people, however, congregate near the
reservoir's shoreline in the southern reaches of the WMA,
leaving the northern forested portion to hikers, bird-watchers,
and photographers.

Fishing and Boating

Fish include largemouth bass; brook, brown, and rainbow
trout; and northern pike. A 30-pound, 2-ounce northern pike
caught here in 1977 is the state record fish for its species.

There is a boat launching ramp in the Spruce Run State
Recreation Area just east of the WMA. Maximum length of
boat allowed is 18 feet, and motors are limited to a maximum
of 10 horsepower. All watercraft must be operated so as not to
produce a visible wake. Boats are available for rent at the
recreation area.

How to Get There: From Exit 17 on I-78, take NJ 31 north to Van
Syckel Rd. Turn left past Spruce Run State Recreation Area (see
description for Round Valley State Recreation Area) to WMA.
   Open daily, year-round, 5:00 A.M.–9:00 P.M. Free.

For Additional Information:
Clinton Wildlife Management Area
Box 409
Hampton, NJ 08827
201-735-8793

Colliers Mills Wildlife Management Area

Colliers Mills Wildlife Management Area near Cassville contains more than 12,000 acres of woodlands, white cedar swamp, open fields, lakes, and ponds. Some 210 acres are grazing fields, excellent for deer; 250 acres are wetlands. The bulk of the upland area is pitch pine and scrub oak forest.

Great deer herds roam the area, and there are plentiful populations of ring-necked pheasant, quail, red and gray fox, raccoon, opossum, squirrel, and grouse. Mallard, black duck, teal, and wood duck use the ponds, many of them nesting in those areas. All of Colliers Mills is excellent for bird-watching, particularly in the spring and early summer, and again in the autumn.

Hiking

A complex of unimproved roads lead through the area, giving the hiker a look at all the various habitats. Bird-watching and wildlife-watching are excellent, particularly early in the morning.

Fishing and Boating

More than 150 acres of water surface in five major ponds and lakes offer excellent bank fishing for bass, pickerel, and perch. Canoes or rowboats may be used but are not available to rent. No motors.

How to Get There: Located in Ocean County northeast of Fort Dix Military Reservation. From Exit 16 on I-195, go southwest on Co. Rd. 537 to Co. Rd. 539 and turn left. Proceed to Colliers Mills Rd., where a left turn will lead you straight to WMA. Look for signs.

Open daily, year-round, 5:00 A.M.–9:00 P.M. Free.

For Additional Information:
Colliers Mills Wildlife Management Area
c/o Nacote Creek Lab
Star Route 9
Absecon, NJ 08201
609-652-9519

Colonial Park

Colonial Park is a popular recreation area offering a number of facilities on its 467 acres. Along its western boundary, the Delaware and Raritan Canal and the Millstone River flow.

An animal display features wild and farm animals. More than 4,000 individual plants make up a large formal rose garden; and there's a Fragrance and Sensory Garden created especially for the handicapped, with wide paths for wheelchairs. Open playfields and numerous picnic sites are available for both family and group use.

Bicycling and Nature Trails

There's a self-guided nature trail within the park, as well as a 1.4-mile paved bike path and a 1.25-mile Parcourse fitness trail.

Fishing and Boating

Some small ponds stocked with bass and bluegill are provided for fishing.

Paddleboat rentals are available during summer months, and there's a public canoe launching ramp on the canal.

How to Get There: Located west of New Brunswick near Millstone. From Millstone, go east on Co. Rd. 514 (Amwell Rd.) to Mettler's Rd. and turn left into park. Park extends both east and west from Mettler's Rd.

Open daily, year-round, 8:00 A.M.–dusk. Free entrance to park.

For Additional Information:
Public Information Officer
Somerset County Park Commission
P.O. Box 837
Somerville, NJ 08876
201-722-1200

Davis Johnson Park and Gardens

The 5½-acre grounds of Davis Johnson Park at Tenafly are a small botanical garden, featuring a conifer rock garden, a beech collection, a spring bulb garden including more than 100,000 tulips, and a rose garden with more than 1,000 plants. The azalea and iris collections are spectacular. During autumn, there's a Fall Festival of Flowers with a special chrysanthemum display. A sign at the park entrance states which flowers are currently in bloom.

Although the gardens have made this park famous, it is outstanding as a peaceful retreat where you may rest on log benches beneath tall pines.

How to Get There: From Tenafly, take E. Clinton Ave. east to Engle St. Turn right and continue to park at 137 Engle St., at corner of Westervelt Ave.

Open daily, year-round, 10:00 A.M.–sunset. Free.

For Additional Information:
Supervisor of Parks
Borough of Tenafly
107 Grove St.
Tenafly, NJ 07670
201-569-7275

Duke Gardens

At Duke Gardens near Somerville, one enters eleven distinctly different botanical environments from around the world, all under one acre of glass. The well-kept gardens range from the lush foliage of a tropical jungle, the arid beauty of a southwest desert, and the precision of a sculptured French parterre garden, to the serene beauty of a well-arranged Chinese garden complete with grotto. The variety of plants and flowers within the glass-enclosed confines of this facility is astounding.

Surrounding these formal gardens are 8½ acres of natural woodlands and lawns, ablaze with color when spring rhododendrons are blooming.

How to Get There: From Exit 10 on I-287, go west on US 22 to US 206, then south to Duke Gardens. Gardens are located on right side of highway 1¼ miles south of Somerset Shopping Center.

Open daily, noon–4:00 P.M., and on Wednesday and Thursday evenings from 8:30–10:30, October 1 to June 1. Advance reservations required for both individuals and groups. Nominal admission charge; special rates for children under 12. No cameras or high heels allowed. Closed New Year's Day, Thanksgiving, and Christmas, and during summer months.

For Additional Information:
Duke Gardens Foundations, Inc.
Route 206 South
Somerville, NJ 08876
201-722-3700

Eagle Rock Reservation

The 400 wooded acres of Eagle Rock Reservation, southwest of Montclair, are managed primarily for such passive recreation as hiking, bird-watching, and nature study. Unbelievably serene for a park located in such a densely populated area, this natural tract features a network of scenic drives. One park road leads motorists to a lookout area some 600 feet above sea level that affords a superb view of the Manhattan skyline between the Verrazano and George Washington Bridges. Rabbits, squirrels, chipmunks, raccoons, and pheasants frolic throughout the park.

Hiking and Horseback Riding

Foot trails 3½ miles long wind through the woodlands in the southwestern part of the park and around the entire perimeter of the area. There are nearly 7 miles of bridle paths; no rentals.

Winter Sports

Sledders and cross-country skiers use the park's hills when there's a good snow cover.

How to Get There: From I-280, go north on Prospect Ave. (Co. Rd. 577) to Eagle Rock Ave. Turn right and proceed to park entrance road on left, just past a playfield and picnic area.

Open daily, year-round, during daylight hours. Free.

For Additional Information:

Essex County Dept. of Parks, Recreation & Cultural Affairs
115 Clifton Ave.
Newark, NJ 07104
201-482-6400

Center for Environmental Studies
621 Eagle Rock Ave.
Roseland, NJ 07068
201-228-2210

East Hill Preserve

Atop the Palisades on the east edge of Tenafly are 274 acres of natural forest, one of the largest tracts of unspoiled woodland in the metropolitan area. Its acquisition in 1976 by the Borough of Tenafly was the culmination of many years of struggling by local conservationists to keep East Hill in its pristine state.

Today, the preserve is the pride of the community, and the public is invited to explore and enjoy this urban woodland via foot trails. A special feature is Hering Rock, a glacial erratic formed from Newark sandstone.

Adjoining East Hill Preserve at its northwest corner is the Tenafly Nature Center, 50 acres of deciduous woodland encompassing a 2-acre pond, a building with live exhibits, and 4⅓ miles of walking trails.

How to Get There: To reach East Hill Preserve, go east from Tenafly on E. Clinton Ave. to preserve on left side of road. No parking except side of road.

To reach Tenafly Nature Center, go east from Tenafly on E. Clinton Ave. to Engle St. and turn left. Go to Hudson Ave. and turn right. Hudson Ave. ends at nature center's driveway.

East Hill Preserve open daily, year-round, during daylight hours. Free. Tenafly Nature Center open daily, year-round, 9:00 A.M.–5:00 P.M., Monday–Saturday, and 10:00 A.M.–5:00 P.M., Sunday. Since staff is limited, it's best to call to check hours first. No entrance fee charged, but membership required after first visit (the one-year rate is very reasonable). First-time visitors are required to check in. Parking on property.

For Additional Information:

East Hill Preserve
Dept. of Parks, Borough of Tenafly
107 Grove St.
Tenafly, NJ 07670
201-569-7275

Tenafly Nature Center
313 Hudson Ave.
Tenafly, NJ 07670
201-568-6093

Flat Rock Brook Environmental Center

Just four miles from New York City is Flat Rock Brook Center for Environmental Study, 75 acres of unspoiled native woodlands. It's owned by the City of Englewood and operated under the auspices of the Flat Rock Brook Nature Association. Stretching along the Palisades ridge east of Jones Road, the grounds have a wide range of geological features, including some 180-million-year-old volcanic bedrock formations. There are also cascading streams, meadows, quarry cliffs, wetlands, and ponds—all set among one of the last remnants of the magnificent Palisades forest, with huge specimens of native trees and a multitude of wildflowers and shrubs.

The beautiful new interpretive building is solar-heated and houses a library, classrooms, and meeting rooms. Other facilities, in the planning stage at this writing, are children's gardens, a variety of wildlife habitat areas, plant succession demonstration fields, wetlands boardwalks, and a historical orchard.

Special programs and lectures, most by noted authorities in various environmental fields, are scheduled periodically.

Hiking
Self-guided trails wind through the woods, and guided nature hikes are frequently scheduled.

How to Get There: From Englewood, go east on Palisade Ave. (Co. Rd. 505) to Jones Rd.; turn right. At Van Nostrand Ave. turn left and go straight to entrance at end of road.

Grounds open daily year-round, 9:00 A.M.–5:00 P.M. The building is open for scheduled programs or by appointment. Parking space on property. Free; memberships available for nominal fee.

For Additional Information:
Director/Naturalist
Flat Rock Brook Center
P.O. Box 571
Englewood, NJ 07631
201-567-1800

Fort Lee Historic Park

See listing under Palisades Interstate Park, page 15.

Franklin Mineral Museum

If you're interested in rocks and minerals, you'll love the Franklin Mineral Museum in Sussex County. Most of the displays here are from the local area. The Franklin Ore Body was the world's richest in zinc before it was depleted of that mineral in 1952. However, the unrefined ore still contains 190 other minerals, 28 of them found nowhere else in the world.

Cases of rocks are identified by a guide, who then takes you into an exhibit room where an ultraviolet light transforms the drab gray of the rocks into spectacular reds and greens.

You may also go to the dumping grounds of the old Franklin Mine to try some prospecting of your own. When the mine was active, workers would toss aside piles of rocks that didn't contain enough zinc or iron to make them profitable. The pile of discards is now bounty for visitors, who are allowed to pick what they want from it. Adults are permitted to take away 25 pounds of rock each; children, 10 pounds. You should bring your own tools—a heavy hammer and chisel work well—and bags or cartons. Safety goggles are a wise precaution.

Your guide will have an ultraviolet light at the dump that you may use to examine your finds.

How to Get There: From Franklin, go north on Main St. to Evans St. and turn right. The museum and dump are located at 6B Evans St.

Open 9:00 A.M.–4:30 P.M., Tuesday–Saturday, and 12:30–4:30 P.M. Sunday, April 1 through November 30; closed Mondays, Easter, and Thanksgiving. Separate admission charge (nominal) for museum and dump; special rates for children and students.

For Additional Information:
Franklin Mineral Museum
6B Evans St.
Franklin, NJ 07416
201-827-3481 or 201-875-6417

The Frelinghuysen Arboretum

Near Morristown is the Frelinghuysen Arboretum, one of the most impressive and well-maintained natural attractions in the state. Formerly a private estate, it was turned over to the Morris County Park Commission in 1969. Its 127 acres sprawl over an undulating terrain of swamp, mature forest, and open field.

Located on the brink of the Wisconsin glacier terminal moraine, the grounds provide varied ecological conditions that support a wide range of native and exotic plants. The arboretum consists of two tracts divided by East Hanover Avenue. The tract in Morris Township includes the great Frelinghuysen family mansion, as well as natural and formal gardens; the other tract, in Hanover Township, serves as a demonstration area for public education. Its rich alluvial soils embrace the banks of the Whippany River.

The grounds surrounding the mansion create a living museum that includes conifers, flowering cherries, magnolias, sweet gums, a lilac garden, rhododendrons, dwarf conifers, pines, spruces, larches, firs, redwoods, tulip poplars, spicebushes, glens of ferns, a skunk cabbage swamp, willows, bald cypresses, and a tract of native woodland. Many of the trees and plants are labeled.

The entire arboretum is also a fine place to look for birds.

The Administration Building (the Frelinghuysen mansion) houses a superb library, open to the public, which includes many volumes on botanical subjects spanning nearly five centuries. It also serves as headquarters for the Morris County Park Commission.

Nature Trails

An excellent trail system totaling about 4 miles takes you through some of the native woodland and along the edge of the swamp. Some trails climb steep hillsides. A Braille Nature Trail only one-sixth-mile long is located in a small wooded hollow east of the main lawn.

How to Get There: From Morristown, take Morris Ave. (Co. Rd. 510) east to a fork in the road and bear left onto Whippany Rd. (Co. Rd. 511). Proceed to E. Hanover Ave. (second traffic light) and turn left. Arboretum entrance is on left, directly across from Morris County Free Library.

Open daily, 9:00 A.M.–5:00 P.M., mid-March to early December; Saturday and Sunday only, 9:00 A.M.–5:00 P.M., rest of year; closed some holidays. Free. Parking on grounds.

For Additional Information:
Superintendent
The Frelinghuysen Arboretum
53 E. Hanover Ave.
P.O. Box 1295R
Morristown, NJ 07960
201-285-6166

Garret Mountain Reservation

Garret Mountain dominates the skyline of Paterson, New Jersey. Atop the mountain, near Lambert Castle, which houses both the Passaic County Park Commission and the Historical Society Museum, an observation tower juts into the sky. From the tower and other spots in the 570-acre woodland park, you get an outstanding view of the Manhattan skyline and the city of Paterson. On clear days, the Great Falls of the Passaic River in Paterson (described elsewhere) create a rainbow, a stunning sight when seen from the mountaintop.

Archaeologists believe Garret Mountain to have been a religious center and perhaps a burial ground for Lenni-Lenape Indians.

Several trails lead through the hilly, wooded terrain.

Winter Sports

During the winter, Barbour Pond is filled with ice skaters, and children of all ages ride their sleds down the park's many hills.

How to Get There: From Exit 57 (Main St. exit) on I-80, go south on Co. Rd. 509 to Valley Rd and turn right. At Mountain Park Rd. turn right again. Proceed to top of hill; a small Garret Mountain Reservation sign and a park road are on the right.

Open daily, year-round, 8:00 A.M.–dusk. Free.

For Additional Information:

Passaic County Park Commission
Lambert Castle
5 Valley Rd.
Paterson, NJ 07503
201-742-6373

Great Adventure Safari

Although Great Adventure Safari is a commercial enterprise (part of the Six Flags Amusement Parks chain), it has lots to offer the nature lover. The wild animals here are not caged; instead, motorists drive their own automobiles over 6 miles of roads through animal habitats. At times, cars must stop for a pride of lions ambling across the road, or patiently wait while curious animals walk up to car windows and peer in. Acclaimed as the world's largest attraction of its kind outside of Africa, the safari has more than 2,000 wild and exotic animals, many of them rare and endangered, roaming some 450 acres. Included are kangaroos, lions, leopards, bears, giraffes, camels, elk, American bison, llamas, white-tailed deer, antelope, and the largest group of Siberian tigers in the world.

Once at the park, tune in your car radio to the Great Safari station and guided tour. The best time to view the animals is early or late in the day, when they're most active.

How to Get There: Located northwest of Lakewood in Ocean County. From Exit 16 of I-195, take Co. Rd. 537 southwest to Great Adventure on left side of road. There are many signs to follow. *By bus*: Buses from Port Authority Terminal in Manhattan go to gate.

Safari is open daily, 9:00 A.M.– 5:00 P.M., late April to early September; open other days, on irregular basis, from early April to late October (advertised in area newspapers). Amusement park is open on same days, but at different hours. Visitors may purchase ticket for safari only, or buy combination ticket for both safari and amusement park at special rate; children 3 and under, free.

For Additional Information:

Public Relations Department
Six Flags Great Adventure
Box 120
Jackson, NJ 08527

201-928-2000
212-472-2000 (New York)
516-829-6966 (Long Island)
201-846-1220 (North Jersey)
609-662-8067 (South Jersey)
215-546-3884 (Pennsylvania)

Great Falls of the Passaic

At the unlikely place of Paterson, near the heart of town, is one of the most spectacular natural attractions of the New York metropolitan area. Known as the Great Falls, it's the second largest waterfall east of the Mississippi. Some 190 million years ago, an earthquake opened up a chasm here, and today the waters of the Passaic River rush through in a powerful torrent. It is a soothing, awesome spectacle to behold, with soft mists rising from the rocky crevices to evaporate in the air around the tall buildings nearby.

The falls also are known as a place of rainbows. They appear regularly, changing here and there as the mists rise in clouds or as the sun shifts in the sky. The rising rock cliffs, the stupendous gorge, the beauty of this place is in many ways as striking as Niagara. It has been considered so through the ages. By the turn of the eighteenth century, knowledge of the falls became widespread, attracting visitors from as far away as Europe.

President Gerald Ford came here in 1976 to dedicate 119 acres surrounding the falls, where an old industrial community has been restored, as a National Historic Landmark. Since 1969, the falls themselves have been a National Natural Landmark.

The ideal time to see the falls is during spring when there are heavy runoffs from rains upstream, but they're magnificent at any time of year. Sometimes, during extremely cold winters, the falls freeze into a superb drapery of ice. The falls are nearly 80 feet tall and 280 feet wide, but they appear taller and narrower because of the closeness of the rock cliffs on either side of the gorge into which they fall.

A footbridge leads across the top of the falls from one part of the park to another. In the Valley of the Rocks, which borders the river's west bank, cliffs reach upward 130 feet; the area is accessible by foot. Numerous Japanese cherry trees turn the landscape into a showplace of blossoms in the spring. A small museum/tour office is located near one end of the footbridge; photographs and exhibits related to the falls may be seen here. Haines Overlook Park, adjacent to the tour office, offers perhaps the best overall view of the falls; it also has a grassy lawn and free parking.

How to Get There: From I-80, take Exit 57 (Main St. exit) to light at end of ramp and turn left onto Main St. Go to Grand St. and turn left. Continue for four blocks to Spruce St., then turn right and go three blocks to McBride Ave. Extension and turn right again. Haines Overlook Park is immediately on left; turn into parking lot. Tour office and footbridge over falls are also on McBride; walk back the way you came.

Park open daily, 7:00 A.M.–11:00 P.M., year-round. Tour office/museum open daily, Monday–Friday, 9:00 A.M.–4:30 P.M., year-round, and when tours are scheduled. Guided walking tours of the Historic District include Great Falls; advance reservations required. No charge, but donations accepted.

For Additional Information:

Great Falls Park
176 Maple St.
Paterson, NJ 07522
201-881-3848 or 201-790-3653

Great Swamp National Wildlife Refuge

Less than an hour's drive from Manhattan is one of the finest wild retreats of the eastern United States—the Great Swamp of New Jersey. The Great Swamp is a place primeval where white-tailed deer roam, Canada geese raise their young, owls penetrate the darkness, and red-shouldered hawks soar in the skies by day. But it is also a botanical paradise where you can wonder on a boardwalk through lush jungle growth.

Comprised of some 7,500 acres, four-fifths of which are included in the Great Swamp National Wildlife Refuge under the management of the U.S. Fish & Wildlife Service, the swamp is an intricate network of streams and rivers, ponds and lakes, grassy marshes and wooded wetlands. About two-thirds of the refuge has been designated wilderness. Green and purple orchids grow among ancient oaks, and each June mountain laurel adorns the swamp with an explosion of blooms.

Along the low banks of the brooks are wetlands which experience recurrent flooding. And in other areas where the elevation is as much as 2 feet higher, handsome hickories, beeches, maples, oaks, and elms grow. The Wisconsin glacier created a transition community of plants both southern and northern. Wild azalea, laurel, pepperbush, and rhododendron grow within a stone's throw of marsh marigold, spatterdock, lizard's tail, and skunk cabbage.

Among the creatures living here are the ubiquitous white-tailed deer and Canada geese, plus mink, striped skunk, red and gray fox, muskrat, beaver, red and gray squirrel, flying

Great Falls of the Passaic *Bill Thomas*

squirrel, opossum, and cottontail rabbit. There are good numbers of colorful wood duck, dove, great blue heron, green heron, and various types of teal. Osprey and peregrine falcon are occasional spring and fall visitors. In the upland parts of the refuge, ruffed grouse are fairly common. Nearly 200 species of birds inhabit the swamp, as well as about 1,000 varieties of plant life.

The refuge is open for public use year-round, but the months of April and May are best for visiting. Wildlife activity is greatest at that time, the insect problem has not yet become severe, and the swamp is verdant with lush spring growth. October, November, and the winter months are also good times to visit. Mosquitoes abound during the months of June, July, and August, so go well prepared, or wait until another season to enjoy the swamp.

Photojournalist Bill Thomas conducts a two-day nature photography seminar in the Great Swamp the last weekend in September. It combines nature study in the field with instructions on the art of photography and how to sell your photos.

Hiking

Although there are roads leading through the swamp, the best way to experience it is on foot. Thousands of acres are included in the wilderness area where no vehicles are permitted. There is a good system of trails, both in the wilderness area and in the management area of the refuge. Boardwalks are provided in some portions of the managed area where you may hike without getting your feet wet. The Wildlife Observation Center off Long Hill Road offers more than a mile of boardwalk, interpretive displays, and an elevated blind from which to observe wildlife activity.

Canoeing

An ideal way to see the swamp is by canoe. Permits can be obtained from Lord Stirling Park (a Somerset County Park described elsewhere) to canoe a 2-mile section of Great Brook and the Passaic River. Other areas are closed to canoeing to protect wildlife habitats. No rentals.

How to Get There: Located south of Morristown, east of Basking Ridge. From Exit 26 to I-287 (Basking Ridge exit), go south on N. Maple Ave. to Madisonville Rd. and turn left. (Along the way, Madisonville Rd. becomes Lees Hill Rd.) At Pleasant Plains Rd., turn right and drive through swamp. Refuge headquarters are on left side of road; you may pick up descriptive literature and maps of swamp here.

Swamp open daily, year-round, during daylight hours. Refuge headquarters open daily, 8:00 A.M.–4:30 P.M., Monday–Friday, year-round. Refuge personnel are also on duty at the Wildlife Observation Center on Long Hill Rd. most weekends.

For Additional Information:

Refuge Manager
Great Swamp National Wildlife
Refuge
RD 1, Box 148
Basking Ridge, NJ 07920
201-647-1222

Bill Thomas
Nature Photojournalism Seminar
Rt. 4, Box 387
Nashville, IN 47448
812-988-7865

Great Swamp Outdoor Education Center

On the northeastern edge of New Jersey's Great Swamp is the Great Swamp Outdoor Education Center. Operated by the Morris County Park Commission, it is one of the best places in the northeastern United States to study a swamp.

Situated on 40 acres of land, the center also makes use of the adjoining Great Swamp National Wildlife Refuge. The public may participate in guided trail walks, attend films and lectures, or simply explore a stunning natural world inhabited by myriads of wildlife and enhanced by the lush array of flora.

For detailed information about the swamp itself, see Great Swamp National Wildlife Refuge (described elsewhere).

Nature Trail

A self-guided loop trail, approximately one mile long, winds through the area; an elevated boardwalk permits you to walk through the swamp without getting your feet wet. A free guidebook may be picked up at the headquarters building.

How to Get There: Located southeast of Morristown. From Morristown, take NJ 24 east. Turn right at Co. Rd. 647 (Green Village Rd. when you turn, and later Southern Blvd.). Center is located at 247 Southern Blvd. on right side of road.

Open Monday–Saturday, 9:00 A.M.–4:30 P.M., and Sunday, 1:00–5:00 P.M., except for July and August when it's closed. Free.

For Additional Information:

Naturalist
Great Swamp Outdoor Education Center
Morris County Park Commission
247 Southern Blvd.
Chatham, NJ 07928
201-635-6629

Greenbrook Sanctuary

Located atop New Jersey's magnificent Palisades are 165 acres of wild woodlands known as Greenbrook Sanctuary. Actually a part of Palisades Interstate Park, the sanctuary is administered as a separate unit by the nonprofit Palisades

Nature Association. Open to the public on a membership basis only, it is a very special place, worth looking into. At few other places in the urban area will you find greater solitude in wilderness surroundings.

The sanctuary, established in 1947, extends across the Alpine-Tenafly borough line and is bordered on the east by the Palisades cliffs and on the west by the Palisades Interstate Parkway. The wild, rugged terrain provides an excellent habitat for wildlife. Raccoon, rabbit, southern flying squirrel, red squirrel, fox, opossum, and more than 230 species of birds have been spotted in the area. In the most secluded areas of a nearly primeval forest, many trees rise to 120 feet, and some exceed 200 years of age. Wildflowers dominate the understory during spring, and at least 20 species of fern are found on the forest floor.

A 5-acre pond with an adjoining bog, some swampy areas, and several brooks that flow through the property increase the great diversity of the sanctuary. Greenbrook Falls, tumbling some 250 feet down ancient cliffs into the Hudson River, creates a spectacular setting above the Hudson River. A view of the waterfall, and of the Palisades and Highlands to the north, is possible from several promontories that look down 350 feet to the river.

In spring, a good place to spend your time is at the pond, bog, and swamps, which are filled with egg masses of spotted salamanders. On spring evenings, toads, pickerel frogs, bullfrogs, and spring peepers chant their mating songs. Copperhead snakes, a few musk turtles, and skink lizards live here and are seen on rare occasions. During the fall, thousands of hawks, even at times an eagle, soar along the cliffs.

Hiking

A number of well-kept trails wind for 6½ miles through and around major habitats such as the pond, bog, and swamp, as well as along the Palisades cliff edges.

How to Get There: From western end of George Washington Bridge in Fort Lee, take US 9W north. Sanctuary entrance is on right side of highway 4.7 miles north of bridge.

Open daily, year-round, during daylight hours. Open to members only. Annual memberships available for individuals and families (at this writing, $12.50 for individuals, $17.50 for families). Guests of members may participate in certain activities and programs.

For Additional Information:
Palisades Nature Association
Box 155
Alpine, NJ 07620
201-768-1360 or 201-569-5698

Greenwood Lake State Forest

See listing under Ringwood State Park, page 105.

Hacklebarney State Park

Approximately 3 miles southwest of Chester, along the banks of the Black River in a wild and lovely gorge, is Hacklebarney State Park. Covering nearly 600 acres of picturesque and largely undeveloped countryside, Hacklebarney is often described as the most beautiful park in the state system. Certainly it is one of the most serene and least crowded. A designated wildlife area, the park is an ideal place for nature study. Indian Mill, a pothole in the Black River, is a noteworthy natural feature.

This is a place to be rather than to do. Facilities are limited, and there are no roads through the park. Be prepared to walk some distance even to a picnic site. Some playground equipment is provided, and a refreshment stand near the park office is open during the summer.

Just north of Hacklebarney, and administered by the same park office, is the state-owned Lamington River Natural Area. Check with the park superintendent for additional information.

Hiking

A network of trails has made this park a favorite with hikers. The lovely wooded hills rise from an elevation of 400 feet along the lower reaches of the Black River as it traverses the park to a peak elevation of 804 feet, and even walking to the choicest picnic spots can be arduous. The topography is rugged; visitors are advised to wear comfortable walking shoes.

Fishing

The Black River, which borders the park for one mile, is a noted trout stream. Fishing is also permitted in two tributary streams, Rinehart and Trout Brooks.

How to Get There: From Chester, take NJ 24 west across the Black River and turn left onto State Park Rd. (it's located between river and Chester Township Municipal Building). Follow State Park Rd. to Hacklebarney Rd. and turn right. Park entrance is on left side of road.

Open daily, year-round, during daylight hours. Free entrance; nominal fee for picnic tables.

For Additional Information:

Superintendent
Hacklebarney State Park
R.R. 2
Long Valley, NJ 07853
201-879-5677

Harmony Ridge Farm and Campground

The Harmony Ridge Campground lies near Branchville, in the Kittatinny Mountains of northwestern New Jersey, and offers pleasant camping, along with an education in the ways of country and farm life.

Besides camping, you can canoe, fish, swim, cross-country ski, ice skate, snowshoe, or go sledding at this 160-acre farm. Children will enjoy petting the farm animals.

Promoted as a step in the back-to-nature movement, the campground is open year-round.

How to Get There: From Branchville, go north on Mattison Ave. Look for campground on left side of road.

For Additional Information:
Harmony Ridge Farm & Campground
RD 1, Box 444
Branchville, NJ 07826
201-948-4941

Hartshorn Arboretum

The Cora Hartshorn Arboretum in Short Hills is located on some 16 acres of wilderness. Stewart Hartshorn willed it so in 1923, when he gave the land to his daughter, Cora, stating that it must be a place where wild things can grow without harm, and where people can come to enjoy them. Cora kept it that way until her death in 1958, when she willed the property to Millburn Township. The stone house on the property is now a museum and nature center. More than 80 species of trees and 175 species of shrubs are found here, in addition to more than 75 species of native fern and a variety of native orchids. New Jersey plants predominate in this arboretum, making it an excellent place to study closely native botanical growth.

Museum exhibits include an active beehive, mounted specimens of native birds and animals, a weather station, and a reference library.

Nature Trails
Roughly 3 miles of trails curve and climb through the arboretum's woodlands, and many trees, shrubs, and plants alongside them are labeled. Guided nature walks available by reservation for groups.

How to Get There: Located west of Millburn. From Millburn, take Old Short Hills Rd. north to Hobart Ave. and turn left. Follow Hobart Ave. to Forest Dr. and turn left. Arboretum is at 324 Forest Dr. South, on left side of road.

Grounds open daily, year-round, during daylight hours. Museum/nature center open Tuesday through Thursday, 2:45–4:45 P.M. and

Saturday, 9:30–11:30 A.M. Some special Sunday hours during certain blooming seasons. Free.

For Additional Information:
Hartshorn Arboretum
324 Forest Dr. South
Short Hills, NJ 07078
201-376-3587

Herrontown Woods Arboretum

Just northeast of Princeton is Herrontown Woods, 147 acres of upland forest preserved in its natural state and administered by the Mercer County Park Commission.

Visitors are free to explore, hike, and bird-watch on their own or request a guided tour with the park commission naturalist. Descriptive literature is available through the county parks office.

A trip here could easily be combined with a visit to the nearby Princeton University campus (described elsewhere).

Hiking
Three miles of hiking trails wind among the hills and along two small streams.

How to Get There: From Princeton, go east on NJ 27 (Nassau St.), through Princeton University campus, to Snowden Rd. Turn left and continue to Herrontown Rd.; another left leads to Herrontown Woods, which borders the road for about half a mile on the left.

Open daily, year-round, during daylight hours. Free.

For Additional Information:
Naturalist
Mercer County Park Commission
640 S. Broad St.
Trenton, NJ 08611
609-989-6532

High Point State Park

Atop the crest of the Kittatinny Mountains, 1,800 feet above sea level, stands a 220-foot-tall obelisk. From this landmark monument, you can see Pennsylvania to the west, the Catskill Mountains of New York to the north, and New Jersey's rugged Sussex County to the south and east. This is the pinnacle of High Point State Park, a wild and beautiful area of nearly 13,000 acres in northwestern New Jersey that encompasses the highest point in the state. This park, along with Stokes State Forest which adjoins it to the south (described elsewhere), offers one of the finest wilderness experiences in the state.

The most noteworthy natural feature of the park is the Dryden Kuser Natural Area, a white cedar swamp noted for the unusual mix of its plant community. Located at an elevation of 1,500 feet, it covers more than 200 acres. Its virgin woodland supports a variety of conifers, including hemlocks, white pine, black spruce, and a fine stand of mature southern white cedar.

Most of the park is undeveloped woodland, and there are scenic drives throughout. The park is beautiful any time of the year, but it's magnificent in the spring when the laurel is in bloom and during fall color.

Hiking

Hikers may follow a portion of the Appalachian Trail (described elsewhere), as it traverses the length of the park, or several shorter park trails, including one that skirts the Dryden Kuser Natural Area. A trail guide is available upon request at the park office.

Fishing and Boating

There are three lakes within the park, and fishing and boating are permitted. Visitors must bring their own boats or canoes; any motors used must be electric.

Camping

A quiet campground surrounding Sawmill Lake provides around fifty sites for tents only; it's open March 1 to November 1. Two remote cabins along the shore of Steenykill Lake, open May 15 through October 15, may be rented, or visitors may enjoy overnight accommodations at the park's lodge and its annex near Lake Marcia.

Winter Sports

Cross-country skiers and snowshoers come during the winter to enjoy both sport and solitude.

How to Get There: From Franklin, take NJ 23 northwest; it passes through the northern part of the park; route is well marked.

Open daily, year-round, during daylight hours, except when weather conditions prevent access. Nominal entrance fee part of year.

For Additional Information:

Superintendent
High Point State Park
R.R. 4, Box 287
Sussex, NJ 07461
201-875-4800

Holmdel Park

Holmdel Park in Monmouth County is a combination natural area and farm. Covering some 330 acres, the park offers scenic views, recreation and conservation activities, and protection for a variety of plant and animal communities. The major portion of the park is heavily forested with mature stands of American beech and a variety of native oaks.

The Holmdel Arboretum, established in 1963, has flowering crabapples, rhododendrons, and a multitude of specimen plantings.

Longstreet Farm, a restored nineteenth-century working farm, lets you experience the sights and sounds of a living farm. You may help with seasonal activities at the farm, such as plowing, harvesting, threshing, blacksmithing, sheepshearing, and ice cutting as they were done nearly a century ago.

Hiking

Some 7 miles of trails provide access to many diverse areas of interest within the park. All trails designed to bring you back to your starting point. Naturalists are available upon request during summer months; guided tours may be arranged.

Fishing

Two fishing ponds are located in the park; largemouth bass, bluegill, and catfish are the principal species taken.

Winter Sports

Lighted sledding slope, and ice skating on fishing ponds.

How to Get There: Located northwest of Red Bank. From Exit 114 on Garden State Pkwy., take Red Hill Rd. southwest to Crawfords Corner–Everett Rd. and turn right. At Longstreet Rd. turn left. Park entrance is on right side of road.

Grounds open daily, year-round, 8:00 A.M.–sunset. Farm open daily, year-round, 9:00 A.M.–5:00 P.M., Memorial Day through Labor Day, and 10:00 A.M.–4:00 P.M., rest of year.

For Additional Information:
Monmouth County Park System
P.O. Box 326
Newman Springs Rd.
Lincroft, NJ 07738
201-842-4000

Hutcheson Forest

One of the finest primeval woodlands in the New York area is the William L. Hutcheson Forest, historically known as Mettler's Woods. Owned by Rutgers University, the 150-acre tract west of New Brunswick is not generally open to the public, but guided tours are offered on a limited basis at various times of the year.

Predominantly composed of oak, hickory, and beech, Hutcheson Forest contains some trees that date back to 1627. The dense woods create a great canopy that keeps out much of the sunlight. Other than various research projects underway there by students and professors at Rutgers, the forest shows little evidence of disturbance by man.

The oaks are the patriarchs of the forest, many reaching heights of nearly 100 feet. An understory made up largely of dogwood trees extends 35 to 40 feet upward. Under the dogwoods are the lesser shrubs and, in places, wet boggy areas where swamp cabbage and ferns grow.

Tours are generally limited to about ten persons and are usually conducted once or twice a month on Sunday afternoons, free of charge, by members of the Rutgers staff. Guided tours can be arranged on other days of the week for a small fee. The university requests that you write rather than phone for a descriptive brochure, schedule, and reservations.

How to Get There: Located a few miles west of New Brunswick in Somerset County. Since the university wishes to protect and preserve the area, specific directions will be given when you inquire about the tours.

For Additional Information:

Director, Dept. of Botany
College of Arts & Sciences
Rutgers University
New Brunswick, NJ 08903

Island Beach State Park

One of New Jersey's most beautiful stretches of seashore dunes is narrow, 10-mile-long Island Beach. Although it's a few miles beyond our 50-mile radius, it's a very special place for nature lovers. The 3,000-acre park is divided into three parts; the upper and lower portions are natural areas, while the middle section is used for recreation.

Groves of beach plum, sand-loving plants like Pine Barrens golden heather and arenaria, and other flora provide a clue to the unusual vegetation that once covered most of the beaches of the New Jersey coast.

Great breakers roll in from the Atlantic Ocean along the island's eastern edge, constantly reshaping the beach, while the western shore on Barnegat Bay is thickly vegetated and interspersed with patches of salt marsh. Birds of nearly every species common to eastern North America use the park as a resting area during migration periods, while songbirds summer amid the brier thickets.

Dunes tower over this barrier beach for almost the entire coastline of the park, and to preserve them visitors must keep off.

Nature Trails

Both guided and self-guided tours are available. Walks through the botanical preserve and wildlife sanctuary make you aware of the unique status of the area, its plant and animal relationships, and the botanical communities peculiar to a barrier beach. Near the visitor's center, a self-guided tour describes the geological origins of the island. During summer, daily naturalist-guided tours are conducted in the afternoon. Special tours may be arranged year-round by prior notice.

Swimming

Two swimming beaches on the ocean offer lifeguard protection, parking areas, bathhouses, and concession stands.

How to Get There: Located near town of Toms River. From Exit 82 on Garden State Pkwy., go east on NJ 37, across Barnegat Bay, to NJ 35; turn right there and proceed to park entrance.

Shuttle Bus Service: Leave Pkwy. at Exit 81 and go left (east) on Water St., following "Island Beach Shuttle" signs to parking lot on right (south) side of Water St. Since access to park is limited by available parking spaces, the state has initiated this service during heavy-use periods; it runs on weekends from late June through early September, July 4, and Labor Day, with a bus leaving Toms River every thirty minutes from 9:00 A.M.–6:00 P.M. Free parking adjacent to shuttle bus stop. Very nominal fee includes admission to park.

Park open daily, year-round, 8:00 A.M.–sunset. Nominal admission fee charged daily throughout year.

For Additional Information:
Superintendent
Island Beach State Park
Seaside Park, NJ 08752
201-793-0506

Jenny Jump State Forest

Just north of the Pequest River at Buttzville, along the Jenny Jump Mountains, lies this forest of more than 1,000 acres. There are several detached parcels of forest land, with only one tract accessible by road for public use.

Jenny Jump Forest is noted primarily for its magnificent views from pinnacles of more than 1,100 feet. Most of the forest is relatively undisturbed.

Hiking and Nature Trails

Hikers will find several woodland trails. The half-mile Notch Vista Trail leads through a nature area that contains at least twenty-three kinds of trees, in addition to several types of woody shrubs and many flowering plants in season. Ferns, mosses, and lichens are abundant, and the outcroppings of bedrock and glacier-tumbled boulders are of geological interest. A trail guide for this area is available from the forest office.

Camping

A small campground provides twenty tent and trailer sites, but there are no hookups. Near the forest headquarters are two camp shelters that may be rented during the same season the campground is open (April 1 through October 31) for a minimum stay of two nights. Fully-enclosed, weather-tight buildings, the shelters have wood stoves for heating, outdoor fireplaces for cooking, and bunk accommodations for four persons; advance reservations are required.

Winter Sports

Cross-country skiing, sledding, and snowshoeing are permitted.

How to Get There: From Exit 12 on I-80, take Co. Rd. 521 south to its juncture with Co. Rd. 519 at Hope. Turn left and go about 4 miles to third road on right. Turn right and continue straight to forest; look for signs.

   Open daily, year-round, during daylight hours. Free.

For Additional Information:

Supervisor
Jenny Jump State Forest
Hope, NJ 07844
201-459-4366

Lewis Morris Park

The Lewis Morris Park, named for the first governor of New Jersey, was the first park established in the Morris County system. At 751 acres, it's also one of the largest. A composite of mixed hardwood forest, open meadow, rolling hills, lake, stream, and pond, it's a great place for bird-watching and wildlife observation.

   The park is adjacent to the Jockey Hollow Natural Area of the Morristown National Historical Park (described elsewhere). Flora and fauna in both parks are similar.

Hiking

A complex of hiking trails over moderately rugged terrain is well maintained and available for use year-round. Some lead into the adjacent Morristown National Historical Park and join an extensive trail system there.

Swimming

There's a swimming beach with bathhouse on Sunrise Lake.

Boating and Fishing

Boat rentals are available at Sunrise Lake, and fishing is permitted.

Winter Sports

When the snow cover is deep enough, the park is used by cross-country skiers, sledders, and snowshoers.

How to Get There: From Morristown, go west on NJ 24 to park entrance on left side of road. Park is also accessible from Morristown National Historical Park, which adjoins it to the south.

Open daily, year-round, during daylight hours. Free.

For Additional Information:

Morris County Park Commission
53 E. Hanover Ave.
P.O. Box 1295R
Morristown, NJ 07960
201-285-6166

Liberty State Park

Across the Hudson from lower Manhattan, where the mighty river meets the sprawling bay, lies Liberty State Park, with one of the finest views of the Manhattan skyline. Directly across the way, on tiny Liberty Island, is the Statue of Liberty.

While much of the state park's 850 acres are designed for cultural activities, relaxation, and waterfront views (benches around the waterfront are crowded on weekends), there are also marshes where wild ducks, rails, and other wetlands birds nest. In autumn, thousands of migrating waterfowl, including half a dozen species of ducks, Canada geese, and brant, rest here on their route south.

Among other birds frequently spotted during spring and summer are great blue herons, common egrets, snowy egrets, glossy ibis, black skimmers, least terns, and black ducks. Raccoons, foxes, cottontail rabbits, and various voles and field mice are residents. Although no entry is permitted into the marshlands, you have an excellent view of them from the visitor's center and at observation points along the waterfront.

During warm weather months, ferryboats carry passengers from the state park to Liberty and Ellis Islands (see Battery Park entry in Part 4 for brief descriptions).

How to Get There: Located in Jersey City. From Exit 14B on NJ Turnpike Extension, follow signs and head east to park entrance.

Park open 8:00 A.M.–10:00 P.M. daily, May through October; 8:00 A.M.–8:00 P.M., rest of year.

For Additional Information:
Liberty State Park
Wolf Drive
Jersey City, NJ 07304
201-435-0736

Loantaka Brook Reservation

Loantaka Brook Reservation is a linear park extending along the corridor of the brook for which it is named. It includes some 560 acres in portions of three Morris County townships and encompasses five separate areas.

The brook is a refreshing, tree-lined stream that meanders through the entire park. One part of the park, known as the Helen Hartley Jenkins Woods, is a natural woodland that has been called one of the finest untouched forests in the nation by several noted ecologists. Only hiking, bicycling, and horseback riding are permitted in this part of the park.

Although it has its own staff, the Great Swamp Outdoor Education Center (described elsewhere) is administered as a unit of this reservation.

The Seaton Hackney Stables, another area, has horseback riding, rentals, and instruction.

Loantaka Brook Recreation Area and Loantaka Brook Park, the remaining two areas, contain such recreation facilities as picnic areas and game fields.

The entire reservation is popular particularly on summer weekends and holidays, with the more developed areas receiving the heaviest use. Nevertheless, the parks are clean and well maintained.

Hiking, Bicycling, and Horseback Riding

Several miles of hiking trails wind through the reservation. Horseback riders (rentals available) and bicyclers each have trails designated for them.

Winter Sports

Cross-country skiers may use the trails when weather conditions permit.

How to Get There: From Morristown, go south on South St. to Seaton Hackney Stables on left. There's a parking lot near stables, also on left side of road. Just beyond stables and oval track is another parking area on left. The remaining areas of the park extend southeast from here along banks of Loantaka Brook.

Grounds open daily, year-round, during daylight hours. Free admission.

For Additional Information:
Morris County Park Commission
53 E. Hanover Ave.
P.O. Box 1295R
Morristown, NJ 07960
201-285-6166

Lockwood Gorge
Wildlife Management Area

The scenic Ken Lockwood Gorge Wildlife Management Area lies along the South Branch of the Raritan River. Part of it has been designated a state natural area because of its wild beauty. Bordering some 2½ miles of the river, the area contains about 260 acres of mixed hardwood forest of oak, beech, tulip poplar, sassafras, and dogwood, with some open fields.

The tract supports considerable populations of deer, cotton-tail rabbit, grouse, and squirrel, as well as raccoon and opossum. Although there are no established hiking trails, this is a beautiful area in which to roam free through the woods.

How to Get There: Located east of Voorhees State Park (described elsewhere) near High Bridge. From High Bridge, go north on Co. Rd. 513 to Hoffmans Crossing Rd. and turn right. Cross Raritan River and proceed to Raritan River Rd. and turn right again. This road runs through WMA.

Open daily, year-round, 5:00 A.M.–9:00 P.M. Free.

For Additional Information:
Lockwood Gorge Wildlife Management Area
c/o Clinton Wildlife Management Area
Box 409
Hampton, NJ 08827
201-735-8793

Lord Stirling Park

In the wetlands of the Great Swamp's western edge is Lord Stirling Park, a Somerset County environmental and conservation facility. Containing nearly 2,500 acres, the park supports five major plant communities and a striking amount of wildlife. Within its boundaries is the La Plus Grande Marsh, where buttonbush, swamp rose, cattails, rushes, and sedges form a veritable green curtain during the summer months. Other parts include Passaic River bottomlands, hardwood forest with pin oak, red maple, and ash, and some abandoned farm fields in various stages of transition back to nature. Pockets of woodlands on higher and drier land are made up of shagbark hickory, black birch, beech, and white oak.

A great variety of wildlife occupies the park lands, but since the majority are nocturnal feeders, they are seldom seen. White-tailed deer are sometimes spotted, however, as well as fox, squirrel, cottontail rabbit, turtles, snakes of half a dozen or more types, Canada geese and other waterfowl, and hundreds of species of songbirds. Sometimes such wading birds as the green heron, great blue heron, and common egret are found here. The shores of two ponds, Branta and Esox, are riddled with the burrowings of muskrat. During spring, the pickerel migrate up the Passaic River and into the shallow swamp waters to lay their eggs.

At the center of the park is the Somerset County Environmental Education Center, the first such center in the nation to be solar-heated and solar-cooled, and for that reason a visitor attraction too. The park is unique in many ways, for few other places have its diversity. It's an ideal place to study wetlands and their ecological value. Marshes, swamps, bogs, river, intermittent streams, springs, floodplain, natural and man-made ponds—all are represented here and are easily accessible via an extensive trail system.

Two buildings at the education center are of particular interest. One houses insects at various stages of development; the other is used for orphaned or injured wildlife brought to the park by conservation officers or veterinarians.

Hiking

A complex of nearly 9 miles of 6-foot-wide trails forms a network through the park. Included is an 8,000-foot-long boardwalk that permits hikers to view the swamp or marsh without getting their feet wet. Along the trails are two observation blinds, one on the western side of Branta Pond, the other on the southern edge of the Lily Pad Pond. Two observation towers give an overview of the Great Swamp basin, of which the park is a part. The taller of the two towers allows visitors to view wildlife in the Great Swamp National Wildlife Refuge (described elsewhere), which adjoins the park.

Permits, either oral or written, are required for hiking on the trails, and groups of eight or more must make advance reservations. Permits are free.

Canoeing

Permits can be obtained to canoe a 2-mile section of Great Brook and the Passaic River. Other areas are closed to canoeing to protect wildlife habitats.

How to Get There: Located southeast of Basking Ridge. From Basking Ridge, go south on S. Maple Ave. to Lord Stirling Rd. at Somerset Hills Airport and turn left. Proceed one mile to park entrance on left. Limited parking.

Trails and office open 9:00 A.M.–5:00 P.M., Monday–Friday, year-round. Trails are also open 10:00 A.M.–4:00 P.M. Saturday and 1:00–5:00 P.M. Sunday. Closed holidays. Permits may sometimes be obtained for use of trails at other times. Free.

For Additional Information:
Lord Stirling Park
Somerset County Environmental Education Center
190 Lord Stirling Rd.
Basking Ridge, NJ 07920
201-766-2489

Lorrimer Nature Center

This small Audubon nature center in Franklin Lakes features a living museum, an observatory, nature trails, a farm, and a book and gift shop.

Since 1955, when Lucine L. Lorrimer, an animal lover, bequeathed her 14-acre estate to the New Jersey Audubon Society, this nature center has attracted thousands of people. A vegetable garden has become a demonstration farm with barns and sheds, chickens and sheep. The spacious lawn is now a foraging field for wildlife. From the observatory one may watch deer, squirrel, rabbit, and occasionally raccoon dining at the feeders. The museum, in the Lorrimer house, contains exhibits of live native reptiles, amphibians, and small mammals.

Numerous natural history courses, programs, and field trips are presented throughout the year, while lengthier "nature vacations" are offered each summer.

Nature Trails
Although the center grounds are not extensive enough to provide a challenging hiking area, there is a self-guided trail system that meanders through field and woodland, farm and garden. Naturalists lead regularly scheduled bird and botany walks. Trail guides are available near the entrance to the trails.

How to Get There: Located southeast of Oakland. From Oakland, take NJ 208 east to Ewing Ave. (Co. Rd. 502). Turn right and continue for about one mile, through first four-corner stoplight. Center is on right side of road.

Trails open daily, year-round, dawn to dusk. Visitor's center open 10:00 A.M.–4:00 P.M., Tuesday–Saturday, and 1:00–5:00 P.M. Sunday.

For Additional Information:
Lorrimer Nature Center
790 Ewing Ave.
Franklin Lakes, NJ 07417
201-891-1211

Mahlon Dickerson Reservation

The largest single facility in the Morris County park system is Mahlon Dickerson Reservation, with nearly 1,300 acres of woodland, streams, and a lake managed primarily as a conservation area. It also includes one of the highest points in Morris County, where 1,300-foot Headley Overlook has been built.

From the overlook, you have a beautiful view of the northern section of Lake Hopatcong and the surrounding hills and wooded countryside. On the northeast side of the reservation, portions of the Great Pine Swamp extend far beyond the county property.

The woodland consists of mixed hardwoods—oak, hickory, tulip poplar, maple, sassafras, dogwood. Numerous wildflowers are evident in the spring and autumn in open areas. Wildlife includes red and gray fox, white-tailed deer, raccoon, opossum, red and gray squirrel, and muskrat. It's also a good bird-watching area with more than fifty species sighted.

Hiking

An excellent rambling trail system extends several miles over all types of terrain. One trail leads to Great Pine Swamp in the northeastern reaches of the park.

Camping

A small campground has five tent sites and eighteen sites for trailers up to 29 feet long; water and electric hookups available. Open all year.

How to Get There: Located north of Dover. From Exit 34 on I-80, go north on NJ 15 to Weldon Rd., which lies northeast of Lake Hopatcong. Turn right on Weldon Rd. and head straight to reservation.

Open daily, year-round, during daylight hours. Free.

For Additional Information:
Morris County Park Commission
53 E. Hanover Ave.
P.O. Box 1295R
Morristown, NJ 07960
201-285-6166

Mills Reservation

A woodland tract of more than 150 acres, Mills Reservation is bordered by Cedar Grove Reservoir on the west and tiny Mountainside Park on the east. This park just north of Montclair has been preserved in its natural state. No roads penetrate the heavily wooded terrain, but there is a parking lot off Normal Avenue at the extreme northern boundary of the park. From there, visitors may enter the reservation on foot. Among the popular features of this park, located on the ridge of First Watchung Mountain, are outstanding vistas of the Manhattan skyline. More than 1,000 irises, usually in full bloom by late May, are displayed in the Presby Gardens in Mountainside Park.

Hiking

Several trails lace through the parkland. Just south of the parking lot is the Crosswoods Interpretive Trail; descriptive pamphlets for Crosswoods, as well as maps of the entire trail system, are available from the Essex County Department of Parks or the Center for Environmental Studies. Eastview Trail leads from the parking lot to a small picnic area in Mountainside Park.

How to Get There: Located north of Montclair in Essex County. From Montclair, go west on Bloomfield Ave. (Co. Rd. 506) to NJ 23 and turn right. Proceed to Ridge Rd. at third traffic light. Turn right and go approximately one mile, past Reservoir Pl., to Reservoir Dr. Turn right and continue around reservoir to Normal Ave. Go right and look for reservation's parking lot on right side of road.

Open daily, year-round, during daylight hours. Free.

For Additional Information:

Essex County Dept. of Parks,
Recreation & Cultural Affairs
115 Clifton Ave.
Newark, NJ 07104
201-482-6400

Center for Environmental Studies
621 Eagle Rock Ave.
Roseland, NJ 07068
201-228-2210

Moggy Hollow Natural Area

A short distance from Far Hills is the Moggy Hollow Natural Area, a place so geographically and ecologically unusual that it has been designated a National Natural Landmark by the U.S. Department of the Interior. Once the drainage point for ancient glacial Lake Passaic, it consists of a deep gorge, upland woodland, and a bog some 100 feet deep. The mixed hardwood forest has probably never been commercially logged, and the bog at the bottom of the steep, rock-strewn walls of the gorge contains a wide variety of plant life. Several hundred plant species, including at least a dozen species of fern, have been catalogued.

Moggy Hollow is a part of the complex of glacial creations in this area that also includes the Great Swamp and Troy Meadows (both described elsewhere).

Although no trails exist, you may walk along the bottom of the gorge. You'll find the going difficult, though.

How to Get There: Located southwest of Bernardsville. From Bernardsville, go southwest on US 202 to Co. Rd. 512 (Liberty Corner

The pioneer homestead at Morristown National Historic Park

Rd.) just east of Far Hills. Turn left and proceed to natural area; it's on right side of road before you reach I-287.

Open daily, year-round, 9:00 A.M.–5:00 P.M. Parking on property. Free.

For Additional Information:

Upper Raritan Watershed Association
Larger Cross Rd.
RD 1, Box 30-W
Gladstone, NJ 07934
201-234-1852

Morristown National Historic Park

Here, within the first National Historic Park established in the United States, is a 1,000-acre oasis of serenity—the remarkably beautiful Jockey Hollow Area approximately 4 miles south of Morristown. History and nature have enriched each other at Jockey Hollow. Since the park was acquired in 1933, the National Park Service has given top priority to historical value in its management of the area, which served as the main encampment for the Continental Army during two critical winters of the Revolutionary War. As a result, most of Jockey Hollow has been tended to by Mother Nature. With the excep-

tion of historical buildings and the grounds surrounding them, this is a wild and verdant place, almost entirely forested. In actual distance barely 30 miles from New York City, it seems light-years removed from the metropolis.

This is a park for all seasons, equally beautiful in each. In spring, the dogwoods bloom, wildflowers carpet the fields with splashes of color, and the fresh green foliage signifies the beginning of a new life cycle. In autumn, dense woodlands are ablaze with brilliant reds and golds. A winter snow drapes the landscape with white velvet. And summer casts a spell of peace and contentment over the forested hills.

More than 300 species of shrubs, trees, and wildflowers, more than 100 species of birds, and some 20 species of mammals have been identified here.

The forest is presently oak dominated, but beech, red maple, and black birch are becoming more prominent. One unusual feature of the park is a small stand of black ash. Generally, trees of this species are found singly and at some distance from each other.

Red and gray fox, white-tailed deer, striped skunk, mink, beaver, southern flying squirrel, woodchuck, bobcat, and the wood turtle, considered a threatened species in New Jersey, all make their home in Jockey Hollow. Occasionally, a black bear wanders through the park.

Wick Farm at Jockey Hollow, used as General Arthur St. Clair's headquarters, still stands. The kitchen garden, with its herbs and rows of quince, gooseberry, and currant shrubs, adjoins a flourishing orchard.

A modern visitor's center dispenses historical literature about Jockey Hollow and other sections of Morristown Historical Park. A road and trail map is available.

The entire park is a serene, uncrowded retreat, where you will always find a quiet corner.

Hiking, Bicycling, and Horseback Riding

Numerous trails wind through the woods, luring hikers and horseback riders (no rentals). Bicyclists follow park roads. Much of the park's flora can be seen along the Primrose Brook Trail, a loop of just over one mile generally considered the loveliest walk in Jockey Hollow. It was formerly known as the Wildflower Trail, but many of the wildflowers have disappeared during the natural encroachment of the surrounding forest. A road and trail map is available at the visitor's center.

Winter Sports

This is an excellent area for cross-country skiers and snowshoers.

How to Get There: From Morristown, go south about 4 miles on US 202 to Tempe Wick Rd., where you will see a park sign. Turn right. Park entrance is on right side of Tempe Wick Rd.

Grounds open daily, year-round, 9:00 A.M.–sunset. Free. Jockey Hollow Visitor's Center open 9:00 A.M.–5:00 P.M. daily except Thanksgiving, December 25, and January 1; Wick House open 11:00 A.M.–5:00 P.M. on same days as visitor's center.

For Additional Information:

Superintendent
Morristown National Historic Park
P.O. Box 1136R
Morristown, NJ 07960
201-539-2016 or 201-539-2017

Norvin Green State Forest

Wilderness hikers will find this undeveloped forest near Wanaque Reservoir in Passaic County a marvelous place to explore. It extends over nearly 3,000 acres of steep hills, and in its dense woodlands you get a sense of isolation. In the southern part of the forest is meandering Posts Brook, which forms Chikahokie Falls along its course. Since the forest's rough terrain has made access somewhat difficult except by foot, it's never crowded.

Hiking

A network of hiking trails is the only sign of man's intrusion here. Terrain is very rugged. A trail map is available from the superintendent's office at Ringwood State Park (described elsewhere).

How to Get There: Located west of Wanaque Reservoir. From town of Wanaque, go north on Co. Rd. 511 (Ringwood Ave.) to Westbrook Rd. and turn left. At Snake Den Rd. turn left again. Access is at end of road. Park along roadside.

Open daily, year-round, during daylight hours. Free.

For Additional Information:

Superintendent
Ringwood State Park
P.O. Box 1304
Ringwood, NJ 07456
201-962-7031

Ocean County Park

Ocean County Park, often called Rockefeller Park, is the oldest and most established facility in that county's park system. Donated to Ocean County by the Rockefeller family in 1940, the park is the former estate of the late John D. Rockefeller, Sr. Though the mansion has been torn down, the more than 150 species of trees and shrubs that Rockefeller brought from around the world remain. Visitors may see white-tailed deer playing among the tall stands of white pine and hemlock. Four miles of roadways wind through the arboretum, and in the summer, you may rent horse-drawn carriages for a ride through the park.

Also on park grounds are shaded picnic groves and three freshwater lakes with a patrolled area for swimming.

On the other side of Ocean Avenue, which runs along the front of the park, is 143-acre Lake Shenandoah Park, situated around a 48-acre, one-mile-long lake that offers some of the best freshwater fishing in the county; no swimming or canoeing is permitted here.

How to Get There: Located east of Lakewood. From Lakewood, go east on NJ 88 (first called Main St., then Ocean Ave.) to park entrance on left side of road.

Open daily, year-round, 8:00 A.M.–dusk. Nominal admission fee for each vehicle on weekends and holidays only from Memorial Day through Labor Day.

For Additional Information:

Ocean County Park System
659 Ocean Ave.
Lakewood, NJ 08701
201-363-8721

Old Troy Park

Here, in a quiet, inconspicuous corner of Parsippany, are nearly 100 acres of unspoiled natural beauty. Wildflowers run rampant in season; then the ground is a multicolored carpet of violets, jacks-in-the-pulpit, mayapples, and wild mustard. The park is perhaps best known, though, for a species of bird that nests here. Birders come from all over the country to find the Lawrence's warbler, a rare hybrid of the blue-winged and golden-winged species that was first sighted here in July 1969. Other birds may be seen as well. In the reeds that thrive on the margin of a 6-acre pond, an American bittern nests. Swallows, the Louisiana water thrush, and an assortment of warblers all live here.

A unit of the Morris County Park System, Old Troy Park has been preserved basically as a passive recreation area. There are a few recreation facilities, such as a ball field and family picnic sites, and a trail leads through the natural area.

How to Get There: From Exit 47 on I-80, go west on US 46 to S. Beverwyck Rd. Turn left and proceed about one mile to fork in road. Bear right onto Reynolds Ave. and go about one mile to park entrance on left. A small parking lot holds thirty-seven cars.

Open daily, year-round, during daylight hours. Free.

For Additional Information:
Morris County Park Commission
53 E. Hanover Ave.
P.O. Box 1295R
Morristown, NJ 07960
201-285-6166

Pinelands National Reserve

Although most of the Pinelands National Reserve in South Jersey, popularly called the Pine Barrens, extends well beyond our 50-mile radius, the area offers such an unexpected and unusual wilderness experience that we felt it should be included. It is an area of strange and haunting beauty not soon forgotten. Covering some 1.6 million acres, a million of which are within the reserve, the Pine Barrens are a forested desert sandwiched between the piedmont and tidal strip of southern New Jersey. Soft white sand is interlaced with natural bogs, swampland, wild streams, and quiet lily ponds. The area once supported much of the state's colonial iron industry, and several towns sprang up, but only ruins remain today. This is a land of legend, few people, abundant small wildlife, and bird life, as well as unusual botanical growth. More than 200 species of wildflowers grow here, and one small grass fern is quite rare.

The forest is made up largely of stunted pitch pine from which the area gets its name. There are places in the barrens such as the Apple Pie Hill fire tower, open April to November, where one can climb up for a bird's-eye view to the horizon. From that perspective, the barrens appear as an unbroken carpet of evergreen forest with a glimmer here and there of a small pond and hardly a hint of human intrusion.

It's possible to hike or canoe on a weekday any month of the year without seeing another person. On summer weekends, the forest is more heavily used, but one may still escape the crowds.

Established by an act of Congress in 1978, the reserve is presently being managed by the Pinelands Commission, composed of federal, state, and county representatives.

Hiking and Backpacking

The major established hiking trail in the Pinelands is the Batona Trail, 30 miles long, stretching generally north from Batsto Fire Tower to Lebanon State Forest. First 6 to 8 miles of the trail north from Batsto follow along the Batsto River, but you'll also cross other streams. There are some water points, but you should carry a good supply. Some of the streams are suitable for drinking; check with a ranger to learn which ones.

The Batona Trail, unquestionably one of the best wilderness trails in the East, was charted and built in 1961 by the Batona Hiking Club of Philadelphia. It has no particular hardships or unusual obstacles and is excellent for all ages. Blaze marks can be readily followed. The trail cuts across a number of roads and thus can be reached by car at many points, making shorter hikes possible.

Only hikers are allowed on this trail, which passes through a diversity of terrain and embraces many attractions—historical, scenic, natural, and man-made. An abundance of wildflowers may be seen in season, particularly during spring, as well as several species of wildlife such as white-tailed deer. You may want to look for the rare Anderson's tree frog, as well as such botanical species as the pitcher plant, sundew, cactus, turkey beard, sheep laurel, and pixie moss. Wild blueberries and huckleberries grow rampant here in many sections.

Nearly 1,000 miles of sand roads and other shorter hiking trails run through the Pinelands Reserve. Hikers may camp along trails in designated areas only. Fire permits are required. Spring and early summer thunderstorms are often violent, so backpackers should be duly prepared.

Canoeing

Some of the most pristine canoe streams in the East flow through the Pinelands. The Mullica and Wading Rivers are especially worth a trip. Information about launch and take-out points, as well as a list of area canoe liveries, can be obtained from the Pinelands Commission.

How to Get There: Located north and east of Hammonton. From Exit 28 on Atlantic City Expwy., head north on NJ 54 to Co. Rd. 542. Turn right and proceed to Batsto within Wharton State Forest. Maps and brochures describing the area are available at Batsto Mansion Visitor's Center. Such highways as US 206 and Co. Rd. 563 also take you alongside or through portions of the Pinelands.

For Additional Information:

Public Information Officer
The Pinelands Commission
Springfield Road
P.O. Box 7
New Lisbon, NJ 08064
609-894-9342

Pinelands National Reserve
c/o Mid-Atlantic Regional Office
National Park Service
143 S. Third St.
Philadelphia, PA 19106
215-597-7018

Supervisor
Wharton State Forest
Batsto, R.D. 4
Hammonton, NJ 08037
609-561-0024

Pleasant Acres Farm Campground

Nestled in the hills of northwestern Sussex County is a recreational campground on a 142-acre working farm where you can become intimately acquainted with all kinds of farm chores and animals.

Here you'll find picturesque views, space, good air to breathe, good water to drink, and a pace of life that's slow and easy. A brook flows through the property, and birds of many varieties enliven the woodlands with song. Free hayrides, dancing, movies, farm demonstrations, live entertainment, games, and even some free meals are part of the outstanding bill of fare.

Most campsites have full hookups, and there are hot showers.

Winter camping is a recently added feature; sleigh riding, tobogganing, cross-country skiing, and ice skating are offered on the grounds, along with a schedule of events as full as the one offered in summer.

Programs of free events are available upon request.

How to Get There: Located northwest of town of Sussex. From Sussex, take NJ 23 north. At DeWitt Rd. turn right. Campground is on the corner of NJ 23 and DeWitt Rd.

For Additional Information:
Pleasant Acres Farm Campground
RD 1, Box 351
Sussex, NJ 07461
201-875-4166

Princeton University Campus

Several natural attractions make the Princeton University campus in Mercer County worth a visit, among them a collection of outstanding trees, well-landscaped grounds, a natural history museum, and a formal garden. Included in the campus arboretum is a great dawn redwood planted in 1948. Before 1942, when a dawn redwood was discovered growing halfway up the Yangtze River in China, this species had been known only from fossil specimens and was thought extinct. Other extraordinary trees include cedar of Lebanon, English yew, red oak, European beech, eastern hemlock, copper beech, hardy rubber trees, Spanish fir, tiger-tail spruce, and giant sequoia. Several trees on and near the campus, including a London plane tree and a blue Atlas cedar from the Atlas Mountains of North Africa, are the largest of their species in the state.

The Arnold Guyot Natural History Museum on campus dates back to 1856 and contains thousands of archaeological, biological, and geological specimens. Named after Princeton's first professor of geology and geography, the museum displays samples of most of the world's minerals and gems, fossils, and such skeletal displays as a saber-toothed tiger, three-toed horse, giant pig, a mastodon, and a 75-million-year-old baby duckbill dinosaur.

You'll want to visit Prospect Gardens, too, while you're on campus. Established in 1849, the garden includes a number of native and exotic trees, as well as an array of flower displays.

How to Get There: Located in the heart of Princeton. Entrances along Nassau St. (NJ 27). *By rail:* Amtrak or New Jersey Transit train from Penn Station in Manhattan to Princeton Junction; shuttle train to Princeton.

Grounds always open. Free. Free guided tours are offered by students during school year, September–June. When guided tours are not available, you may pick up a published self-guiding tour booklet in Stanhope Hall, at the Princeton University Store, or at the University Art Museum for a very nominal fee.

For Additional Information:
Director of Communications
Princeton University
Stanhope Hall
Princeton, NJ 08544
609-452-3600

Ramapo Mountain State Forest

Extending about 6 miles along the ridge of the Ramapo Mountains in north central New Jersey, this long, narrow forest of more than 2,300 acres is particularly attractive to hikers. It is considered one of the most desirable areas for passive recreation in the metropolitan area.

Approximately half of the forest lands are included in the Ramapo Mountain Natural Area. At 120 acres, spring-fed Ramapo Lake within the natural area is the largest body of water in the forest, but there are four other small ponds.

Scenic Skyline Drive winds along the eastern border of the natural area.

Hiking

A network of trails crisscrosses the forest, one leading to and around Ramapo Lake. The trail system here links up with the one at Ringwood State Park (described elsewhere). A trail map is available from the forest headquarters.

How to Get There: Located west of Oakland. From Oakland, go west on W. Oakland Ave. to Skyline Dr. Turn right and continue a short distance to first parking lot on left side of road. From here, a trail leads to Ramapo Lake. Another parking lot is available farther up Skyline Dr.

Open daily, year-round, during daylight hours. Free.

For Additional Information:
Supervisor
Ramapo Mountain State Forest
P.O. Box 225
Oakland, NJ 07436
201-337-0960

Ramapo Valley County Reservation

This surprisingly rugged wilderness park, located in northwest Bergen County, contains a mix of tall timber, mountainous terrain, swampy areas, two small lakes, and a waterfall in its 1,400 acres. This is an area primarily for hikers; visitors must park at the entrance and walk into the reservation. Canoe and raft owners have portage access to the Ramapo River, which flows through the reservation near the parking area. Tent camping is allowed at designated sites beside the river and around Scarlet Oak Pond, but it's necessary to obtain a permit in advance. The park also has a picnic area and natural science displays.

Hiking

Trails in the reservation vary in length from ⅓ mile to 2 miles; most are of moderate difficulty and require some climbing.

Sketch maps of the hiking trails are available from the ranger at the Ramapo Park Office (near parking area), the Bergen County Wildlife Center (described elsewhere), and the Bergen County Park Commission headquarters. Public walks and hikes, guided by staff naturalists, are offered some weekends.

How to Get There: Located north of Oakland. From Oakland, take US 202 north, past Campgaw Mountain County Reservation on right, to Ramapo Reservation on left. It's located just south of the point where Darlington Ave. joins US 202 from the east. The entrance is a bit inconspicuous; look for a phone booth, a parking lot, and a Ramapo Reservation sign.

Open daily, year-round, from sunrise to a half hour after sunset.

For Additional Information:

Bergen County Wildlife Center
Crescent Avenue
Wyckoff, NJ 07481
201-891-5571

Bergen County Park Commission
327 Ridgewood Ave.
Paramus, NJ 07648
201-646-2680

Reeves-Reed Arboretum

The Reeves-Reed Arboretum boasts 12½ acres of natural hardwood forest, open fields, formal gardens, and lawns, and features a glacial punch bowl that becomes a daffodil garden each spring. A natural foil for the daffodil plantings, the punch bowl was formed when a great chunk of ice broke free from the melting Wisconsin glacier, was buried, and later melted to form the depression. There are similar kettle ponds at other places, but few, if any, have become daffodil beds.

Special programs are offered throughout the year, including workshops, lectures, and field trips. Owned by the City of Summit, the arboretum is maintained and operated by the Reeves-Reed Arboretum, Inc., a nonprofit organization.

Nature Trails

Two three-quarter-mile nature trails invite nature study; excellent printed trail guides add to enjoyment along the way.

How to Get There: From junction of Broad St. (Co. Rd. 512) and Summit Ave. in the town of Summit, go north on Summit Ave. to Franklin Place and turn right. Go to Hobart Ave. and turn left. Arboretum is at 165 Hobart Ave. Parking on property.

Arboretum open daily, year-round, dawn to dusk; office open Tuesday and Thursday, 9:00 A.M.–3:00 P.M., in spring and fall; Tuesday and Thursday, 10:00 A.M.–3:00 P.M., other seasons. Free.

For Additional Information:

Reeves-Reed Arboretum
165 Hobart Ave.
Summit, NJ 07901
201-273-8787

Riker Hill Park

This Essex County park north of Livingston is made up of three connected units that total over 200 acres. It appeals particularly to those interested in archaeology and geology.

The Riker Hill Visitor's Center is in the southernmost unit of the park. Once a U.S. Army Nike base, this 42-acre tract atop Riker Hill offers a diversity of ecosystems suited for wildlife and nature study. Visitors will find upland forests, secondary thickets, old fields, wetlands, and grassy areas. Just off the north edge of the parking lot at the visitor's center is a grassy slope that houses a colony of woodchucks in half a dozen tunnels. Raptors may be observed at the park's 460-foot summit, and American kestrels hunt over the area. Deer, rabbits, squirrels, owls, and an abundance of songbirds live along the entire park corridor. Also in the Nike base unit is the Geological Museum, with exhibits related to the geology of Essex County. A geologist is on hand to answer questions. This museum serves as an educational support facility for the Walter T. Kidde Dinosaur Park, another unit of Riker Hill Park.

In Dinosaur Park, visitors may search through pieces of talus (rubble) for fossils and dinosaur footprints. The dinosaurs that once roamed this area were not the gigantic type; some were barely the size of chickens. Other fossil finds include fish, insects, and plants. Because of the abundance and diversity of fossils, the park has been designated a National Natural Landmark. The igneous and sedimentary rock formations combined with glacial deposits also make Kidde Park an excellent site for geological investigations.

Largest of the three units is the 147-acre Becker Tract, a combination of woods, grassland, and farm fields, some under cultivation. Once part of a large dairy farm, the Becker Tract lures trail-walkers and picnickers. Bobwhite quail, striped skunk, gray fox, white-tailed deer, and numerous species of birds have been seen here.

Hiking

The Riker Hill Interpretive Trail leads down a steep hill from the Nike base unit to Dinosaur Park. The gate at the trail head near the Geology Museum is open between 9:00 A.M. and 4:30 P.M. only. Along the way, you'll see rock outcroppings, a glacial erratic, various types of vegetation, and an area that was burned by a natural fire in 1977, and is now in the process of revegetating itself. Within Dinosaur Park, you may follow the self-guided Dinosaur Quarry Trail. The Farm Woodlot Interpretive Trail winds through the Becker Tract. Check at the visitor's center for maps and descriptive pamphlets.

How to Get There: From Exit 4 of I-280, just east of the Passaic River, take Eisenhower Pkwy. south. Proceed to Beaufort Ave. entrance on left side of parkway. Follow Beaufort Ave. to Riker Hill Park sign on left and turn left into park. This will lead you to the visitor's center. Inquire there for exact directions for reaching the Becker Tract and Kidde Dinosaur Park.

Grounds open daily during daylight hours. It's best to call the Geological Museum (201-992-8806) for the exact hours and days it's open; schedule varies from season to season. Free.

For Additional Information:

Essex County Dept. of Parks, Recreation & Cultural Affairs 115 Clifton Ave. Newark, NJ 07104 *201-482-6400*

Center for Environmental Studies 621 Eagle Rock Ave. Roseland, NJ 07068 *201-228-2210*

Ringwood State Park

Ringwood State Park contains four contiguous units totaling more than 3,500 acres in a sparsely populated part of northern Passaic County.

Most of the Ringwood Manor section is made up of lovely wooded hills, and there are secluded picnic areas along the banks of the Ringwood River. This section is rich in Revolutionary War history, and Ringwood Manor itself has been designated a National Historic Landmark. Visitors today can see a replica of a waterwheel on a site once occupied by an iron forge. George Washington often headquartered at Ringwood. In a small cemetery here is the burial plot of Robert Erskine, surveyor general for the Continental Army; the tree that marks his gravesite was planted in his memory by his friends George and Martha Washington. The 1810 mansion is now a museum, and the beauty of the grounds is enhanced by formal gardens and two ponds.

Another historic mansion, open for tours on certain days, stands in the Skylands section, one of the most beautiful tracts of parkland in the state. On this 1,100-acre preserve, the gardens are the star attraction. Covering approximately 300 acres, they include unusual botanical treasures brought from around the world. They are interspersed with many native species, and something is in bloom at all times of the year. An alley of crabapple trees extends for half a mile, and there are more than 400 varieties of lilacs, azaleas, and peonies. There are both formal plantings (such as a pinetum and a rhododendron display garden) and informal plantings (such as a heather and heath garden and a bog garden). A greenhouse that supplies flowers for Morven, the governor's mansion, is open to visitors. Four trees at Skylands—the silver bell, the paulownia, the Jeffrey pine, and the golden rain tree—are acknowledged to be the largest of their species in New Jersey. Surrounding the manor house and its extensive gardens are some 800 acres of wooded hills and ponds. Skylands is little known and never crowded.

Perhaps the remotest unit of Ringwood is the undeveloped Bear Swamp Lake section, tucked away in the southeast corner of the park, accessible by foot from the Skylands section.

The 541-acre Shepherd Lake section is the center of recreation activities for the park. Rowboats may be rented for use on the 74-acre spring-fed lake; other activities include fishing, lake swimming, picnicking, trap and skeet shooting, ice skating, and sledding.

A visitor's center is located in the Skylands section, and the park office is in the Ringwood Manor section. Maps are available for each section of the park. Naturalists are on duty during peak tourist seasons to answer questions and conduct special programs and tours.

Not far west of Ringwood State Park is a 3,000-acre tract of undeveloped land. Eventually, this area will be known as Greenwood Lake State Forest. At present, it is a large open space, administered by Ringwood State Park and used by hunters, fishermen, and nature lovers. A fine trout stream, a small lake, and an upland wooded area where deer are fairly plentiful lie within its boundaries. The Wanaque Wildlife Management Area, which encompasses an additional 1,400 acres of woodlands drained by the Wanaque River and several tributary streams, adjoins Greenwood Lake State Forest to the north.

Hiking

All sections of the park may be explored via a network of trails; their routes are shown on an overall map of the park available at the visitor's center or park office. From here, it is possible to link up with the trail system in Ramapo Mountain State Forest (described elsewhere) to the south.

How to Get There: Just south of the town of Browns, located at the southern end of Greenwood Lake, head east on Co. Rd. 511; approximately one mile from Browns you will pass through Greenwood Lake State Forest, which meets the road on both sides. Continue east to Sloatsburg Rd. and turn left. The Ringwood Manor section borders Sloatsburg Rd. on the left just before you reach the New York State line.

To reach the Skylands section, turn right off Sloatsburg Rd. onto Morris Ave. shortly before you reach the Ringwood Manor section. Follow Morris Ave. to its intersection with Shepherd Lake Rd. Continue on Morris to reach Skylands; turn left on Shepherd Lake Rd. to reach the Shepherd Lake section. It is somewhat difficult to find the way to this park. If possible, obtain a map from the park office or a Passaic County map before going there.

Park grounds open daily, year-round, during daylight hours. Nominal admission fee at Ringwood Manor, Skylands, and Shepherd Lake sections, daily from Memorial Day through Labor Day, and Saturday and Sunday from May 1 to Memorial Day and from Labor Day through October.

For Additional Information:

Superintendent
Ringwood State Park
Box 1304
Ringwood, NJ 07456
201-962-7031 or 201-962-7047

Wanaque Wildlife Management
Area
c/o Clinton Wildlife
Management Area
Box 409
Hampton, NJ 08827
201-735-8793

Round Valley and Spruce Run
State Recreation Areas

Nestled in the crater of Cushetunk Mountain near Clinton, 2,350-acre Round Valley Reservoir is the second largest reservoir in the state. A narrow strip of land that completely surrounds it adds another 1,270 acres to the park. Also within the immediate area are Voorhees State Park, Clinton Wildlife Management Area, Lockwood Gorge Wildlife Management Area (all described elsewhere), and Spruce Run State Recreation Area, which borders another reservoir often called Round Valley's twin. Altogether, they create a prime outdoor recreation area in Hunterdon County.

Round Valley, surrounded by steep, tree-covered hills, is fine for bird-watching and other types of nature study. Numerous dogwood trees make the park particularly attractive in the spring, when they seem to fill the landscape with their blooms.

Both Round Valley Reservoir and Spruce Run Reservoir to the northwest are state-owned. Although Spruce Run is more developed than Round Valley, there are some nice areas for walking.

Hiking

A hiking trail, nearly 10 miles in length, completely encircles Round Valley Reservoir and includes many scenic views. There is some hilly terrain.

Swimming and Scuba Diving

Approximately 3 acres of white sand beach line the shore near Round Valley's main entrance area at the southern end of the reservoir. There's also a swimming beach at Spruce Run, and bathhouses at both.

Scuba diving is permitted in both reservoirs, but proper permits must be obtained first.

Fishing and Boating

Round Valley Reservoir yielded the state record rainbow trout in 1979 and is noted as the finest trout lake in the state. It's stocked with brown trout on a regular basis, and lake trout have been released on an experimental basis. Other species include largemouth and smallmouth bass, brown bullheads, black crappie, and white perch. There's a launch ramp at the northern end of the reservoir; motors up to 10 horsepower are permitted.

Rowboats, sailboats, canoes, and paddleboats are available for rent at Spruce Run. For fishing at Spruce Run, see description for Clinton Wildlife Management Area, which borders the same reservoir.

Winter Sports

Cross-country skiing, snowshoeing, and sledding are permitted in appropriate areas.

Camping

More than 100 wilderness campsites, accessible only by hike-in (backpack) or small boat, have been established along the southern shore of Round Valley Reservoir; sites are open year-round, but advance reservations are necessary.

About seventy family campsites for tents and trailers up to 24 feet are available at Spruce Run, April through October, and more sites are planned. Showers may be hot or cold, depending on budget allocations at the time.

How to Get There: To reach Round Valley SRA: From Exit 24 on I-78, take Co. Rd. 523 south past US 22 to Dreahook Rd. and turn right. At Round Valley Rd. turn right again and continue to park.

To reach Spruce Run SRA: From Exit 17 on I-78, take NJ 31 north to Van Syckel Rd. and turn left. Proceed to park.

Recreation areas open daily 8:00 A.M.–8:00 P.M., year-round. Nominal admission fee charged daily, Memorial Day through Labor Day; on Saturday and Sunday only, May 1 to Memorial Day and Labor Day through October.

For Additional Information:

Round Valley State Recreation Area
R.D. 1, Round Valley Rd.
Lebanon, NJ 08833
201-236-6355

Spruce Run State Recreation Area
Box 289A, Van Syckels Rd.
Clinton, NJ 08809
201-638-8572 or 201-638-8573

Rutgers University Campus

The Rutgers University campus near New Brunswick has two attractions of interest to nature lovers.

The 41-acre Frank G. Helyar Woods are managed and maintained by the Forestry and Wildlife Section of Cook College at Rutgers. Although it adjoins one of the most heavily traveled highways in the nation (US 1), the forest provides a refreshing atmosphere of serenity. It has been called a "miracle of survival" because it was threatened upon several occasions by the construction of the highway and because it thrives in spite of the heavy fumes from passing automobiles and trucks. It's a good example of how nature and development can coexist.

Among other attractions, it includes a swamp with swamp white oak, red maple, red gum, black gum, and hornbeam, as well as greenbrier, arrowwood, wild elderberry, cinnamon fern, and skunk cabbage. There's also a graveyard of American chestnut stumps with markers posted where the great trees once grew.

An old-growth oak forest here is considered one of the finest such stands in the East, and more than ninety species of birds have been sighted within and adjacent to the woods.

Although used primarily for research, the Rutgers Display Gardens are of interest to anyone who likes plants and trees. The gardens include plots of Japanese holly, dogwood, American holly, a holly orchard, a rhododendron and azalea garden, a shrub garden, an evergreen garden, an annual garden, a yew garden, and a couple of ponds. Also located here are a number of horticultural research plots.

Scattered about the university grounds are several trees that are the largest of their species in New Jersey; among them are a Japanese pagoda, ponderosa pine, pecan, Chinese elm, and Bartram oak.

Nature Trails

A nature trail about two-thirds of a mile long loops through Helyar Woods and takes about forty-five minutes to walk. Labels depict points of interest along the way. Paths and roads through the gardens lead to thirteen different areas.

How to Get There: From US 1, which passes through eastern New Brunswick, take Ryders Lane exit onto the campus. Display Gardens and Helyar Woods adjoin each other in the southeast corner of this intersection. Follow Ryders Lane southeast to gardens entrance on left side of road. Drive through gardens to parking lot near Helyar Woods.

Woods and gardens open daily, 8:30 A.M.–dusk, May through

September; 8:30 A.M.–4:30 P.M., October through April. Closed on Saturday during hunting season. Both free.

For Additional Information:

Helyar Woods
Forestry & Wildlife Section
Cook College
Box 231
Rutgers University
New Brunswick, NJ 08903
201-932-8915

Tours & Information Office
Van Nest Hall
College Avenue Campus
Rutgers University
New Brunswick, NJ 08903
201-932-7799

Rutgers Display Gardens
College of Agriculture & Environmental Science
Rutgers University
New Brunswick, NJ 08903
201-932-8915

Sandy Hook

See listing under Gateway National Recreation Area, page 8.

Sawmill Creek Wildlife Management Area

Sawmill Creek Wildlife Area, made up entirely of tidal marsh and shallow bays, is an excellent place for crabbing from June through mid-September. And it lies just 6 miles west of New York City, in the towns of Lyndhurst and Kearny.

Made up of some 1,000 acres, the salt marsh is a noted birding area, one of the principal reasons why the marsh was purchased and set aside by the state. It was one of the first in a series of steps being taken by the state to bring about an environmental rebirth of the once-beautiful Hackensack Meadowlands, currently a much-abused garbage dump.

Shorebirds such as the stilt sandpiper, Hudsonian godwit, American avocet, and Wilson and northern phalarope are just a few of the uncommon species sighted here. Black duck, mallard, pintail, blue- and green-winged teal, canvasback, and gadwall use the area. A common nesting bird is the Florida gallinule. The least bittern, redwing blackbird, and long-billed marsh wren are also residents.

Plans call for this WMA eventually to be included in a new state park that is to be created within the next decade. The WMA lies along the Hackensack River.

Canoeing

The shallow bays and connecting tidal creeks are best suited for canoeing or very small boats with electric motors (to eliminate as much noise as possible).

How to Get There: Located about 6 miles west of Manhattan, the area encompasses the lower reaches of Sawmill Creek, a tributary of the Hackensack River. The WMA is bound on the east by the Hackensack River and lies between the east and west branches of the New Jersey Turnpike, north of NJ 7 and just east of Kearny. The west branch of the Turnpike cuts through the WMA near its western border, and a sign identifying the area can be seen from the Turnpike. There is no direct access to the area at this writing, but efforts are being made to provide one as soon as possible. Private boat launches do exist upstream, such as Sky Harbor Marina (end of Paterson Plank Rd., Carlstadt) and Tony's Old Mill (at the end of Mill Ridge Rd., Secaucus).

Open daily, year-round, 5:00 A.M.–9:00 P.M. Free.

For Additional Information:
Sawmill Creek Wildlife Management Area
c/o Clinton Wildlife Management Area
Box 409
Hampton, NJ 08827
201-735-8793

Scherman-Hoffman Wildlife Sanctuaries

These twin sanctuaries, holdings of the New Jersey Audubon Society, combine some 250 acres of woodlands, streams, and fields at the headwaters of the Passaic River along the Morris-Somerset County line. The adjoining sanctuaries, of particular interest to bird-watchers, are home to more than sixty resident bird species and numerous migrating birds during the spring and fall months. The pileated woodpecker nests here, and ten species of warblers have been seen. Best birding time is during the months of April and May and again in late September and October.

Frogs, salamanders, and six species of snakes share this sanctuary with the birds. From spring through early fall, hundreds of wildflowers enliven the landscape and several varieties of ferns thrive throughout the year.

Facilities include a small museum with specimen collections, a library, and a sales desk. Seasonal field classes are held on natural history subjects.

Other services the Audubon Society provides include an Owl Information Service and the Voice of New Jersey Audubon telephone report. The former (201-766-5787) answers questions by phone about orphaned and injured wildlife, places to go, bird identification, and natural history. The latter (201-766-2661) is a tape recording that gives up-to-date information on birds and birding in New Jersey; it's changed every Wednesday evening. Calls can be made any time of day or night.

Hiking and Nature Trails

A complex of trails includes the Dogwood Trail, a one-hour walk around both sanctuaries. The Museum Trail and Nature Trail offer glimpses at a few rare introduced plant species, such as twinleaf and bee balm. Self-guided trail leaflets are available.

How to Get There: From N. Maple Ave. exit on I-287 (Exit 26), head west on N. Maple Ave. to traffic light near Old Mill Inn (at intersection with US 202). Continue west, crossing over 202; Maple Ave. becomes Childs Rd. immediately after crossing 202. Follow Childs Rd. about 100 yards to Hardscrabble Rd. and turn right. Sanctuary parking lot is about 1 mile on right side of road.

   Trails open daily, Tuesday–Sunday, year-round during daylight hours. Office and museum open Tuesday–Saturday, 9:00 A.M.–5:00 P.M.; closed Sunday and Monday, major holidays, second half of June, and December. Free to individuals and families; groups must pay small fee and make advance reservations.

For Additional Information:
New Jersey Audubon Society
Hardscrabble Road
P.O. Box 693
Bernardsville, NJ 07924
201-766-5787

Shark River Park

Shark River Park, established for the dual purpose of conservation and recreation, lies adjacent to the Garden State Parkway in Monmouth County. It provides a study in geology, dating back to the days when the coastal plain of New Jersey was at the bottom of the ocean. Ancient fossils, including sharks' teeth and vertebrae and shellfish impressions dating back some 80 million years, have been found. From a later era, there are such Native American artifacts as arrowheads, potsherds, hammerstones, and tomahawks.

   Within the park's 760 acres are abandoned fields where many types of berry-producing plants grow, including blackberry, strawberry, and wild cherry, which feed the resident populations of ring-necked pheasant, bobwhite quail, goldfinches, and many other birds. Much of the plant life, such as pitch pine and scrub oak, is more typical of the Pine Barrens (described elsewhere under Pinelands National Reserve). Trailing arbutus, lady's slippers, and turkey beard are a few of the wildflowers that thrive where the undergrowth is thickest. Cottontail rabbit, raccoon, opossum, white-tailed deer, and woodchuck all live here. Tidal marshlands and the river's wooded shorelines provide additional areas for ecological studies.

Recreation facilities include a fishing and ice skating pond, playfields, picnic sites, an eighteen-hole golf course, and courts for horseshoes and shuffleboard.

Hiking

A network of hiking trails extends through the park's various ecological zones. The most mature forest in the park, consisting of oaks, tulips, and maples, is found along the floodplain of the river; it's alive with birds during spring and fall migrations. Violets, spring beauties, and jacks-in-the-pulpit flourish in the rich floodplain soil. Trails lead through this area, as well as to swamps and bogs, where visitors can see frogs, turtles, and snakes, along with cranberries, insectivorous sundew and pitcher plants, and rare Hartford climbing ferns.

How to Get There: From Exit 100 on Garden State Pkwy., take NJ 33 east. At Schoolhouse Rd. turn right and continue to park entrance.
Open daily, year-round, 8:00 A.M.–8:30 P.M. Free admission.

For Additional Information:
Monmouth County Park System
Newman Springs Rd.
Lincroft, NJ 07738
201-842-4000

Somerset County Environmental Education Center

See listing under Lord Stirling Park, page 89.

South Mountain Reservation

Sprawling over more than 2,000 acres just north of Millburn, South Mountain Reservation is the largest park in the Essex County park system. Paved roads wind through this hilly and wooded tract and lead to scenic lookouts along Crest Drive near the southern boundary. One panoramic view may be seen from Washington Rock, where George Washington surveyed the countryside during the Revolution. On clear days, you can see Manhattan's skyline.

The Rahway River winds through the reservation, forming two small ponds along the way and feeding the City of Orange Reservoir, all within park boundaries. Other smaller streams wander down hillsides and form natural waterfalls. Perhaps the most picturesque is Hemlock Falls, accessible by a short foot trail.

A deer paddock encloses a large herd of deer in a natural

setting, while in another part of the park there's a 15-acre zoo. Perched on the side of South Mountain, Turtle Back Zoo displays exotic and farm animals. Dogwood Hillside is popular from late April to early May, when the slope is vibrant with blossoms. Nighttime visitors may view this floral display under lights. Other facilities within the park include several picnic areas, a cross-country run, an archery range, and game fields.

Hiking and Horseback Riding

Numerous foot and bridle trails crisscross the reservation, about 20 miles of each in total; no horse rentals in park. A printed brochure, available from the Essex County Department of Parks or the Center for Environmental Studies, describes the Turtle Back Rock Interpretive Trail, a circular foot path named for an interesting rock formation seen along the way.

Winter Sports

In the winter, both downhill and cross-country skiers use South Mountain, as do sledders. An indoor ice skating rink offers "Learn to Skate" programs. The ice skating arena is generally open about seven months each year, beginning in mid-September.

How to Get There: Located west of South Orange. Take Garden State Pkwy. south from I-280 to South Orange Ave. Follow South Orange Ave. (Co. Rd. 510) west into park. *By rail:* Conrail's Erie-Lackawanna Railroad stops at Millburn Station, just opposite Locust Grove Picnic Area at park's southern boundary.

Grounds open daily, year-round, during daylight hours. Zoo is closed some holidays.

For Additional Information:

Essex County Dept. of Parks,
Recreation & Cultural Affairs
115 Clifton Ave.
Newark, NJ 07104
201-482-6400

Center for Environmental Studies
621 Eagle Rock Ave.
Roseland, NJ 07068
201-228-2210

Spruce Run State Recreation Area

See listing under Round Valley and Spruce Run State Recreation Areas, page 107.

Stephens–Saxton Falls State Park

See listing under Allamuchy Mountain State Park, page 55.

Stokes State Forest

Extending over nearly 15,000 acres in Sussex County, Stokes State Forest includes some of the loveliest country northern New Jersey has to offer. Its dense woodlands, mountainous terrain, clear streams and lakes, freshwater springs, sweeping views, and miles of scenic roads and trails have made this one of the most popular facilities in the state system.

In the southwestern part of the forest is the Tillman Ravine Natural Area, where visitors may enter only on foot. Masses of rhododendron cover the steep banks of the ravine beneath a canopy of old-growth hemlocks. Tillman Brook, rising from springs along the side of the Kittatinny Mountains to the east, forms picturesque waterfalls as it tumbles over huge boulders and seeks its way through the gorge. The unusual varnish conk fungus, so named because it appears to have been coated with dark varnish, is occasionally found on fallen hemlock. Other vegetation includes the wild indigo, sheep laurel, moccasin flower, meadow buttercup, and red pine. Throughout the forest, mountain laurel grows abundantly, coloring the landscape with its spectacular pink and white blossoms in mid-June.

Stokes State Forest adjoins High Point State Park (described elsewhere) to the north and the 2,334-acre Flatbrook-Roy Wildlife Management Area to the west.

Hiking and Horseback Riding

Both Sunday afternoon strollers and experienced hikers will find trails to their liking in Stokes State Forest. A 9-mile stretch of the Appalachian Trail follows the ridge for the length of the forest and takes about six hours to hike at a moderate rate. Other trails vary in length from $\frac{1}{2}$ to nearly 4 miles, and range in difficulty from easy walks to those over hilly, rocky terrain. An excellent trail guide is available at the forest office.

Bridle paths are also provided, but there are no horse rentals in the park.

Swimming

At Stony Lake Recreation Area is a sand beach for swimmers, with a lifeguard on duty and bathhouse nearby.

Fishing and Boating

Stony Lake, Lake Ocquittunk, and forest streams yield trout, largemouth and smallmouth bass, and perch. Small, nonpowered boats may be launched at Lake Ocquittunk.

Winter Sports

This is one of the best areas around for cross-country skiing and snowshoeing; ice skating also permitted.

Camping

Three camping areas offer seventy primitive family campsites for tents and small trailers up to 24 feet in length. Some sites have lean-to shelters. Open mid-March through October. At the Lake Ocquittunk campground, cabins for four to twelve persons may be rented from April through mid-December.

How to Get There: From Branchville, head northwest on US 206 to the forest. Forest lands adjoin both sides of highway. The forest office is located on right side of US 206 approximately 4½ miles from Branchville.

Forest open daily, year-round, during daylight hours. Free entrance. There is a nominal admission fee at Stony Lake Recreation Area daily from Memorial Day through Labor Day; Saturday and Sunday, May 1 to Memorial Day and Labor Day through October. Also a nominal charge for picnic tables in some sections.

For Additional Information:

Supervisor
Stokes State Forest
R.R. 2, Box 260
Branchville, NJ 07826
201-948-3820

Tenafly Nature Center

See listing under East Hill Preserve, page 68.

Tourne Park

One of the most unspoiled areas in the Morris County park system is Tourne Park, established in 1960. These sprawling 460 acres of rugged, wooded hills and hollows abound with wildlife and wildflowers. On clear days, from the park's peak elevation, you can see the skyscrapers of Manhattan.

White-tailed deer, grouse, red and gray fox, raccoon, opossum, and eastern cottontail rabbit like this park, too; you're most likely to see them at dawn or sunset, particularly during spring and fall months.

Partridge and wood duck nest in a one-acre bird sanctuary within the park, and occasionally a pileated woodpecker appears.

Trees include a mixed hardwood forest of oak, tulip poplar, sweet gum, hickory, sassafras, dogwood, and sycamore, as well as a fine stand of hemlock

Hiking and Nature Trails

A trail up to the lookout is strenuous enough to challenge most hikers. The Hemlock Trail leads through a fine stand of towering hemlock trees, and there's a wildflower trail developed by various garden clubs of the Boonton area. More than 250 plants that are native to Morris County have been placed along the trail. Other shorter trails wind through various picnic areas, as well as the recreation area.

Winter Sports
Cross-country skiing, sledding, and tobogganing are popular in the winter.

How to Get There: Located northeast of Denville and north of Mountain Lakes. From Mountain Lakes, go north on The Boulevard (Co. Rd. 618) to a fork in the road. Turn left at fork onto Powerville Rd. Proceed to McCaffery Ln., the park access road, and turn left.
   Open daily, during daylight hours, year-round. Free.

For Additional Information:
Morris County Park Commission
53 E. Hanover Ave.
Box 1295R
Morristown, NJ 07960
201-285-6166

Troy Meadows

Near Manhattan, New Jersey has several great meadows of freshwater wetlands where nature predominates over rows of houses and office buildings. One such place is Troy Meadows, a vast green oasis in Morris County. The major portion—1,500 of the area's 2,000 acres—is owned by Wildlife Preserves, Inc., a private nonprofit organization that depends upon donors for its existence. Another 300 acres of Troy Meadows have been acquired by the state through its Green Acres program.

   Although constantly endangered by impinging development on and pollution from its periphery, Troy Meadows is a refreshing place where one may find raccoon, fox, muskrat, a few dozen reptile species, many amphibians, and white-tailed deer. The meadows are justly famous as a bird-watching area. You may see or hear such birds as the wood duck, Virginia rail, king rail, common gallinule, great blue heron, the pied-billed grebe, long-billed marsh wren, American and least bitterns, the swamp sparrow, and several species of waterfowl. It is possible to sight 100 species on some May days.

   While most of Troy Meadows consists of cattail marsh, there are some hardwood groves in the uplands. Troy Brook winds through the sanctuary, and the Whippany River edges its eastern boundary. Wildflowers are abundant during the spring and throughout the summer. Also growing here are wild strawberries, blueberries, and a few raspberries.

Full-time wardens keep an eye out for poachers. Absolutely no hunting is permitted, and no plants may be removed for any reason.

The ecological importance of Troy Meadows has been recognized by the U.S. Department of the Interior, which has designated it a National Natural Landmark.

Hiking

A 2½-mile boardwalk trail, partially underwater, leads directly through the meadows under the Public Service power line. The boardwalk was constructed by the power company to provide maintenance access, but the public is welcome to use it for hiking and nature study. High boots are advisable.

How to Get There: Located northeast of Morristown. From Exit 4 of I-280, just east of the Passaic River, take Eisenhower Pkwy. south to Eagle Rock Ave. and turn right. At Ridgedale Ave. turn left and go to Willow Place (near huge power line towers that cross road); turn right and proceed to small parking lot at dead end. Walk a few yards back toward Ridgedale Ave. to path on right. Follow path to construction area beneath power lines. Cross construction area and pick up boardwalk on other side. Be sure to look carefully; the beginning of the boardwalk is sometimes overgrown. Keep your eyes on the power lines; the boardwalk parallels them on the north.

Open daily, year-round, during daylight hours. Free.

For Additional Information:

Chief Ranger, Troy Meadows
Wildlife Preserves, Inc.
Box 194
Hopatcong, NJ 07843
201-398-5318

Wildlife Preserves, Inc.
154 E. Clinton Ave.
Tenafly, NJ 07670
201-569-0892

Turkey Swamp

When New Jersey's countryside was first settled, the scrub oak and pine area just north of the Pine Barrens was known as Turkey Swamp. Today, portions of the swamp have been set aside in a state wildlife management area (1,855 acres) and in a Monmouth County Park (498 acres). The two adjoin each other in places, providing a complex of public-use land that sprawls for quite a few miles. And since there's a good deal of water—including a 13-acre lake in the center of the county park, sphagnum swamps, and bogs—as well as vast stretches of forest land and open meadow for grazing, a multitude of wildlife lives here. White-tailed deer, cottontail rabbit, pheasant, quail, grouse, gray squirrel, woodcock, and various kinds of waterfowl, including mallard ducks and Canada geese, stay year-round. Additional rafts of ducks and geese settle down on the lake during fall migration.

Children canoeing at Turkey Swamp lake   *Bill Thomas*

Common egrets, green heron, great blue heron, and numerous songbirds are also here during the summer months, making it a great place to bird-watch from March until October.

Hiking

Excellent hiking trails throughout both the park and the wildlife area total several miles in length. Most are wooded or run along the edges of open fields; those in the WMA follow dirt roads.

Camping

No camping permitted in the WMA, but the county park has an excellent campground; sixty-five tent and trailer sites, with water, electricity, and hot showers. There's also a wilderness campground for group use, available by reservation only.

Boating and Canoeing

Canoeing is permitted on the county park lake; canoes, rowboats, and paddleboats are rented at the park.

How to Get There: From Freehold, take US 9 south to Co. Rd. 524 and head west. To reach Monmouth County's Turkey Swamp Park, turn left onto Georgia Rd.; park entrance is on right side of road. To reach Turkey Swamp WMA, continue west on 524 past Georgia Rd. to Co. Rd. 537 (Freehold–Mt. Holly Rd.); turn left and proceed to Co. Rd. 527 (Siloam Rd.), and turn left again. WMA access roads lead off to the left; the management area is divided into several parcels of land. One unimproved road leads through both the county park and a portion of the WMA that immediately adjoins it, but it's not open at all times.

Park open daily 8:00 A.M.–8:30 P.M., year-round. WMA open daily, year-round, 5:00 A.M.–9:00 P.M. Free admission to both.

For Additional Information:
Superintendent
Turkey Swamp Park
Box 86C, Nomoco Rd., RD 4
Freehold, NJ 07728
201-462-7286

Van Saun Park

This Bergen County park of some 100 acres is a special delight for children. It contains a children's zoo, a re-created 1860s farmyard, a walk-through aviary that presents a look at the state's famous Hackensack Meadowlands marsh area, pony rides, and a duck pond whose inhabitants like to be fed. A shaded garden surrounds historic Washington Spring, from which George Washington is believed to have drunk when he visited a Continental Army encampment here in 1780. Other facilities include tennis courts, sled runs, a lake for fishing in summer and ice skating in winter, and a bicycle trail/footpath. Picnic tables and some shelters are provided. This park is one of the most popular in the Bergen County system and often becomes very crowded in nice weather, particularly on Sundays.

How to Get There: From Hackensack, go north on Co. Rd. 503 (first called River St., then Kinderkamack Rd.) to Howland Ave. and turn left. At Forest Ave. turn right. Park is on right side of Forest Ave., between Howland and Continental Aves.

Grounds open daily, year-round, from sunset to a half hour after sunset. Admission to grounds free.

For Additional Information:
Bergen County Park Commission
327 E. Ridgewood Ave.
Paramus, NJ 07652
201-646-2680

Voorhees State Park

This small but rugged park includes about 500 acres of densely wooded hills that visitors may roam at will. Deer inhabit the hardwood forest, and hundreds of flowering plants delight the eye from spring through fall.

For those who prefer to drive through the park, there are roads leading to scenic views. An easily accessible picnic area has drinking water and a playground.

Voorhees Park is the site of the New Jersey Astronomical Association's observatory. Officially named the Edwin Aldrin Astronomical Observatory, in honor of the New Jersey native who was the second U.S. astronaut to set foot on the moon, it contains the largest refractory telescope lens ever constructed by amateurs. Check at the observatory or at the park office for a schedule of special programs open to the public.

Hiking and Nature Trails
Well-marked hiking trails take visitors through several miles of the park, while nature trails follow the banks of Willoughby Brook. Guided nature tours, conducted by a park naturalist, are available by reservation.

Camping
A family campground, with about thirty primitive sites for tents and trailers up to 24 feet, is open all year.

How to Get There: Located in Hunterdon Co. From High Bridge, go north on Co. Rd. 513 (High Bridge–Long Valley Rd.) to park entrance on left side of road.

Open daily, year-round, during daylight hours. Free admission.

For Additional Information:
Superintendent
Voorhees State Park
RD 2, Box 80, Rt. 513
Glen Gardner, NJ 08826
201-638-6969

Watchung Reservation

In the Watchung Mountain range of New Jersey lies the Watchung Reservation, often called a children's paradise. This 2,200-acre natural area is the largest in the Union County park system, an incredibly beautiful place apart from the urban areas surrounding it. A special feature of the reservation is the Trailside Nature and Science Center, an environmental education facility where weekend fairs, lectures, field walks, and courses are given to interested individuals and groups.

Among the buildings at the Trailside Center is one that houses a live exhibit of native snakes of New Jersey. There is also a planetarium that presents shows to the public at 2:00 and 2:30 P.M. on Saturdays and Sundays, and at 8:00 P.M. on Wednesdays; the show is not recommended for children under 8.

More than 6,000 specimens of minerals, shells, birds, reptiles, insects, and plants are displayed in a natural history museum. In a children's garden, you will see wild madder, feverfew, Venus's looking-glass, purple bergamot, apple mint, confederate violet, common yarrow, Roman wormwood, mugwort, and other herbs and flowers. You'll also find a path with animal track imprints in the pavement—casts of tracks made by bear, muskrat, mink, white-tailed deer fawn, gray fox, African lion, moose, woodcock, laughing gull, turkey, vulture, wood duck, great blue heron, and plover.

In season, usually near mid-May, there's a fabulous display of rhododendron. A 575-foot-high observation tower provides fine views and is an excellent spot from which to watch bird migrations.

Hiking and Horseback Riding

The Watchung Reservation has miles of hiking trails. Much of the park has been left in its natural state, and many of the trails follow old Indian paths through these sections.

There are 20 miles of scenic horseback trails, and rentals are available at Watchung Stable within the reservation.

Boating

At narrow, one-mile-long Surprise Lake, you can rent a rowboat from the end of March through October.

Winter Sports

Ice skating is permitted at both upper and lower Surprise Lake, and the longest cross-country ski trail in the county park system (nearly five miles) is here. There's also a shorter trail for beginners.

How to Get There: From US 22 near Mountainside, take "Mountainside, New Providence Road" exit. Go north on New Providence Rd. into park.

Park open 8:00 A.M.–11:00 P.M. daily, year-round. Center and museum open 1:00–5:00 P.M. daily, year-round, except for major holidays. Free (except very nominal charge for planetarium shows).

For Additional Information:

Director
Trailside Nature & Science Center
Coles Ave. & New Providence Rd.
Mountainside, NJ 07092
201-232-5930 (Center)
201-273-5547 (Stable)

Union County Department
of Parks & Recreation
P.O. Box 275
Elizabeth, NJ 07207
201-352-8431

Wawayanda State Park

Lying atop the Northern Highlands sections of New Jersey, Wawayanda State Park straddles the Sussex-Passaic county line near the New York border. Included within its 10,000 acres of wonderfully wild terrain are cedar swamps, northern hardwood forests, hemlock groves, ponds and streams. Three state-designated natural areas make up nearly half of the park's total acreage.

The largest body of water in the park is 255-acre Wawayanda Lake. At any given time, it is an entrancing sight. Four islands adorn the water's surface, pine trees edge its banks, and water lilies create floating gardens in its coves. But in mid-June, when the mountain laurel blooms, it is breathtaking.

Just east of Wawayanda Lake, up a hillside, is Laurel Pond. Its waters, partially spring-fed, are pure, and its shores are made beautiful by banks of tall pine and rhododendron. At the southeast end of the pond is a virgin stand of hemlock. So wild is this area that signs of bear have occasionally been spotted, and there is always the possibility of seeing a deer bound through the woods.

Farther to the east is a swamp with an extensive stand of southern white cedar, unusual because of its location. Such a stand is generally found along seacoast marshes. Interspersed among the trees are masses of rhododendrons, alive with pink blossoms in July.

Wawayanda State Park's northeast boundary adjoins Abram

S. Hewitt State Forest (described elsewhere). So atypical is this area that you may forget for a while that you're in one of the most industrialized states in the union.

Hiking

The Appalachian Trail cuts through the northern half of Wawayanda Park for about 4 miles, and additional trails totaling about 20 miles lace through all parts of the park. A free trail map is available at the park office.

Fishing and Boating

At the north end of Wawayanda Lake is a day-use area. A small boat launch is provided, and there are rowboats for rent; any motors used must be electric. Park waters open for fishing include Wawayanda Lake, Wawayanda Creek, and Laurel Pond; lurking in the depths are brown and rainbow trout, largemouth and smallmouth bass, and perch.

Swimming

A swimming beach with bathhouse is located at the north end of Wawayanda Lake.

Winter Sports

Winter visitors enjoy cross-country skiing, snowshoeing, sledding, and ice skating.

Camping

At this writing, group camping only is available, but family sites are being designed.

How to Get There: From West Milford, go north on Co. Rd. 513 (Union Valley Rd.) to Warwick Turnpike and turn left. Follow Warwick around southern end of Upper Greenwood Lake and then northward to Wawayanda Park's East Entrance Rd. Turn left into park; park office is located along this road.

Open daily, year-round, during daylight hours. Nominal admission fee daily, Memorial Day through Labor Day; Saturday and Sunday only, May 1 through Memorial Day and Labor Day through October.

For Additional Information:
Superintendent
Wawayanda State Park
P.O. Box 198
Highland Lakes, NJ 07422
201-764-4120

Weis Ecology Center

On Snake Den Road near Ringwood is the Weis Ecology Center, a private, nonprofit educational facility dedicated to increasing awareness and appreciation of the natural environment. Located on 120 acres in the north Jersey highlands adjacent to the 4,000 acres of wild woods in Norvin Green State Forest (described elsewhere), the center offers not only nature studies but also outdoor activities, and enthusiastically encourages interest in wildflowers, trees, shrubs, wildlife, and the land. Special weekend programs are offered year-round; groups may request custom-tailored environmental education programs. There is lodging on the grounds for overnight and extended periods.

The center is also popular with day visitors who come to swim, picnic, and use the playfields as well as to explore the natural world.

Hiking and Nature Trails
Several miles of hiking trails extend into Norvin Green State Forest. There are also some self-guided nature trails on the center grounds.

Swimming
Swimming in a 100-foot-by-200-foot, naturally-fed swimming pool; admission fee covers use.

How to Get There: From Oakland, go west on W. Oakland Ave. to Skyline Dr. Turn right and follow Skyline Dr. to its end at Co. Rd. 511. Turn left, go 1.8 miles south to Westbrook Rd., and make sharp turn to right. Proceed, bearing to left, and turn at second uphill left turn (Snake Den Rd.). Center is located near end of road.

At this writing, the center is undergoing transition from seasonal to year-round facility; hours and days open to be determined. Check before going. Nominal admission charge; children's rates.

For Additional Information:
Executive Director
Weis Ecology Center
150 Snake Den Rd.
Ringwood, NJ 07456
201-835-2160

West Essex Park

Comprising three separate units, each bordering the east bank of the Passaic River, this Essex County park of some 1,400 acres is the second largest in the county system and is preserved as a natural area.

The Center for Environmental Studies, located in the northernmost and largest section, is the hub of nature-oriented activities in Essex County. A greenhouse near the center provides a year-round haven for ferns, herbs, hanging baskets, and a wide variety of plants from all over the world. Visitors to the center also have access to a secluded picnic area and to an extensive environmental reference library.

The predominant feature of this park, though, is the Passaic River. Hatfield Swamp, part of which lies within the park, is among the most significant freshwater wetland tracts in northern New Jersey. Long known as a paradise for bird-watchers, the swamp regularly attracts individuals and organized groups. More than 150 species of birds have been sighted there over the years, including great blue herons, Canada geese, sandpipers, and a variety of ducks. Such wildlife species as the blue-spotted salamander, bog turtle, bald eagle, peregrine falcon, osprey, and Cooper's hawk—all listed as endangered in New Jersey—have been seen here.

The center can also supply information about other parks in the Essex County system.

Nature Trails

Two foot trails are maintained within the park—the Swinefield Interpretive Trail near the Center for Environmental Studies and the Cedar Ridge Interpretive Trail in the southernmost section of the park. Pamphlets for a self-guided tour of each may be picked up at the center. Also found on the center grounds is a Sensitivity Trail; a tape-recorded message guides blindfolded visitors along the trail and stresses the beauty of the sound, smell, and feel of nature.

Canoeing

Among the most popular programs offered in the park are the naturalist-guided canoe trips on the Passaic River and, when water levels permit, into Hatfield Swamp. Since the river is normally slow-moving in this area and drops an average of only 2 inches to the mile, even beginners are welcome. All necessary equipment and shuttling are provided, and participants will receive instructions on canoeing techniques. Trips for the general public, some half-day and some full-day, are scheduled every Saturday and Sunday from April to November; groups may make special arrangements for weekday trips. Registration forms are available from the center; advance registration and payment of fees required.

Since much of this park consists of wetlands, the canoe is an ideal vehicle for exploring it. Though the center will not rent its canoes for self-guided trips, visitors are welcome to bring canoes along and launch them from special access areas at the center and in other parts of the park.

How to Get There: From Exit 4 of I-280 just east of the Passaic River, take Eisenhower Pkwy. south to Eagle Rock Ave. and turn right. Proceed to the Center for Environmental Activities. It's located at 621 Eagle Rock Ave. on left side of road.

Grounds open daily, year-round, during daylight hours; free. Hours for center may vary, depending upon special programs being offered; a nominal fee may be charged for some programs.

For Additional Information:

Center for Environmental Studies
621 Eagle Rock Ave.
Roseland, NJ 07068
201-228-2210

Essex County Dept. of Parks,
Recreation & Cultural Affairs
115 Clifton Ave.
Newark, NJ 07104
201-482-6400

Whittingham Wildlife Management Area

In mountainous Sussex County is the Whittingham Wildlife Management Area, some 1,500 acres of woodland, marsh, and open field. Four hundred of those acres have been set aside as a nature sanctuary and designated as a state natural area.

White-tailed deer, rabbit, grouse, woodcock, squirrel, pheasant, beaver, otter, wood duck, mallards, and black ducks live here. The forest consists of mixed hardwoods, and along the open fields are hedgerows maintained for the shelter and cover of wildlife. Headwaters of the Pequest River form here.

Hiking
Dirt roads double as trails and lead into parts of the tract, including the Whittingham Natural Area.

How to Get There: From Newton, go south on US 206 to Springdale. Then go west (right turn) on Springdale-Fredon Rd., which passes through the northern part of the WMA, or go southwest (right turn) on Springdale-Tranquility Rd. along WMA's eastern border. Look for signs.

Open daily, year-round, 5:00 A.M.–9:00 P.M. Free.

For Additional Information:

Whittingham Wildlife Management Area
c/o Clinton Wildlife Management Area
Box 409
Hampton, NJ 08827
201-735-8793

Wilderness Survival and Tracking School

Although Tom Brown, Inc., has its headquarters a few miles beyond our 50-mile radius, this company offers a unique service worth including.

Tom Brown, Jr., author of a fast-selling autobiography called *The Tracker,* has launched the nation's largest wilderness survival school from his home near Milford. Although he teaches courses all over the country, he also holds classes on his own 500-acre farm and in the depths of New Jersey's Pine Barrens (described elsewhere as Pinelands National Reserve). So phenomenal has been his success that courses at this writing are booked solid a full year in advance.

In addition to basic survival skills, Brown teaches his students Indian philosophy and technique in the hope of preserving the Native Americans' heritage. The big attraction for many students, though, seems to be the instruction on tracking animals. Brown's tracking methods are so highly regarded they are currently being used in universities across the country, and Cornell will publish his book on the subject.

Brown currently offers five basic survival courses: a weekend mini-course, a week-long standard, the advanced (seven days in the New Jersey Pine Barrens), the expert (twenty-one days in Montana's Bob Marshall Wilderness Area), and a children's weekend course for ages 6 to 12. Brown will also arrange special outings, such as wilderness canoeing and camping trips that focus on survival.

For Additional Information:

Tom Brown, Inc.
P.O. Box 318
Milford, NJ 08848
201-993-7211

Willowwood Arboretum

In the Hacklebarney hills of north central New Jersey is Willowwood Arboretum, comprising some 130 acres of rolling land in a shallow valley. Established in 1950 as a private arboretum, this unit of the Morris County Park System includes many specimens of plants and trees that date back to 1908.

Today, about 3,500 kinds of native and exotic plants are found there and are used for classes in identification and landscape design. There are two small formal gardens, but the pervading feeling at Willowwood is of pleasant, informal walks in open areas and woodland.

Systematic collections now include about 30 kinds of oaks, 52 of maples, 110 of willows, a single superb redwood now more than 70 feet tall, hillsides of pink lady's slippers, masses of ferns, and drifts of flowering dogwood. Fine collections of lilacs, magnolias, hollies, cherries, and conifers are also featured, along with a cottage herb garden and a Japanese-style pool garden.

A number of gardening workshops are held at the arboretum throughout the year for a nominal charge.

How to Get There: Located near Hacklebarney State Park (described elsewhere) in Morris County.

Open daily, year-round, at all times, by appointment only. Detailed directions will be given when appointment is made. Free.

For Additional Information:

Willowwood Arboretum
c/o Morris County Park Commission
53 E. Hanover Ave.
P.O. Box 1295R
Morristown, NJ 07960
201-285-6166

Part 4

Bill Thomas

Natural Attractions in
New York
City

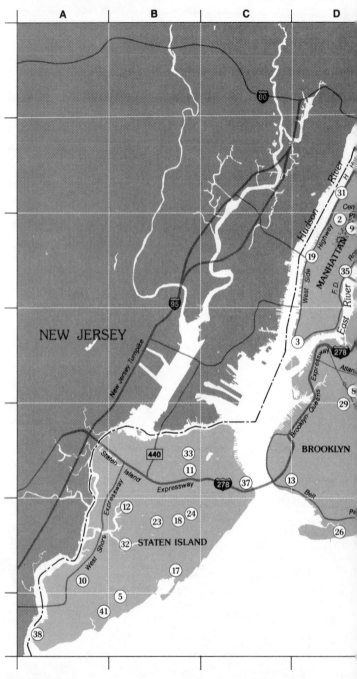

NEW YORK CITY

1. Alley Park **G-3**
2. American Museum of Natural History and Hayden Planetarium **D-3**
3. Battery Park **D-4**
4. The Biblical Garden of the Cathedral of St. John the Divine **D-2**
5. Blue Heron Park **B-7**
6. Breezy Point **E-6**
7. Bronx Zoo **E-2**
8. Brooklyn Botanic Garden **D-4**
9. Central Park **D-3**

10. Clay Pit Ponds State Park Preserve **A-6**
11. Clove Lakes Park **B-5**
12. Davis Wildlife Refuge **B-6**
13. Dyker Beach Park **C/D-5**
14. Flushing Meadows–Corona Park **F-3**
15. Forest Park **F-4**
16. Fort Tryon Park and the Cloisters **E-1**
17. Great Kills Park **B-6**
18. High Rock Park Conservation Center **B-6**
19. Hudson River Dayline Cruise **D-3**
20. Inwood Hill Park **E-1**

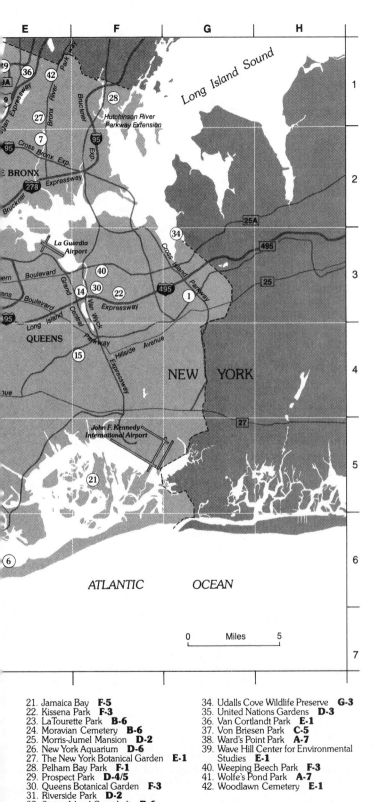

One
The Bronx

Bronx Zoo

One of the most impressive zoological parks in the nation is the Bronx Zoo, a 232-acre woodland sanctuary where more than 3,000 wild animals live. The atmosphere is pleasant, generally spacious, and uncrowded, for both visitors and zoo residents. Many animals live in settings so natural you sometimes find it hard to remember this actually is a zoo. Wolves and Kodiak brown bears roam virtually free. There are ponds and lakes where numerous waterfowl swim unrestrained, and there are sloughs so realistic they might be in some distant southern swamp. Open fields, meadows, woodlands, and rock cliffs provide the settings.

It's possible to take a one-day trip around the world here. Thematic displays include the African Plains, where herds of antelope graze and great cranes call forlornly, where prides of lions laze in the shade of trees. Buffalo, or American bison, elk, wolf, and bear make up part of a North American display. Wild Asia, open May through October, duplicates the environment of the great Asian heartland, where the rare Siberian tiger is king of all he surveys.

In the Rare Animals Range are creatures already extinct in the wild. The zoo, of course, tries to breed rare species and carefully raise their young. Some 600 babies of various species are born here each year.

The innovative Children's Zoo enables youngsters to imitate as well as see animals. They can crawl into a child-size prairie dog burrow, learn a form of animal escape by sliding down a hollow tree, and listen as a fox does through oversize replicas of fox ears. A house of nocturnal animals and rides on camels and elephants add excitement to a zoo visit.

And when it all becomes too much for you, you can stop to rest on a carpet of green grass under sprawling locust and oak trees with canopies so dense that the sun seldom breaks through even on the hottest summer day. This is a place to enjoy in all seasons. Come here in autumn to glory in the fall color or in winter to photograph snow scenes. In the spring, the landscape is adorned by blossoming trees and plants.

How to Get There: Located in central part of the Bronx. From Cross Bronx Expwy. (I-95), go north on Bronx River Pkwy. to zoo. Follow signs to parking area. *By subway*: #2 to Pelham Pkwy., or #2 or 5 to E. Tremont Ave. *By bus*: Pelham Pkwy. Bus Service, Inc., provides

Alaska brown bears frolic at the Bronx Zoo.   *Bill Thomas*

express service from midtown Manhattan Monday through Saturday, except holidays.

Open daily, year-round, at 10:00 A.M. Closes at 5:30 P.M., Sunday and holidays; at 5:00 during warm weather months, other days; and at 4:30 during winter months, other days. Nominal admission fee Friday through Monday; free, Tuesday through Thursday. Nominal parking fee at all times.

For Additional Information:
The New York Zoological Society
185th St. & Southern Blvd.
Bronx, NY 10460
212-220-5100 or 212-220-5121

The New York Botanical Garden

One of New York's most fascinating green oases is the New York Botanical Garden, a paradise of some 250 acres in north central Bronx. Among the delights are open meadows, virgin woodland, a rushing white-water stream, brooks, two ponds, and millions of plants (the Herbarium alone has nearly 4 million plant specimens).

The garden is known around the world for its research and field expeditions into all parts of the globe. Among the variety of environments that have been re-created are wetlands, upland forest, tropical jungle, and desert. The library of some 400,000 volumes is the largest of its kind in the world.

One of the main attractions at the gardens, one that dominates the landscape, is the great glass castle called the Enid A. Haupt Conservatory. It houses eleven large galleries, including a central palm court with a 90-foot dome. A palm grove, fern jungle, Old World and New World deserts, an orangerie, a collection of plants important for their economic value, and a tunnel filled with plants that thrive in subdued light are among its attractions.

Other major attractions are the Bechtel Memorial Rose Garden, with more than 150 varieties of tea roses, floribundas, grandifloras, and other hybrids; the Jane Watson Memorial Garden with a systematic collection of flowering herbaceous and woody plants; the Herb Garden; the Rock Garden; the Native Plant Garden; Pine Hill, with more than fifty species of pines from all parts of the world; and the Hemlock Forest.

The latter is one of the most amazing natural attractions in New York. Consisting of 40 acres of virgin forest, it is possibly the only woodland in New York City left uncut since Native American days. It is also the southernmost natural stand of Canadian hemlock on the eastern coast. Besides hemlock, the other predominant trees are cherry birch, tulip tree, white ash, American beech, and red oak. Growing in the understory are Solomon's seal, ironwood, American graffiti tree, coltsfoot (a fern with leaves shaped like a horse's foot), and arrowwood. Along the west end of the forest is a flourishing stand of orange and lemon trees.

The forest teems with animals, too, such as red and gray squirrels, southern flying squirrels, rabbits, raccoons, opossums, and small reptiles and amphibians. Enhancing the forest ecosystem is the Bronx River, which flows through it. The river itself, except for some debris lodged along part of the way, is mostly pristine within the botanical garden and even has a small but lovely waterfall.

The garden also features botanical intrigue. Just left of the entrance to the main building is a nondescript plant whose behavior has baffled even botanists. Called the Glastonbury thorn, a species of hawthorn that has become a legend in England where it is believed to have originated, it puts out small white blossoms not only in the spring but also, mysteriously, at Christmas. Just why it does this no one knows.

Walkways lead throughout the grounds. This is also one of the finest places in New York City for nature and plant photography. Bring some fast film for the dark forested areas.

How to Get There: From Cross Bronx Expwy. (I-95), take Jerome Ave. north to Fordham Rd. and turn right. At Crotona Ave. turn left and proceed to where Crotona joins Southern Blvd. Follow Southern Blvd. north to entrance on right side of road near intersection with Bedford Park Blvd. Many signs to follow. *By subway:* #2 or 5 to 149th St.–Third Ave., then free transfer to bus Bx 55; D to 161st St., then free transfer to Bx 55; #4 or D to Bedford Park, then Bx 17. *By rail:* Conrail Harlem Line to Botanical Garden.

Open daily, year-round; 8:00 A.M.–7:00 P.M. in summer, 10:00 A.M.–5:00 P.M. in winter. Free admission. Nominal parking fee.

For Additional Information:
The New York Botanical Garden
Bronx, NY 10458
212-220-8777—General Information
212-220-8700—Administration

Pelham Bay Park

One of the most magnificent wild parks within New York City is Pelham Bay, some 2,100 acres of natural complexities. One neither expects nor can quite believe such a place exists within the confines of such a sprawling metropolitan area. Acclaimed as the most diverse city park in America, it encompasses woodland, marsh, meadow, 13 miles of saltwater shoreline, rivers, estuaries, lagoons, coves, upland woods, and even islands.

The largest city park in New York, Pelham Bay contains great expanses of marshland. Tall salt meadow cord grass grows in the soggy areas, along the marsh streams that feed the creeks, and along the mosquito ditch embankments. On drier ground the short salt meadow cord grass takes over, while farther upland black grass or juncus (actually not a grass, but a member of the lily family) appears as a deeply contrasting green.

You can sun on glacial boulders and gneiss outcroppings, remnants of the last Ice Age; view the vast expanse of Long Island Sound; dig for clams in inlets whose character changes daily with the ebb and flow of the tide; watch fiddler crabs lay eggs on gravelly beaches; or monitor the seasonal changes in the marsh, as it evolves from the verdant green of spring and summer to winter's chocolate brown.

Pelham Bay contains a variety of rocks, many of which have never been identified. Some have been carried downriver from New England and the Canadian Shield south of Hudson Bay. There are unexpected formations and configurations of rocks not seen anywhere else in the mid-Atlantic states, some of historical significance, others used by the Siwanoy Indians for worship. The coves and beaches of Hunter's Island yielded shells the Siwanoy transformed into ornamental beads and money. In the tidal inlet west of Orchard Beach, once accessible to Long Island Sound, the Siwanoy established a large fishing camp, and occasionally artifacts dating back to that era are still found.

Two woodlands in the park are within the Hunter Island Marine Zoology and Geology Sanctuary. Both areas were once islands themselves, known locally as Twin and Hunter's Islands; today, they are part of the mainland. Red and white oak, chestnut oak, pin oak, hickory and maple, dogwood, sassafras, wild cherry, and winged sumac make up the forest. Food-producing plants such as crabapple trees, Juneberry bushes, honey locust, chestnut oaks, hickory, black locust, and black cherry provide forage for the vast wildlife population. Squirrel, raccoon, muskrat, opossum, white-tailed deer, barn and barred owls, hawks, and hundreds of songbirds and waterfowl inhabit the area. Among the waterfowl are Canada and snow geese, razorbills, red-breasted mergansers, American widgeon, goldeneye, buffleheads, mallards, black ducks, horned grebes, and wood duck. Some are migrants, but many stay year-round. Great blue heron, green heron, common egret, and an occasional snowy egret fish in these waters.

The Thomas Pell Wildlife Refuge is a 50-acre remnant of what was once a 5,000-acre salt marsh in the East Bronx. Other smaller segments of marsh can be found near Bartow Creek on the southern end of Rodman's Neck and on the northern portion of Hunter's Island.

Mollusks cover the banks of Goose Creek at low tide, and a multitude of crabs live in this watery world. Eels and other fish are found in the creek, and woodcocks, bitterns, and sandpipers dwell in the adjacent marshlands.

The park has its formal side, too. On Shore Road in Pelham Bay are the Bartow-Pell Mansion and Gardens, numbered among the most beautiful landscaped spots in the city. The immaculate grounds, terraced gardens, rhododendron walk, and nineteenth-century mansion are reminiscent of what life once was here, in a serene past filled with birdsong and murmuring brooks. Today, they're maintained by the International Garden Club, which has its headquarters here.

Although hordes of people throng here on summer weekends, you can usually find a quiet, out-of-the-way corner away from the recreation areas.

Hiking and Horseback Riding

Miles of park trails are open to hikers and horseback riders. Horses may be rented in the area; among stables are Cy's Pelham Parkway Riding Academy (212-822-8510) and Pelham Bit Stables (212-885-9848).

Swimming

The extensive waterfront includes Orchard Beach, well known for its fine swimming.

Fishing and Boating

From the outermost rocks of Hunter's and Twin Islands, fishermen catch striped bass, tomcod, kingfish, flounder, and black bass. Sailboats and motorboats may be rented at nearby City Island.

How to Get There: Located along Westchester County border in northeast corner of the Bronx. From New England Thruway (I-95), which passes through part of the park, take Orchard Beach exit and head northeast into park. Follow signs. *By subway*: #6 to last stop, Pelham Bay Park.

Grounds open at all times. Some fee areas.

For Additional Information:

Supervisor
Urban Park Rangers—Bronx
Van Cortlandt Stadium
Van Cortlandt Park South
Broadway & 242nd St.
Bronx, NY 10471
212-822-4336

Supervisor
Parks & Recreation Department
Bronx Headquarters
Bronx Park East & Birchall Ave.
Bronx, NY 10462
212-828-3200

International Garden Club, Inc.
Pelham Bay Park
Shore Rd.
Bronx, NY 10464
212-885-1461

Van Cortlandt Park

In the Bronx is one of New York City's most diverse parks, huge Van Cortlandt, which sprawls over 1,146 acres of mixed hardwood forest, swamp, marsh, and lake. Rugged, hilly, and in places heavily wooded, it was once a popular hunting ground of the Mohicans. While it possesses some of the wildest terrain in New York City, it also provides many recreational facilities. Runners find it challenging; archers come for organized shoots; swimmers enjoy the pool; picnickers, golfers, ball players, hikers, bird-watchers, and those who just want to escape the pressures of the city all come here.

A swamp adjacent to a 36-acre lake is kept alive by Tibbetts Brook, a little stream that meanders down from Yonkers. The swamp, the wooded portions of the park, and a small cattail marsh that has been granted State Wetland status to insure its protection attract a variety of birds and have earned for this park the reputation as one of the best bird-watching areas in the city. On spring weekdays, you may occasionally see green and great blue herons. The fish crow, wood duck, long-billed marsh wren, Traill's flycatcher, rusty blackbird, swallow, and warbling vireo come here, and sometimes Virginia rail and sora are seen. In winter, the common snipe and rusty blackbird may linger until January. The wooded slopes of the park are excellent for viewing migrating birds in the spring. In the northeastern corner of the park is a sycamore swamp filled with spring warblers, including such rare species as the golden-winged and cerulean. There are also two designated bird sanctuaries in the park.

Squirrel, rabbit, muskrat, pheasant, red fox, raccoon, chipmunk, and turtle thrive in the varied surroundings here.

Van Cortlandt Mansion, built as a Colonial farmhouse in 1748, is maintained as a museum by the Colonial Dames. A formal Dutch garden surrounds it.

Hiking and Horseback Riding

An extensive, well-marked trail system leads throughout the park. The rugged 5-mile varsity cross-country course here is famous among runners-in-the-know as the first such course in the country; nearly every famous runner in the United States has tried this course at one time or another. The Old Croton Aqueduct hiking trail, which runs north into Westchester County, has its beginning in this park.

A 7-mile-long bridle trail, longest in the city park system, is located here; horses may be rented at the park stable (212-549-6200).

Fishing and Boating

Fishing for largemouth bass, carp, catfish, and bluegill is permitted; rowboats may be rented at the park's 36-acre lake.

Winter Sports

Ice skating is allowed on the park's larger lake, and there are some fine hills for sledding.

How to Get There: Exit 18 on Henry Hudson Pkwy. (NY 9A) is near center of park, which is in northwestern part of the Bronx along Westchester County border. *By subway:* #1 to last stop, Van Cortlandt Park at W. 242nd St.

Park open at all times. Free admission. Some fee areas.

For Additional Information:

Supervisor	Supervisor
Urban Park Rangers—Bronx	Parks & Recreation Dept.
Van Cortlandt Stadium	Bronx Headquarters
Van Cortlandt Park South	Bronx Park East & Birchall Ave.
Broadway & 242nd St.	Bronx, NY 10462
Bronx, NY 10471	*212-828-3200*
212-822-4336	

Wave Hill Center for Environmental Studies

On a high bluff overlooking the Hudson River are the magnificent grounds of an unusual nature preserve. Known as Wave Hill, it encompasses wild woods, formal gardens, sweeping lawns dotted with huge old trees, and a majestic nineteenth-century mansion. The former estate has served as home to Mark Twain, Arturo Toscanini, and, when he was 12, Teddy Roosevelt, who gained a love for birds here that remained with him throughout his life. Today, Wave Hill remains a living laboratory, where raccoons and opossums den in hollow oaks, mourning doves nest in mountain maples, and voles can be seen skittering around the grounds.

Now a designated National Environmental Educational Landmark, Wave Hill has wild as well as formal gardens and three greenhouses, one a smaller version of the Palm Court of the New York Botanical Garden. Thousands of plants are nurtured, both indoors and out, ranging from native American elms to exotic South African specimens, as well as succulents and cacti. Also found here are a lily pond, an herb garden with more than 150 varieties, a wildflower garden traversed by a nature trail, and a collection of about 125 trees like those that grow on George Washington's plantation at Mount Vernon. Across the river, you can see the New Jersey Palisades.

Wave Hill offers an outstanding variety of programs and field trips.

How to Get There: Located in northwest corner of the Bronx. From Henry Hudson Pkwy. northbound (NY 9A), exit on 246th St. and continue north on service road that parallels Pkwy. to 252nd St. At 252nd St., turn left over Pkwy. and immediately turn left again. At 249th St., turn right and proceed straight to Wave Hill gate. *By subway:* #1 to 231st St., then M100 bus up to 252nd St. Or A to last stop (207th St. and Broadway), then M100 bus up Broadway to 252nd St. *By express bus:* Mid-Manhattan Riverdale Express (phone 212-881-1000 for schedule).

Grounds open daily, year-round; 10:00 A.M.–4:30 P.M. weekdays, 10:00 A.M.–5:30 P.M. Saturday and Sunday. Greenhouses open daily, 10:00 A.M.–noon and 2:00–4:00 P.M. Free on weekdays; nominal admission, Saturday and Sunday; under 14 free.

For Additional Information:

Wave Hill Center for
Environmental Studies
675 W. 252nd St.
Bronx, NY 10471
212-549-2055

Woodlawn Cemetery

Founded in 1863 as a rural burial ground, at a time when the Bronx was mostly farmland, Woodlawn Cemetery has managed to remain an island of serenity in a sea of development to this day. It is justifiably known as one of the most beautiful cemeteries in the world.

Although more than 250,000 people are buried here, the grounds also serve as a park, an arboretum, and a bird sanctuary. Woodlawn Lake attracts mallard ducks and Canada geese; and occasionally a sea gull drops by to survey the pastoral scene. More than 100 species of birds have been sighted here.

Throughout Woodlawn's 400 acres of meadows and gentle hills are 3,500 trees. About 50 of them are replaced each year to help maintain the cemetery's well-cared-for look. Among the species to be seen are hemlock, ash, cherry, dogwood, catalpa, cypress, beech, and sycamore.

Many historical figures—politicians, military men, writers, musicians, entertainers, and businessmen—are buried here. Memorials range from elaborate mausoleums to simple headstones, and the diversity of artistic and sculptural styles is astonishing.

How to Get There: Located in northern Bronx near Westchester County border, just east of Van Cortlandt Park (described elsewhere). From Major Deegan Expwy. (I-87), exit at E. 233rd St. Go east on 233rd St. to entrance road near Webster Ave., and turn right into cemetery. Or, from same Deegan Expwy. exit, pick up Jerome Ave. south to cemetery entrance on left side of road. *By subway:* #4 to Woodlawn station opposite Jerome Ave. entrance.

Open daily, year-round, 9:30–4:30. Free. Map of grounds and other literature available at Jerome Ave. gate.

For Additional Information:

Main Office	Executive Office
Woodlawn Cemetery	Woodlawn Cemetery
233rd St. & Webster Ave.	20 E. 23rd St.
Bronx, NY 10470	New York, NY 10010
212-547-5400	*212-254-4470*

Two
Brooklyn

Brooklyn Botanic Garden

The Brooklyn Botanic Garden is not one, but many gardens. Situated in the most populous borough of the most densely populated city in the nation, the garden is an oasis, a great touch of green expanse amid a sea of development. It is only 50 acres in size, but because of its diversity and the sense of spaciousness achieved by its excellent design, it seems considerably larger. Some 12,000 plants, representing every part of the world, grow here.

Among some of the special collections here are the Rhododendron Garden, Rose Garden, Rock Garden, Herb Garden, Iris Garden, Children's Garden, a Fragrance Garden for the blind, a Shakespearean Garden, and two lily pools. Perhaps the loveliest of all is an exquisite Japanese Garden, where five cascading waterfalls empty into a lake reflecting evergreens and weeping Higan cherry trees; many authorities rate it as the most beautiful garden in the Western Hemisphere.

A conservatory features a tropical rain forest, a desert house, a fern house, a bromeliad (air plant) house, and one of the world's finest bonsai collections, with specimens from 50 to 800 years old.

Noted as much for its trees as for its flowers, the garden includes nearly 250 tree monarchs, of which three are national champions (largest of their species in the United States).

Spring is unquestionably the best time of year to visit the garden, but it's open and worthwhile all year. Blooming periods extend from late winter through November. From April into May, when hundreds of cherry trees are in bloom, the garden sponsors a Cherry Blossom Festival.

A superlative educational program offers courses related to horticulture, botany, and conservation.

Brooklyn Botanic Garden also has two branches within the 50-mile radius prescribed for this book that are open to the public: the 12-acre Clark Garden at Albertson, N.Y., and the Kitchawan Research Station near Ossining, N.Y., 233 acres of natural woodlands, meadows, and demonstration gardens. Visitors to the latter will find 5 miles of trails to explore.

How to Get There: Located at 1000 Washington Ave. within Prospect Park (described elsewhere), on west side of street. From Atlantic Ave. in northern Brooklyn, go south on Washington Ave. to garden.

A serene oasis at the Brooklyn Botanic Garden

By subway: #2, 3, or 4 train to Eastern Pkwy.–Brooklyn Museum Station; D, M, QB, or SS trains to Prospect Park.

Open 8:00 A.M.–6:00 P.M., Tuesday through Friday, May through August; 10:00 A.M.–6:00 P.M. weekends and holidays (including Monday holidays). 8:00 A.M.–4:30 P.M., Tuesday through Friday, September through April; 10:00 A.M.–4:30 P.M., weekends and holidays (including Monday holidays). Conservatory open 10:00 A.M.–4:00 P.M., Tuesday through Friday; 11:00 A.M.–4:00 P.M. weekends and holidays. Free admission. Nominal entrance fee for conservatory and some special gardens on weekends and holidays only.

For Additional Information:

Brooklyn Botanic Garden
1000 Washington Ave.
Brooklyn, NY 11225
212-622-4433

Dyker Beach Park

One of the least known of all city parks, Dyker Beach covers 217 acres in southwest Brooklyn. Although part of the park has been developed for recreation, most of it is a vast expanse of lawns and trees, enhanced by a small lake with marsh plants. There are fine views of Gravesend Bay and the Verrazano-Narrows Bridge, and delightful breezes from the water to cool you. Sea gulls fly about, from ocean to meadows and back again. In autumn, various species of land birds migrate above you. A pedestrian walkway over the Shore Parkway (also called Belt Parkway and Leif Ericson Drive) from Bay 8th Street and Cropsey Ave. leads to the waterfront, where fishermen may try their luck. In other parts of the park, people play golf, tennis, soccer, baseball, and football; but the southern portion is an ideal place for peace, quiet, and relaxation. Dyker Beach has been a park since July 24, 1895, and famed park architect Frederick Law Olmsted predicted that "it will be the finest seaside park in the world . . ."

How to Get There: From Brooklyn-Queens Expwy. (I-278) in southwest Brooklyn, take the 92nd St. Exit and go east on 92nd St. to park. 92nd St. ends at Seventh Ave., along western border of park. *By subway:* RR to 86th St. and Fourth Ave.

Open daily, year-round, at all times. Free.

For Additional Information:

Supervisor
Urban Park Rangers—Brooklyn
NYC Dept. of Parks &
Recreation
95 Prospect Park West
Brooklyn, NY 11215
212-856-4210

Director, NYC Dept. of Parks &
Recreation
Brooklyn Headquarters
Litchfield Mansion
Prospect Park West & 5th St.
Brooklyn, NY 11215
212-768-2300

Jamaica Bay

See listing under Gateway National Recreation Area, page 6.

New York Aquarium

A grand opportunity to explore the enchanting underwater world of the ocean without great expense or hassle awaits visitors to the New York Aquarium, one of the finest in the nation. A popular attraction is the shark exhibit, where some forty species of sharks and rays swim about in a 90,000-gallon tank. There are also exotic tropical fish, horseshoe crabs, fiddler and ghost crabs, penguins from the Antarctic, eels, piranhas, white beluga whales, and dolphins.

Many displays re-create the natural environment of their inhabitants. Some of the mid-Atlantic and New England states' prime sport and table fish—striped bass, summer flounder, pickerel, pike, and sea bass—are displayed. Visitors may also peer beneath the surface of a typical Long Island freshwater pond to see the surprising number of creatures living there or look into the recesses of an Indo-Pacific reef and see the deep, dark cavern home of a giant Pacific octopus.

How to Get There: Located at Coney Island in south Brooklyn. From Exit 7 on Belt Pkwy. (Shore Pkwy.), take Ocean Pkwy. south. Ocean Pkwy. curves right into Surf Ave. Proceed west to aquarium parking lot on left side of road. *By subway:* D, F, M, or QB to W. 8th St.; B or N to Coney Island.

Open daily, year-round, 10:00 A.M.; closes 6:00 P.M., Monday through Friday, and 7:00 P.M., Saturday, Sunday and holidays, during summer months; closes 5:00 P.M. rest of year. Nominal admission charge; special rates for senior citizens (certain hours only) and children 12 and under. Also parking fee.

For Additional Information:

The New York Aquarium
c/o The New York Zoological Society
Bronx, NY 10460
212-266-8500

Prospect Park

In the heart of Brooklyn is 526-acre Prospect Park, containing a number of different ecosystems. Only one of them is completely natural—a 20-acre tract of undisturbed forest. This pre-Colonial woodland has remained intact as a memorial to a Revolutionary War battle fought here in 1776.

The Camperdown elm, located at the foot of the northeast slope of Breeze Hill, is described in *Tree Trails in Prospect Park* as the "most distinguished tree in the city and possibly in the state." It is a rare weeping variety of Scotch elm with intricate, sprawling branches. Standing on the Nethermead is the largest tree in the park, an American elm more than 300 years old. A Saul oak in the park ranks as a national co-champion; it and a tree in Roslyn, Pennsylvania, share the honor of being the largest of this species in the United States.

Generally speaking, the largest trees in the park, many of them nearly 200 years old, are found among the mixed hardwoods that make up the pre-Colonial woodland mentioned above. White, red, and black oak, along with hickory, black birch, black beech, tulip, and sweet and sour gum dominate this section, spreading their branches over an understory of creepers and glens of ferns.

Also in the park is a system of interconnecting pools, streams, and 60-acre man-made Prospect Lake, dotted with islands. Several meadows provide grassy open space in the park. The largest, Long Meadow, stretches across the northern section. In the central section, the more protected Nethermead (Lower Meadow) nestles between wooded hills.

All these habitats combine to make Prospect Park one of the best bird-watching areas in the metropolitan region. More than 250 species have been sighted here, among them the northern phalarope, prothonotary warbler, Townsend's warbler, Bachman's sparrow, Caspian tern, Henslow's lark, Swainson's warbler, cattle egret, scissor-tailed flycatcher, tufted titmouse, and the clay-colored sparrow.

Prospect Park also has a small zoo with exotic animals and a re-created farmyard; a gardenlike area known as the Vale of Cashmere, currently being restored; an environmental center; and many recreational facilities.

The Urban Park Rangers (described elsewhere) have their Brooklyn office in this park. In addition to providing information about borough parks, they offer guided tours and workshops on the environment, history, and horticulture. They also conduct guided tours through the salt marsh in Brooklyn's Marine Park and hope to extend programs to other borough parks in the near future.

Hiking and Horseback Riding

A complex of foot and bridle trails (no rentals) weaves through the park.

Boating

Pedal boats may be rented for use on Prospect Lake.

Winter Sports

Ice skating at an outdoor rink, as well as sledding and skiing on park slopes, are all enjoyed here in the winter.

How to Get There: From Brooklyn-Queens Expwy. (I-278) in northwest Brooklyn, go southeast on Flatbush Ave. to park entrance at Grand Army Plaza, located at park's northern boundary. *By subway:* #2, 3, or 4 to Grand Army Plaza.

Open at all times. Free.

For Additional Information:

Supervisor
Urban Park Rangers—Brooklyn
NYC Dept. of Parks & Recreation
95 Prospect Park West
Brooklyn, NY 11215
212-856-4210

Director, NYC Dept. of Parks & Recreation
Brooklyn Headquarters
Litchfield Mansion
Prospect Park West & 5th St.
Brooklyn, NY 11215
212-768-2300

Three

Manhattan

American Museum of Natural History and Hayden Planetarium

Visiting the American Museum of Natural History is akin to taking a one-day trip around the world—and through time as well. It encompasses what seems to be every aspect of the natural sciences on all continents, not only in contemporary time, but in ages past. Founded in 1869, it and its satellite, the Hayden Planetarium, which opened its doors in 1935, cover more than 25 acres on the west side of Manhattan. The two are unquestionably major tourist attractions.

A total of twenty-two buildings, all connected, house the museum and planetarium. There are thirty-eight exhibition halls currently open to viewing, in addition to many corridors used as display areas. No other museum of its kind in the world has more exhibition space.

The variety of displays is overwhelming. You'll see an ancient armadillo the size of a pony, precious gems such as the Star of India sapphire, a gigantic model of a blue whale. The dioramas are impressive in their realism; with a little imagination you can share the world of a water buffalo, smell the plains grasses in the air, stand atop a cliff high above the Bering Sea alongside puffins and auklets.

You'll find more than 34 million artifacts and specimens, among them some 15 million insect specimens, more than 400,000 specimens of fish, and more than 250,000 of mammals.

The huge Ahnighito meteorite at the planetarium is the largest on display anywhere; it weighs nearly 70,000 pounds. On a special scale, you may calculate your "space weight" and learn what you'd weigh on other planets and the moon. Through the magic of a huge projector, the auditorium's dome is transformed into a night sky—filled with the wonders of the universe.

How to Get There: Located on Central Park West between W. 77th St. and W. 81st St. *By subway:* #1 to 79th St. and Broadway; AA, B, or CC to 81st St. and Central Park West. *By bus:* M7, M10, M11, M17, M104.

Museum open daily, 10:00 A.M.–4:45 P.M., Monday through Saturday, until 9:00 P.M. Wednesday; 11:00 A.M.–5:00 P.M., Sunday and holidays; closed January 1, Thanksgiving, December 25. Admission by contribution (suggested amount is nominal). Planetarium open in conjunction with daily programs at varying times. Fixed admission fee also allows free admission to museum; children under 5 are discouraged from attending planetarium shows.

For Additional Information:

American Museum of Natural History and Hayden Planetarium
Central Park West at 79th Street
New York, NY 10024
212-873-4225
212-873-8828 (Planetarium Show Information)

Battery Park

At the southernmost tip of Manhattan, where the Hudson and East Rivers merge into New York Bay, is an arc of greenery that has always held a special place in the hearts of New Yorkers. It is a pleasant expanse of lawns and trees and waterfront promenade, where sea breezes cool the land and where the distant horizons of New York Harbor set one to dreaming.

Battery Park represents the roots of New York City. It was near here that the city's history began, when Italian navigator Giovanni da Verrazano first set foot ashore in 1524 after discovering New York Harbor. Much history has occurred in this area in the centuries since then, and there are numerous statues and memorials throughout the park that commemorate these events. Also in the park and open to the public free of charge is the Castle Clinton National Monument, a restored fort built between 1807 and 1811 in anticipation of the War of 1812.

On a lawn adjoining Castle Clinton is a cluster of trees known as the Jerusalem Grove. The fifteen blue Atlas cedars were presented to the people of New York City in 1976 on behalf of the people of Jerusalem.

From South Ferry, at the foot of Whitehall Street just east of Battery Park, one of the most famous ferries in the world departs for thirty-minute trips across Upper New York Bay to Staten Island—an ocean voyage in miniature for a bargain price (twenty-five cents a round trip for pedestrians at this writing). The sea air is invigorating, and the view of the Manhattan skyline is magnificent, particularly at dusk. Since the city-owned ferry runs year-round, twenty-four hours a day, seven days a week, on an average of every twenty minutes on weekdays and every half hour on weekends, it's a trip that can be experienced anytime you choose. For an additional fee, you can take your car along, and, of course, you can also board the ferry at the Staten Island terminal (foot of Bay Street in St. George). En route, you may see loons, grebes, a variety of waterfowl, and several species of gulls. The rare little gull has been spotted here in April and May amid flocks of Bonaparte's gulls.

Another ferry, equally well known because of its destination, takes visitors to the awe-inspiring Statue of Liberty on 12-acre Liberty Island. Within its base is the American Museum of Immigration. To create an appropriate setting for the statue, the entire island has been beautifully landscaped with grassy lawns, beds of flowers, and tree-lined walkways, some at the water's edge. For the most magnificent view, you can go to the top of the 152-foot-high statue. Ferries usually depart from Battery Park every hour on the hour, 9:00 A.M.–4:00 P.M. daily, year-round, with additional sailings sometimes offered on Saturday, Sunday, holidays, and afternoons in spring and summer.

Since 1976, 27-acre Ellis Island, just north of Liberty Island, has also been open to the public. Until April of that year, ever since the island closed in 1954 after sixty-two years of service as the busiest immigration center in history, the haunting red brick buildings stood silent. They have been renovated now, and the land surrounding them is being converted into a park, landscaped with trees and lawns. Visitors are taken on one-hour guided tours. Ferry service from Battery Park is available four times daily, at 9:30 and 11:45 A.M., 2:00 and 4:15 P.M., late April through late October.

Both Liberty and Ellis Islands are administered by the National Park Service as part of the Statue of Liberty National Monument. (They may also be reached by ferry service from Liberty State Park in New Jersey, described elsewhere.) There is a modest fee for the ferry ride to each island (both ferries are operated by the Circle Line), as well as a small charge for riding an elevator within the Statue of Liberty; everything else is free.

One of the most unusual ways to spend your lunch hour if you work in Manhattan (and even if you don't) is aboard a 1938-vintage yawl that sets sail twice daily, mid-April through mid-October, for forty-five-minute lunch cruises. The 70-foot *Petrel*, accommodating up to thirty-four passengers, leaves from Battery Park at noon and again at 1:00 P.M. Be sure to bring a picnic lunch along; only drinks are served on board. You may also join the *Petrel* for a Happy Hour Sail on most weekday afternoons at 5:30 or a two-hour harbor sail on weekends. Reservations are definitely advised, as these excursions are very popular. In spring and summer, sailing lessons are given on a group basis. For details and rates, contact Bring Back Sailing, Inc. (address and phone number below).

How to Get There: Located at the southernmost tip of Manhattan Island; Battery Pl. and State St. meet at its northeast corner. *By subway*: #1 or 5 to South Ferry; #4 or SS to Bowling Green; RR, N to Whitehall St. *By bus*: M1, M6, M15; B88, Stop 28.

Always open. Free entrance.

For Additional Information:

Urban Park Rangers—Manhattan
NYC Dept. of Parks & Recreation
16 W. 61st St.
New York, NY 10023
212-397-3087

Director, NYC Dept. of Parks &
Recreation
Manhattan Borough
16 W. 61st St.
New York, NY 10023
212-397-3100

Superintendent
Castle Clinton National Monument
National Park Service
Manhattan Sites
26 Wall St.
New York, NY 10005
212-344-7220

Superintendent
Statue of Liberty National Monument
Liberty Island, NY 10004
212-732-1236 or 212-732-1286

Statue of Liberty/Ellis Island
Ferries
The Circle Line
Battery Park, South Ferry
New York, NY 10004
212-269-5755

Public Information Officer
Staten Island Ferry
Battery Park, South Ferry
New York, NY 10004
212-248-8097
or 212-248-8093

Public Information Officer
Staten Island Ferry
Bay St., St. George
Staten Island, NY 10301
212-727-2508

The *Petrel*
Bring Back Sailing, Inc.
1 Broadway
New York, NY 10004
212-825-1976

The Biblical Garden of the Cathedral of St. John the Divine

One of the more unusual gardens in greater New York City is the exquisite Biblical Garden, which lies in the shadow of the world's largest Gothic cathedral—the Cathedral of St. John the Divine. Every plant in the garden is mentioned in the Bible.

Closed off from the rest of the world by borders of tamarisks, cedars of Lebanon, and tall willows, this quarter-acre plot is a refreshing refuge from the city's pavements and rushing traffic. It is secluded and quiet here, though thousands of persons come to visit each year. Fruit trees, vegetables, herbs, and flowers fill it to overflowing, and plaques identifying each plant cite the particular Biblical verse in which it is mentioned.

The fig and the grapevine, named several times, and the apricot, which botanical historians have described as the forbidden fruit of the Garden of Eden, all grow here. Others include aloe, almond, anemone, carob, bay tree, crocus, dandelion, flax, frankincense, redbud or Judas tree, narcissus, holly oak, lentils, oleander, onion, star-of-Bethlehem, and more.

In a pond in the corner of the garden grows papyrus, the material used to make the basket that hid baby Moses and also to make paper and mats. Tamarisk trees in the past were a source of a honeylike substance called manna. What looks like ordinary corn growing in the garden is actually sorghum, or Jerusalem corn, used in biblical times as a cereal grain.

How to Get There: Located at Amsterdam Ave. and W. 112th St., just northwest of Central Park. *By subway*: #1 to 110th St. and Cathedral Pkwy. *By bus*: M4, M5, M7, M11, M104; M41, Stop 11.

Open daily, year-round, 7:00 A.M.–7:00 P.M. Free. Best time to view garden is May through October.

For Additional Information:
Joan Evanish
Program Coordinator
The Biblical Garden of the Cathedral of St. John the Divine
1047 Amsterdam Ave. at 112th St.
New York, NY 10025
212-678-6886

Central Park

The classic urban park of New York City, perhaps the entire nation, is Central Park. Not because it's traditional, not because it's ideal or the ultimate in park design, but because it is there, highly visible, highly usable green space in the middle of one of the world's most densely populated cities. Millions of people visit Central Park each year, a good proportion of them out-of-towners who consider it as much a part of getting to know New York as riding the observation elevator to the top of the Empire State Building or taking the ferryboat out to the Statue of Liberty. Central Park, it's claimed with some degree of credibility, is the most used park in the nation.

Extending from 59th Street on the south to 110th Street 2½ miles to the north, the 840-acre park reaches from the plushest sanctum of the city into the southern quarters of Harlem and occupies more than 5 percent of Manhattan Island. It encompasses a number of diverse habitats—lakes and ponds, swamp, marsh, woodland, and meadow. Thousands upon thousands of gray squirrels live here, sometimes migrating in great numbers between Central Park and Theodore Roosevelt Park just to the west at the Museum of Natural History.

The New York City Department of Parks & Recreation claims some 15 million visitors annually. And there may be half that many birds pausing here, too, as they migrate north in the spring and south in the autumn. Some 250 species have been sighted in the park, more than a third of all the species known to appear on our continent north of Mexico. Four areas are particularly good for bird-watching—the Ramble, a small wilderness between 72nd and 79th Streets; a fenced-in bird sanctuary near the southeastern corner of the park; the 90th Street Reservoir; and the Loch, a marshy brook at 104th Street. Rare species on the park list include the snowy owl, purple gallinule, and Townsend's warbler.

The park offers much to those interested in rocks and geology. Boulders more than a billion years old are found here, as well as some of the finest ice-polished rock anywhere. Layers of bedrock under the park, known as the Manhattan foundation, were formed 480 million years ago. It's that same rock that makes it possible to build huge skyscrapers without their foundations giving way.

Garnets can be found in some of the exposed striated rock. At other places there are *roches moutonnées*, French for "sheep rock," which resembles a recumbent sheep. There are unquestionably fossils in the park, too, perhaps even the skeletons of mastodons, but since no excavations can be made, they will likely never be recovered. Some of these mighty artifacts of the Pleistocene Age have been discovered by workmen excavating less than two blocks away.

As interesting as the rocks are the trees. Some are old, some huge in size, and there are a number of different species, native as well as exotic. The oldest small-leafed Chinese elm in the United States is located a few yards from Fifth Avenue, near the 72nd Street entrance. It is also believed to be the largest.

The Arthur Ross Pinetum, an extensive collection of pine trees from all over the world, edges the Great Lawn near 85th Street. Found here are pines whose ancestors developed on the mountain slopes of Japan, in Austria, and in the Himalayas.

Perhaps the most interesting natural area in the park is the Ramble between 72nd and 79th Streets, just to the northeast of the lake there. Essentially a knoll of some 30 acres, the Ramble contains some of the highest land in this hilly park (although the actual high point is farther north at Summit Rock, 137½ feet above sea level). It shelters a maze of macadam walks that encompasses such man-made features as the Summerhouse, Azalea Pond, and the Swamp. A few native oaks, elms, and locusts have stood here for more years than this land has been a park. Exotic flora, too, flourish here—the Chinese pagoda tree, Korean mountain ash, and English holly, among others. A word of caution: don't venture into the Ramble alone at any time, and even on days when the park is filled with people, take along some friends.

Besides the multitude of birds and squirrels in the park,

The lake in Central Park   Bill Thomas

there are ducks and sometimes geese on the ponds, pools, and lake. Snakes, wood mice, moles, rabbits, and raccoons dwell in the byways.

Two lovely formal gardens grace the park. The Shakespeare Garden, located near the Delacorte Theatre at West 81st Street, contains hawthorn and mulberry trees grown from seeds and cuttings from the same trees Shakespeare himself once tended in his own English garden at Stratford-on-Avon. In the northeast corner of the park, between East 104th and East 105th Streets, is the Conservatory Garden, a gift from the Vanderbilt family in the late nineteenth century; irises, roses, and daffodils grow here in profusion.

A small 6½-acre zoo is located in the southeastern section of the park. In recent years, it's been the target of much criticism as being outdated and run-down, but a 1980 agreement calls for the New York Zoological Society (which operates the greatly acclaimed Bronx Zoo, described elsewhere) to take over management of this area of the park, as well as the municipal zoos at Prospect Park in Brooklyn and Flushing Meadows–Corona Park in Queens.

The Urban Park Rangers (described elsewhere), part of a new and innovative program in city parks, have their Manhattan office in Central Park. They offer many nature-oriented programs and activities free of charge, and are also on hand to answer your questions about all parks in Manhattan.

Hiking, Bicycling, and Horseback Riding

As a crow flies, it's 2½ miles from south to north in the park, but within that space are 28 miles of walkways. A roadway measuring more than 6 miles circles through the park, but it is periodically closed to motor vehicles (every weekend, year-round, and eight hours of every weekday from May through October). Trees shade most of the trails in the park, and water fountains are scattered throughout. The maze of paths through the Ramble alone provides hours of interest if you combine your walk with nature study along the way. The Central Park Heritage National Recreation Trail leads past major features and celebrates the concept of urban parks. To keep you posted as to your whereabouts in the park, each lamp post should have a plate with four numbers on it. No. 8033 tells you 80th Street is closest. If the last two digits are odd, you are on the west side; even digits mean you're on the east side. Free naturalist-guided walks are conducted on weekends from The Dairy.

A special bike path 1.7 miles long may be used anytime, but bicyclists use all park roads when they're closed to cars. Bikes may be rented at Loeb Boathouse from April through September. Daylight horseback riding is permitted over 6 miles of bridle paths; rentals at Claremont Riding Academy, 175 West 89th Street.

Along with most of the rest of the country's population, you may already know that Central Park is one of the most famous jogging areas anywhere.

Boating

Rowboats may be rented at Loeb Boathouse.

Winter Sports

Two outdoor ice skating rinks are available, and cross-country skiers take to the park's trails. Four areas, one specifically for smaller children, are used by sledders.

How to Get There: Central Park is located between 59th St. on the south and 110th St. on the north, and is bound on the east by Fifth Ave. and on the west by Central Park West, an extension of Eighth Ave. *By subway:* #1, A, D, AA, B, or CC to Columbus Circle; AA, CC, or B to 72nd St., 81st St., 86th St., 96th St., or 103rd St.; RR or N to Fifth Ave. *By bus:* M1, M2A, M3, M4.

Open at all times. Free. A public information center is located at the Dairy, at 65th St. between the zoo and the carousel.

For Additional Information:

Urban Park Rangers—Manhattan
NYC Dept. of Parks & Recreation
16 W. 61st St.
New York, NY 10023
212-397-3091

Director, NYC Dept. of Parks
& Recreation
Manhattan Borough
16 W. 61st St.
New York, NY 10023
212-397-3100

Fort Tryon Park and the Cloisters

A combination of nature and art make this park, situated on the highest point in Manhattan, unusually attractive. It sits atop a rock ledge, opposite the magnificent New Jersey Palisades, overlooking the Hudson River. Within the park is the Cloisters, an art museum that houses a fabulous medieval art collection given to the Metropolitan Museum of Art by John D. Rockefeller, Jr.

One of the most prized exhibits in the collection, a blend of artistic beauty and skilled craftsmanship, is of absorbing interest to horticulturists (and art lovers) throughout the world. Six handwoven fifteenth-century tapestries known as the Unicorn Tapestries, each about 150 feet square, depict plants from all over Europe. They are so precisely detailed that they look almost real, and after all these centuries, the vegetable dyes remain vibrant and colorful. The craftsmen who so intricately fashioned them have never been identified, but their accuracy astonishes many experts in the field.

Rockefeller also donated 62 acres of land for Fort Tryon Park, and then acquired land along the Palisades across the Hudson to keep the view intact.

Operated as a branch of the Metropolitan Museum of Art, the Cloisters is a living reconstruction of the French monasteries of the Middle Ages. Five different cloisters (unroofed spaces) are connected by covered walkways, and interspersed throughout are gardens containing more than 140 varieties of plants used in the Middle Ages. Some of the most unusual herb gardens in the country are here.

The park also has other gardens, planted with heathers and perennials and maintained by the city parks department. Sprinkled over the wooded hills are some noteworthy specimens of trees and shrubs.

Fort Tryon Park is extraordinarily beautiful, some say the most beautiful park in America. Certainly it is serene, a world apart, totally unrelated to the teeming metropolis just outside its gates.

Hiking

Eight miles of paths, including a promenade, lead through the park. Terrain is wooded and hilly.

How to Get There: Located in the northernmost reaches of Manhattan, along the banks of the Hudson River, it lies between 190th St. on the south and 201st St. on the north. Access is from the east side of Riverside Dr., or from the corner of Fort Washington Blvd. and W. 193rd St. *By subway:* A train to 190th St. *By bus:* M4, M100; M41, Stop 10, free transfer privileges to and from M41 with ticket.

Park open at all times. Free. The Cloisters is open Tuesday through Saturday, 10:00 A.M.–4:45 P.M.; Sunday and holidays, noon–4:45 P.M., May 1 through September 30. Same rest of year, except Sunday and holidays, 1:00–4:45 P.M. Closed January 1, Thanksgiving, and December 25. Nominal admission charge; special rates for students.

For Additional Information:

Urban Park Rangers—Manhattan
NYC Dept. of Parks & Recreation
16 W. 61st St.
New York, NY 10023
212-397-3087

The Cloisters Museum
Fort Tryon Park
New York, NY 10040
212-923-3700

Director, NYC Dept. of Parks & Recreation
Manhattan Borough
16 W. 61st St.
New York, NY 10023
212-397-3100

Hudson River Dayline Cruise

See listing on page 10.

Inwood Hill Park

A naturalist's paradise at the extreme northern tip of Manhattan, 196-acre Inwood Hill Park is a tiny gem of wilderness in the most densely populated city in America. This sheer escarpment of bedrock towering above the Hudson River attracts geologists, bird-watchers, historians, archaeologists, botanists, and nature lovers who come to study its treasures and escape the pressures of city life. Within Inwood Hill's boundaries is the last tract of original woodland in Manhattan.

Algonquin Indian caves were discovered here during the latter part of the nineteenth century, and many yielded artifacts. At a spot near the cliffs, Peter Minuit is believed to have purchased Manhattan Island from the Indians in 1626 for trinkets and beads worth then about twenty-four dollars. Hessian soldiers occupied the hill during the Revolutionary War, and occasionally buttons from their uniforms are found.

Glacial kettle holes and schist outcroppings, reminders of the last great glacier, are located in many parts of the park.

An area called the Clove is considered the best bird-watching area, and more than 150 species of birds have been sighted there over the years. The indigo bunting is plentiful, and green herons can be spotted beside Spuyten Duyvil Creek, which flows through the park. When it's not frozen over, a lagoon in the park hosts waterfowl during the winter.

The park has retained its wilderness character. Nature trails lead through forests of great deciduous trees and a few hemlocks. At least six species of maple grow here, and five of oak. There are hackberries and wild cherry, birches and hickories. Huge tulip trees with columnar trunks rise nearly 80 feet above the ground.

Hiking
A network of hiking trails traverses all sections of the park, uphill and downhill, most of them in wooded areas.

How to Get There: Located at northernmost tip of Manhattan, where the Harlem and Hudson Rivers meet. Bound by Dyckman St. on south, Payson Ave. on east, Harlem River on north, and Hudson River on west. *By subway:* A train to Dyckman St. or 207th St. *By bus:* M100 to Dyckman St. or 207th St.

Park open at all times. Free.

For Additional Information:

Urban Park Rangers—Manhattan
NYC Dept. of Parks & Recreation
16 W. 61st St.
New York, NY 10023
212-397-3087

Director, NYC Dept. of Parks
& Recreation
Manhattan Borough
16 W. 61st St.
New York, NY 10023
212-397-3100

Morris-Jumel Mansion

Perched on the crest of a steep slope known as Honey Hill, the Morris-Jumel Mansion, a magnificent colonial residence, commands a sweeping view of the Harlem River. It is the focal point of tiny Roger Morris Park, a bit of greenery in northern Manhattan.

The grounds of the park are laden with lilac and magnolia trees, making it a lovely spot in blooming season. Alongside the house, a sunken garden displays roses and nearly fifty varieties of perennials. Hollyhocks and nasturtiums bloom here also, and a colonial herb garden is filled with old-fashioned herbs.

The mansion itself, the oldest house remaining in Manhattan, dates back to 1765. It has been called the handsomest and most interesting Colonial home in the city as well. George Washington made it his headquarters for about a month in the fall of 1776; it was later captured and held by the British for seven years.

How to Get There: Located in Roger Morris Park at the corner of W. 160th St. and Edgecombe Ave., slightly north of Macombs Dam Bridge. *By subway:* #1 to 157th St.; AA, B to 163rd St. *By bus:* M2, M3, M4, M5, M100, M101; M41, Stop 10A.

Park open at all times. Free. Mansion open Tuesday through Sunday, 10:00 A.M.–4:00 P.M. Nominal admission charge.

For Additional Information:

Curator
Morris-Jumel Mansion
W. 160th St. & Edgecombe Ave.
New York, NY 10032
212-923-8008

Director, NYC Dept. of Parks
& Recreation
Manhattan Borough
16 W. 61st St.
New York, NY 10023
212-397-3100

Urban Park Rangers—Manhattan
NYC Dept. of Parks & Recreation
16 W. 61st St.
New York, NY 10023
212-397-3087

Riverside Park

A long, narrow green stretch of hills and hollows, extending for about 3 miles along the east bank of the Hudson River, Riverside Park is noted primarily for its beauty and its serenity. From its rocky eastern boundary, it slopes gradually down to the riverbank. The park consists of three levels, and walkways traverse the park on each. Along historic Riverside Drive, which borders the highest level on the east, the sidewalk is wide, and the elm-shaded promenade has a gracious European look to it. Down the hillside, the middle level, known as the Terrace, leads along an esplanade through gardens and alleys. The lower level path, which follows the river's edge, is the quietest and least frequented. In its northern reaches, the park is most isolated and picturesque. Use greater caution, however, the farther north you venture. It's safest on crowded days or weekends.

Approximately 13,000 trees adorn Riverside's 267 acres. In the spring, the many flowering species color the landscape and perfume the air. Numerous birds nest here during the spring, summer, and fall, and migratory species stop by to rest.

People of all ages come here to play as well as to relax. There are many play areas, including tennis courts, and kids especially love to wet a fishing line in the Hudson; but most people come to stroll, bike, or jog in a cool oasis with a river view. Riverside is also a fine place in which to sled or cross-country ski during winter snows.

The park is noted, too, as the site of many important monuments. One of the best known is Grant's Tomb, a massive ornate memorial reminiscent of Napoleon's Tomb in Paris, even to the tinted light. The bodies of General and Mrs. Grant lie in lonely grandeur within. Officially called the General Grant National Memorial, the tomb is administered by the National Park Service. It's located on the west side of Riverside Drive at West 122nd Street.

How to Get There: Located along the east bank of the Hudson River, extending northward from W. 72nd St. to W. 125th St., it abuts Riverside Dr. on the east. Henry Hudson Parkway (also known as the West Side Highway and NY 9A) runs through the park in a north-south direction, but no cars are allowed within the park itself. There is some parking on streets around the park. *By subway*: #1, 2, or 3 to 72nd St. or 96th St. and Broadway; #1 to 79th St., 86th St., 103rd St., 110th St., or 116th St. and Broadway. *By bus*: M5 bus runs along entire length of Riverside Dr.

Open daily at all times. Free.

For Additional Information:

Ms. Clara Cayman
Friends of Riverside Park
309th W. 104th St.
New York, NY 10025
212-749-8454

Urban Park Rangers—Manhattan
NYC Dept. of Parks & Recreation
16 W. 61st St.
'New York, NY 10023
212-397-3087

Director, NYC Dept. of Parks
& Recreation
Manhattan Borough
16 W. 61st St.
New York, NY 10023
212-397-3100

Superintendent
General Grant National
Memorial
National Park Service
Manhattan Sites
26 Wall St.
New York, NY 10005
212-666-1640 or 212-264-8711

United Nations Gardens

Situated on a tract of 18 acres donated by John D. Rockefeller, Jr., facing the East River in Manhattan, is the United Nations, one of the foremost tourist attractions in New York City. More than three-quarters of the acreage is devoted to superbly land-scaped and maintained grounds and gardens, and up to 4 million visitors come to see them annually, along with the United Nations Building itself.

The gardens include more than 2,500 rose bushes in forty-seven varieties, more than 180 flowering cherry trees, 52 dwarf fruit trees, and hundreds of ornamental trees, including haw-thorn, sweet gum, pin oak, sycamore, and feathery honey locust. The shrubbery—ilex, myrtle, wisteria, California privet, lawns of selected touch grasses, as well as ground covers of English ivy and vinca minor—was selected both for its beauty and its ability to withstand pollution, soot, wind, and harsh variations of weather.

Against the left wall of the garden are espaliered formations of apple, crabapple, and pear trees in fifty-six separate varie-ties. These trees, in the tradition of a living art borrowed from the French, have been trained to grow in various patterns against wooden diagonals supported by pipe frames.

The special glory of the United Nations gardens is its rose collection, in bloom from late May through mid-November. Varieties are changed from time to time as new and better roses are developed. Among the displays is the delicate and famous (and in this case symbolic) Peace Rose. The head gardener (it takes twelve year-round gardeners and five or six seasonal ones to maintain the gardens) says it doesn't fare well most years.

Many of the monuments and fountains in the gardens are contributions from various nations around the world.

How to Get There: Located between First Ave. and the East River, the United Nations is bound on the north by E. 48th St. and on the south by E. 42nd St. *By subway*: #4, 5, 6, 7, S to Grand Central Terminal. *By bus*: M15, M27, M101, M104, M106; M41, Stop 21; B88, Stop 17.

Gardens open daily, 9:00 A.M.–5:30 P.M. from April 15 through late fall. They are also included in guided tours of the United Nations Building; open daily, year-round, 9:00 A.M.–4:45 P.M., except January 1, December 24, and December 25; nominal fee for guided tours, children under 5 not permitted.

For Additional Information:
Department of Public Information
United Nations
New York, NY 10017
212-754-1234 or 212-754-5292

Urban Park Rangers Program

There's something new in New York City—a unique urban park ranger program that provides ranger-guided environmental tours and workshops for individuals, schools, and groups. Specialists in such fields as ornithology, geology, and biology are on hand to provide information about parks in their respective boroughs. In addition to conducting regularly scheduled tours, the rangers will endeavor to tailor programs to your specific needs. Offices are located in each of the five boroughs.

The park rangers also enforce park rules. At present, they are working primarily in Central Park in Manhattan, Van Cortlandt Park in the Bronx, Flushing Meadows–Corona Park in Queens, Clove Lakes/Silver Lake on Staten Island, and Prospect Park in Brooklyn.

This is a relatively new program, established in 1979 and modeled after the National Park Service. If it is successful and budget permits, services will be extended to other parks.

A schedule of activities is available upon request. Rangers are on duty twenty-four hours a day, seven days a week.

For Additional Information:

Executive Director
Urban Park Rangers Program
NYC Dept. of Parks &
Recreation
The Arsenal, Central Park
830 Fifth Ave.
New York, NY 10021
212-360-8181

Urban Park Rangers—Manhattan
NYC Dept. of Parks & Recreation
16 W. 61st St.
New York, NY 10023
212-397-3087

Urban Park Rangers—Bronx
Van Cortlandt Stadium
Van Cortlandt Park South
Broadway & 242nd St.
Bronx, NY 10471
212-822-4336

Urban Park Rangers—
Brooklyn
NYC Dept. of Parks &
Recreation
95 Prospect Park West
Brooklyn, NY 11215
212-856-4210

Urban Park Rangers—Queens
Flushing Meadows–Corona Park
Administration Building
Corona, NY 11368
212-699-6722

Urban Park Rangers—Staten Island
Clove Lakes/Silver Lake Parks
1150 Clove Rd.
Staten Island, NY 10301
212-442-1304

Four

Queens

Alley Park

In the northeastern part of the borough of Queens on Long Island is Alley Park, once known as Alley Pond Park. The great pond for which it was named has long since been filled in to create a path for two superhighways, but there are still natural wonders here—glacial kettle ponds, vast woodlands, meadows where wildflowers grow, and little streams where frogs croak from the rushes and cattail marshes. Though damaged, it has not been destroyed; and it remains the most rustic and secluded area in this borough.

The park is composed of both saltwater and freshwater marsh and a mixed hardwood forest of beech, oak, sassafras, dogwood, hickory, and tulip poplar. Alley Creek runs directly through the park and is largely surrounded by marsh.

More than 175 species of birds have been sighted here, and the park is also home to numerous small mammals. You will find raccoon, squirrel, rabbit, muskrat, opossum, and numerous rodents of the marsh. A 23-acre bird sanctuary is home to such species as pheasant, scarlet tanager, woodpecker, and quail. Other birds that have been sighted in the area include various warblers and, occasionally, hawks, black-crowned night herons, and great blue herons. Each spring and fall, thousands of migrating wild ducks settle down on Little Neck Bay, which borders the extreme northern reaches of the park, and green-winged teal come to spend the winter.

The Alley Pond Environmental Center, located at 228-06 Northern Boulevard, provides an interpretive look at the environment of the area. Special nature studies are a part of the center, and a recycling center for glass, aluminum, newspapers, and corrugated paper has been set up to help cover operating expenses.

Urban Park Rangers, whose Queens headquarters is at Flushing Meadows–Corona Park (described elsewhere), conduct environmental tours through the park.

Hiking, Horseback Riding, and Nature Trails

Many miles of hiking paths are in the park. The 2-mile Pitobik Trail loops through the woodlands in the southern part of the park, and there's an interpretive trail that encircles Turtle Pond. Printed guides are available for each. A trail in the northern part of the park provides the "wildest" experience.

Chunks of the trail sometimes collapse into gully washouts, and low-lying sections must be forded with care. In the steaming heat of summer, luxuriant growths of brambles and poison ivy reach across your path.

There are also 2 miles of bridle trails, but no horse rentals.

Winter Sports

Cross-country skiing here is some of the best and most challenging in the city park system, but wait for a deep snow. Some of the hilly paths are rocky in places.

How to Get There: Located in northeastern Queens. From Exit 30 of Long Island Expwy. (I-495), go south on Cross Island Pkwy. to Grand Central Pkwy. (Exit 29). Turn west to park entrance road on right side of Grand Central Pkwy. Environmental center is at 228-06 Northern Blvd. in northern part of park. *By subway:* E or F to Kew Gardens station, then Q44 bus to Winchester Blvd.

Park open daily, year-round, at all times. Environmental center open daily, 9:00 A.M.–5:00 P.M., Monday through Saturday, and 11:00 A.M.–4:00 P.M., Sunday, July and August; same hours other months, but closed on Monday. Also closed Christmas and occasionally other holidays. Free.

For Additional Information:

Alley Pond Environmental Center
228-06 Northern Blvd.
Douglaston, NY 11363
212-229-4000

Urban Park Rangers—Queens
Flushing Meadows–Corona Park
Administration Building
Corona, NY 11368
212-699-6722

NYC Dept. of Parks &
Recreation
Queens Borough
The Overlook
Park Lane & Union Turnpike
Kew Gardens, NY 11415
212-544-4400

Breezy Point

See listing under Gateway National Recreation Area, page 5.

Flushing Meadows–Corona Park

Sprawling over nearly 1,300 acres in north central Queens, Flushing Meadows is New York City's third largest city park. It was first a tidal marsh, then it became a dumping ground (the Valley of Ashes described by F. Scott Fitzgerald in *The Great Gatsby*), and finally it was converted into a suitable site for the 1939–40 and the 1964–65 World's Fairs. For a few years between fairs, the United Nations General Assembly met on the site. Today, it is mainly a giant playground for children of all ages. There are rows of trees, vast expanses of lawn, a

Mallard ducks are abundant throughout the New York area. *Bill Thomas*

freshwater lake, and shaded picnic areas, but primarily the park offers a plethora of year-round recreational activities.

At the 18-acre Queens (or Flushing Meadows) Zoo, black bears, timber wolves, river otter, American bison, and other animals indigenous to the North American continent can be seen in natural settings of rolling hills, rocky dens, and freshwater pools. An outstanding feature of the zoo is the aviary dome, one of the largest ever built, landscaped with trees, shrubs, pools, and waterfalls; herons, ring-necked pheasants, sparrows, doves, and robins are equally at home here. The New York Zoological Society will take over management of this zoo within the next few years.

Next door is the Heckscher Children's Farm, where children may pet the animals and ride the ponies.

The Hall of Science of the City of New York is one of the largest science and technology centers in the world. It includes a small planetarium, a hatchery where you can watch baby chicks being born, a weather station, and many exhibits related to our environment.

There's a game field for practically every sport, including baseball, football, cricket, soccer, and hockey. There are also boccie courts, indoor rinks for ice skating (November through April) and roller skating, and the park's famous tennis courts, both indoor and outdoor, established by the U.S. Tennis Association. Additional facilities are described below.

Urban Park Rangers (described elsewhere) are on hand to conduct guided environmental and historical tours in Flushing Meadows, as well as in Alley Park (described elsewhere). One of their walks acquaints visitors with the wildest remaining part of Flushing Meadows, Willow Lake near the southern boundary. The rangers, whose Queens headquarters is in this park, are also an information source for all city parks in Queens.

Hiking, Bicycling, and Running Trails

Hikers, bikers, and joggers may follow a pathway that circles Meadow Lake. Total distance is approximately 2½ miles, and the terrain is fairly flat. The lake is located near the southern, least developed part of the park. There is also a Perrier Parcourse here, designed to encourage physical fitness. Starting near the public swimming pool off Meadow Lake, you go from sign to sign, stopping to do the exercises illustrated on each one.

Swimming

A 70-foot outdoor pool is just north of Meadow Lake. It's open daily, 11:00 A.M. to 7:00 P.M., June through Labor Day. Nominal fee.

Fishing and Boating

Fishing permitted in Meadow Lake. Rowboats and pedal boats may be rented for a nominal charge from the Meadow Lake boathouse; the lake, about three-quarters of a mile long and a quarter-mile wide, was created for the 1939–40 World's Fair. Rentals available 10:00 A.M. to 5:00 P.M. weekdays, 9:30 A.M. to dusk weekends, when weather permits. Hourly charge plus deposit.

How to Get There: Located in north central Queens, between Flushing and Forest Hills. Use Long Island Expwy. (I-495), which goes through center of park, to exits at Grand Central Pkwy. or Van Wyck Expwy. (I-678), which border park on the west and east respectively. Parking around park's perimeter. *By subway:* #7 stops at Willets Point–Shea Stadium near the park's northern boundary, and at 111th St. near park's western boundary.

Park open at all times. Free. Zoo open 10:00 A.M.–4:00 P.M. daily, year-round. Free; small charge for animal rides. Hall of Science open Wednesday through Friday, 10:00 A.M.–4:00 P.M.; Saturday, 10:00 A.M.–5:00 P.M.; Sunday, 11:00 A.M.–5:00 P.M.; closed major holidays; nominal admission charge; special rates for children; 4 and under free.

For Additional Information:

Urban Park Rangers—Queens
Flushing Meadows–Corona Park
Administration Building
Corona, NY 11368
212-699-6722

NYC Dept. of Parks &
Recreation
Queens Borough
The Overlook
Park Lane & Union Turnpike
Kew Gardens, NY 11415
212-544-4400

Hall of Science
111th St. & 48th Ave.
Queens, NY 11368
212-699-9400

Queens Zoo
111th St. & 54th Ave.
Queens, NY 11368
212-699-4275

Forest Park

In west central Queens near the Brooklyn border is 508-acre Forest Park, which offers one of the last natural mature oak forests in the city. Although this primeval forest was periodically burned by the Indians who occupied Long Island before the European settlers arrived, it remains pristine in appearance, a veritable green wilderness in the midst of the city.

The types of trees found here are no different from those that grew here 350 years ago. Great white oaks, from 70 to 90 feet tall, dominate the forest although they are slowly succumbing to air pollution. Around them are black birch, wild black cherry, Norway maple, yellow poplar, sweet gum, shagbark hickory, ailanthus, and sassafras; the canopy they create in the summer is so dense that sunlight cannot penetrate it.

The wildlife has not survived as well. Few species of animals found in Colonial times remain today. But eastern gray squirrels nest ten or fifteen to an acre, and eastern cottontails scamper through the woods.

Forest Park is also an excellent place to see evidence of the terminal moraine created by the Ice Age's Wisconsin glacier— low hills interspersed with steep-sided pits, flat plains, and an unsorted mixture of rock fragments from New England and the northern Appalachian Mountains. A number of the kettle pits visible today were formed when chunks of ice were overridden and buried by glacial debris. When they melted, the debris above them sank, creating the kettles.

The park is a good spot for bird-watching, with more than fifty species living in the area. Among them are eastern and accipiter hawks, two species of woodpeckers, blue jays, mourning doves, yellow-bellied sapsuckers, great-crested flycatchers, Acadian flycatchers, white-breasted nuthatches, ruby-crowned kinglets, cardinals, warblers, and vireos.

Hiking, Bicycling, and Horseback Riding

A complex of trails leads through the park. You can easily spend an entire day hiking them, studying and photographing nature, and looking for wildlife. A particularly quiet area is south of Forest Park Drive and west of Woodhaven Boulevard. One of the most popular activities in the park is horseback riding (no rentals) along 2.4 miles of meandering bridle paths. Bicyclists enjoy following Forest Park Drive through the entire length of the park.

Winter Sports

Both cross-country skiing and sledding are popular.

How to Get There: From Long Island Expwy. (I-495), go south on Woodhaven Blvd. to Forest Park Dr., which runs through the park both east and west from Woodhaven. Street parking available. *By subway:* GG or QJ to Woodhaven Blvd. station; Q11 bus to park.

Park open at all times. Free.

For Additional Information:

Urban Park Rangers—Queens
Flushing Meadows–Corona Park
Administration Building
Corona, NY 11368
212-699-6722

NYC Dept. of Parks &
Recreation
Queens Borough
The Overlook
Park Lane & Union Turnpike
Kew Gardens, NY 11415
212-544-4400

Jacob Riis Park

See listing under Gateway National Recreation Area, Breezy Point Unit, page 5.

Jamaica Bay

See listing under Gateway National Recreation Area, page 6.

Kissena Park

Kissena Park combines formally landscaped acreage and swampy, untouched land in its 238 acres. Spring-fed Kissena Lake is located within the park, and there are about 20 acres containing the last vestiges of the Parsons Nursery, famous for its introduction of many new species to the United States. A magnificent specimen of Carolina silver bell, measuring some 60 feet tall and about 4½ feet in diameter, may be the biggest in the East. In the spring it's a mass of white blossoms.

Also in this refuge for tree giants are thirty-one other monarchs, the largest of their species on Long Island. Among them are the Lenne saucer magnolia, weeping larch, Japanese hornbeam, and the eagle-claw Norway maple, with its curious semiclenched leaves. None of the trees is labeled, however.

The many trees and a marsh in the southern portion of the park attract numerous land birds.

In the park's developed areas, it is possible to enjoy tennis, fishing, boating, and shuffleboard. The kite flying is great, and there's also a model-boat pond. Winter lures ice skaters, sledders, and cross-country skiers.

Just west of the park is a narrow stretch of greenery that

links Kissena with the Queens Botanical Garden (described elsewhere). Adjoining Kissena on the east is a similar green ribbon of parkland that extends to Cunningham Park, a large forested area of about 600 acres crisscrossed with a network of trails. All together, this continuous strip of parks forms a greenbelt known as the Kissena Corridor, with Kissena Park at its center.

How to Get There: Located just north of the Long Island Expwy. (I-495) in Flushing. Go north from Long Island Expwy. at 164th St. exit. Continue north on 164th St., past Booth Memorial Blvd., to the park entrance on the left side of the road at the corner of 164th and Oak Ave. *By subway:* #7 to Main St. station; then Q17 bus to park. E or F train to 169th St. station; then Q17 bus to park.
   Open at all times. Free.

For Additional Information:

Urban Park Rangers—Queens
Flushing Meadows–Corona Park
Administration Building
Corona, NY 11368
212-699-6722

NYC Dept. of Parks &
Recreation
Queens Borough
The Overlook
Park Lane & Union Turnpike
Kew Gardens, NY 11415
212-544-4400

Queens Botanical Garden

One of the city's newer botanical gardens, Queens Botanical Garden occupies land that was once a garbage dump. Originally an exhibition at the 1939–40 World's Fair, it was so popular that New York City's park commissioner decided to continue the garden on a permanent basis. It was 1963 before it could be completed, however.

Fifteen of the 38 acres here are devoted to gardens, while the rest is an arboretum that features 150 evergreen trees.

The pride of the garden is the Perkins Memorial Rose Collection of more than 4,000 bushes. Near the entrance is a huge circle of 40 different kinds of petunias. Other areas include a rock garden, herb garden, a collection of dwarf conifers, and more than 200 varieties of azalea, heather, rhododendron, and other ericaceous plants. The grounds are brightened in the spring by flowering cherry trees, crabapple trees, and 250,000 tulips; and during the fall, there's a spectacular display of 10,000 chrysanthemums. A fragrance garden for the blind is under construction as of this writing.

A shop on the grounds sells indoor and outdoor plants for very reasonable prices, usually less than they would cost anywhere else.

How to Get There: Located at 43-50 Main St., Flushing, just east of Flushing Meadows–Corona Park (described elsewhere). From Main

St. Exit on Long Island Expwy. (I-495), go north to garden on left side of road at corner of Main and Dahlia; watch for signs. *By subway:* #7 to Main St. station, then Q44 bus to Elder Ave. *By rail:* LIRR to Main St. station, then Q44 bus to Elder Ave.

Open Wednesday through Sunday, 9:00 A.M.–dusk, year-round. Free.

For Additional Information:
Queens Botanical Garden
43-50 Main St.
Flushing, NY 11355
212-886-3800

Udalls Cove Wildlife Preserve

One of the newest additions to the New York City park system is the result of a cooperative effort between the city and the Village of Great Neck Estates in Nassau County. More correctly, it is a wildlife preserve rather than a park, a salt marsh teeming with marine life and waterfowl, surrounded by sand ridges covered with scrub oak and pitch pine.

Udalls Cove Preserve covers some 90 acres, 33 of them within New York City and the rest in Nassau County, just outside city limits on Long Island. (The Nassau County portion is owned by the Village of Great Neck Estates.) It was established as a result of the untiring efforts of Aurora Gareiss, a Queens resident who lives near the marsh and who led a campaign for many years to have it preserved. Her efforts led to a direct confrontation, with the citizens of Douglaston, Queens, and other neighborhoods forming a body chain across the road to prevent dump trucks from filling the marsh.

The cove, edged by Douglaston and Great Neck Estates, supports migrating waterfowl and a host of native birds. American and snowy egrets, as well as great blue herons, are seen here. Redwing blackbirds come to nest in the spring. Dense stands of spartina salt grass provide both cover and nutrients for marine life and land animals.

Although the marsh is not yet readily accessible, visitors may enjoy it from the perimeter with a pair of binoculars or join Arthur Kelley of the Udalls Cove Preservation Committee on one of the field trips he leads into the marsh. Future plans call for the development of self-guided nature trails and construction of a boardwalk.

How to Get There: Udalls Cove is a tiny inlet off Little Neck Bay in the northeastern corner of Queens. The Queens-Nassau County boundary line runs through it. From Northern Blvd. (NY 25A), just west of the Queens-Nassau County line, head north on Little Neck Pkwy. all the way to a cut-stone parking lot at the tip of the parkway.

A large expanse of the cove and marsh can be seen from here. *By rail:* LIRR to Douglaston station.

For Additional Information:

Aurora Gareiss, President
Udalls Cove Preservation
Committee, Inc.
3107 Douglas Rd.
Douglaston, NY 11363
212-229-4809

Urban Park Rangers—Queens
Flushing Meadows–Corona Park
Administration Building
Corona, NY 11368
212-699-6722

Arthur Kelley
Education Chairman
Udalls Cove Preservation
Committee
325 Beverly Rd.
Douglaston, NY 11363
212-225-7050

NYC Dept. of Parks &
Recreation
Queens Borough
The Overlook
Park Lane & Union Turnpike
Kew Gardens, NY 11415
212-544-4400

Weeping Beech Park

In the heart of Flushing, surrounded by an iron fence, stands a tree so special that the City of New York purchased the land around it and made the tract into a park just to preserve the tree. The magnificent weeping beech that thrives here was the first and thus far only tree ever designated by the New York City Landmarks Preservation Commission as an official landmark. More than 60 feet tall, with a trunk that measures nearly 15 feet in circumference, it forms an immense canopy of drooping branches with a spread of nearly 85 feet. Although not the largest of its species, it is extraordinarily beautiful.

It came to Queens at a time when Flushing was a noted center for nurseries in this country. Samuel Parsons, a local nurseryman who supplied Central and Prospect Parks with many of their trees and shrubs, grew it from a shoot he brought back from Europe in 1847. Today it is recognized by several noted horticulturists as the finest tree of its kind in the world, and cuttings from it have started countless new trees all over our country.

The weeping beech tree shares its small tract of parkland with another lovely tree, a golden larch that is the largest of its species on Long Island.

Also in Weeping Beech Park is the historic Kingsland Homestead. An example of Dutch Colonial and English architecture, it is the second oldest house and the only remaining eighteenth-century dwelling in Flushing. It serves as the headquarters for the Queens Historical Society and may be toured. The society also provides information about the beech tree.

The block on which Weeping Beech Park is located has been made into a cul-de-sac with a small playground area at the closed end of the street. Right next to the swings, surrounded by an iron fence, is a cedar of Lebanon; like the golden larch, it's the largest of its species on Long Island.

How to Get There: Located at 143-35 37th Ave., between Parsons Blvd. and Bowne St. From the Main St. Exit on Long Island Expwy. (I-495), go north on Main St. to Northern Blvd. and turn right. Continue to Parsons Blvd., and turn right again. Proceed to 37th Ave., then make another right turn onto 37th. This block of 37th is a cul-de-sac; park along street. *By subway:* #7 to Main St. station.

Park open daily, year-round, 8:00 A.M. to sunset. Tree may be viewed at any time through fence. Free. Kingsland Homestead open Tuesday, Saturday, and Sunday, 2:30–4:30 P.M., year-round. Donations accepted.

For Additional Information:

Urban Park Rangers—Queens
Flushing Meadows–Corona Park
Administration Building
Corona, NY 11368
212-699-6722

Queens Historical Society
Kingsland Homestead
143-35 37th Ave.
Flushing, NY 11354
212-939-0647

NYC Dept. of Parks & Recreation
Queens Borough
The Overlook
Park Lane & Union Turnpike
Kew Gardens, NY 11415
212-544-4400

Five

Staten Island

Barrett Park Zoo

See listing under Staten Island Zoo, page 185.

Blue Heron Park

Consisting of Blue Heron Pond, Spring Pond, adjacent marshes, two woodland tracts, and the Meadow of 10,000 Lilies, Blue Heron is one of New York City's newest parks. Its function as a valuable ecosystem resulted in its designation as a State Freshwater Wetland in 1975. The largest concentration of the protected Turk's Cap lilies within the New York metropolitan area is here, and when they burst into bloom during the early summer, the landscape is stunning.

Made up of 130 acres, the park gives visitors a sweeping vista of sun-dappled ponds and lush marshland where great and little blue heron, wood duck, osprey, and woodcock feed and sometimes nest. The wetlands are also inhabited by painted turtles, wood turtles, box turtles, raccoons, and opossums. People come to fish for catfish and red-eared sunfish in a pond adorned with water lilies; if you keep your back to the road that borders it, you might feel that you've been transported to a primeval swamp.

Access to the area (sometimes referred to as the Poillon Avenue Wetlands) is limited at the moment, but part of it may be seen from the street, and trails are planned for the near future. The park will be managed by High Rock Park Conservation Center (described elsewhere).

How to Get There: Parklands lie on both sides of Poillon Ave., between Amboy Rd. and Hylan Blvd. in Annadale on south Staten Island. From Staten Island Expwy (I-278), take Hylan Blvd. south to Poillon Ave. and turn right. Poillon leads through part of park. Park along road. *By rail*: SIRT to Annadale station. *By bus*: #103 down Hylan Blvd.

Open at all times. Free.

For Additional Information:

High Rock Park Conservation Center
200 Nevada Ave.
Staten Island, NY 10306
212-987-6233

Urban Park Rangers—Staten Island
Clove Lakes/Silver Lake Parks
1150 Clove Rd.
Staten Island, NY 10301
212-442-1304 or 212-442-7640

Clay Pit Ponds State Park Preserve   *Bill Thomas*

Clay Pit Ponds State Park Preserve

A tract of undeveloped land encompassing about 260 acres, Clay Pit Ponds State Park Preserve is a rare combination of ponds, bogs, swamps, sand barrens, marshes, mature woodlands, and intermittent spring-fed streams. Portions of it resemble New Jersey's Pine Barrens (described elsewhere under Pinelands National Reserve). The State Department of Environmental Conservation has designated about 90 acres of the park site as State Freshwater Wetlands. Another 70 acres were designated a Unique Natural Area with the highest statewide rating under the State Nature and Historical Preservation Trust.

According to the New York City Parks Department, this section of Staten Island harbors the most diversified geological

features in the metropolitan area. Deposits of cretaceous sands and clay, laid down some 70 million years ago, are still visible. In the latter part of the nineteenth century, some commercial clay mining resulted in abandoned pits of various sizes that soon filled with water. That, of course, attracted birds and wildlife.

Clay Pit Ponds is also noted for its resident reptiles and amphibians. Fowler's toads live here, as do the fence lizard, red-backed salamander, spring peeper, and green frog.

There are birds too, of course—hundreds of them. The great blue heron, green heron, ring-necked pheasant, barn owl, marsh hawk, and downy woodpecker are but a few of the species you might see. The mammal population includes muskrat, opossum, raccoon, deer mouse, and eastern cottontail rabbit.

Several varieties of berries provide forage for wildlife, while among the trees growing here are the sweet gum, black cherry, tulip poplar, American beech, cottonwood, tupelo, and black locust.

The park exists today mainly because a 20-year-old Brooklynite named Joe Fernicola was interested in lizards. He had gone all over New York City looking for them, without success, until a map led him to this part of Staten Island in 1973. His "discovery" led to the preservation of this unique wilderness.

Individuals and groups may participate in natural-history-related field trips, lectures, and workshops at the state park.

Hiking and Horseback Riding

Hikers and horseback riders (no rentals) currently explore the site on sandy, forested trails. One trail leads to Clay Pit Pond about 400 yards north of Clay Pit Road.

How to Get There: Located in southwestern Staten Island. It extends east from Charleston and north about half the distance to Rossville. Arthur Kill Rd. borders the area on the west, the West Shore Expwy. is to the east, and Clay Pit Rd. runs through the park in an east-west direction. There are three separate areas: Five Lakes lies between Clay Pit Rd. on the north and Sharrotts Rd. on the south; Clay Pit Pond is north of Clay Pit Rd. about 400 yards; and Sharrotts Pond lies just south of Sharrotts Rd. From Staten Island Expwy. (I-278), take West Shore Expwy. south to Bloomingdale Rd. and turn left. Continue on Bloomingdale Rd. to Sharrotts Rd. Turn right onto Sharrotts Rd. and proceed to Carlin St. Turn right on Carlin St. and proceed to Neilsen Ave., where you turn left to park headquarters. *By bus:* S113 bus to Clay Pit Rd. or Sharrotts Rd.

Park open at all times. Free at this writing; some nominal fees may be instituted as facilities are added.

For Additional Information:

Superintendent	General Manager
Clay Pit Ponds State Park Preserve	State Parks & Recreation
83 Neilsen Ave.	New York City Region
Staten Island, NY 10309	1700 Broadway
212-967-1976	New York, NY 10019
	212-977-8240

Clove Lakes Park

Across Clove Road from the Staten Island Zoo (described elsewhere) is Clove Lakes Park, lying along an ancient glacial valley bisected by a small stream connecting three man-made lakes—Brooks Lake, Martling's Pond, and Clove Lake—whose impoundments create overflow waterfalls.

On a serpentine rock ledge near the southwestern corner of the park is a small stand of ebony spleenwort, one of the rarer of the small ferns. A mixed hardwood forest of beech, oak, hickory, and tulip lies along the western slope and there is also an impressive specimen of a Bartram oak.

Some of the city's prime mulberry orchards are near Brooks Lake in the northwestern part of the park. In June, you may indulge yourself.

The Urban Park Rangers (described elsewhere) have their Staten Island headquarters at Clove Lakes Park. They offer nature-oriented programs and workshops and conduct environmental tours in Clove Lakes and adjacent Silver Lake Park, a 10-acre mix of natural woodlands and manicured lawns with tennis courts and a golf course. Another function of the rangers is to provide information about all city parks on Staten Island.

Hiking, Bicycling, and Horseback Riding

Walks wind around the lakes, and footpaths take hikers to hilly, wooded sections of park. A figure-eight bike path circles around and across the park's interior lake for .9 mile. Check for hours open to cyclists. Bridle trails (3.8 miles) are also available; privately owned Clove Lake Stables at 1025 Clove Road has rentals.

Fishing and Boating

You may fish for largemouth bass, bluegill, and golden carp. Rowboats may be rented at Clove Lake boat house.

How to Get There: Located in north central Staten Island. From the Clove Rd. exit on Staten Island Expwy. (I-278), follow Clove Rd. north to park on left side of road. Besides Clove Rd., it's bound by Victory Blvd. on the south, and Martling Ave. crosses it. *By bus*: S6, S7, S106, S107, S110, or S112.

Open at all times. Free.

For Additional Information:
Urban Park Rangers—Staten Island
Clove Lakes/Silver Lake Parks
1150 Clove Rd.
Staten Island, NY 10301
212-442-1304 or 212-442-7640

Conference House Park

See listing under Ward's Point Park, page 187.

Davis Wildlife Refuge

The William T. Davis Wildlife Refuge, established in 1933, was the first such sanctuary in New York City. To this day, it remains a placid green haven for wildlife and people. Covering 260 acres near the center of Staten Island, the refuge serves as a vital link between city dwellers and their natural heritage. Wading birds such as the great blue heron and the common egret are found here, along with hundreds of other species of wildlife. Along the banks of several brooks in the refuge, muskrats have built their homes.

Named after a prominent naturalist and entomologist who once lived on Staten Island, the Davis Wildlife Refuge centers around New Springville Creek, which drains a huge portion of sanctuary lands. Most of it is marsh, but there are areas of dry and wet woodlands, freshwater swamps, and open meadows as well, giving it a distinct variety of habitat. Ironweed, pokeweed, white ash, wild black cherry, arrowwood, Japanese honeysuckle, sweet gum, and a multitude of other plant species are found in the upland sections of the refuge.

Nature Trails

A 1½-mile nature trail wends its way through 80 acres of the refuge, with several observation points over the swamp and marsh. Field trips are conducted during the spring and fall by the staff of the Staten Island Institute of Arts and Sciences, which co-administers this area with the New York City parks department.

How to Get There: From the Richmond Ave. exit on Staten Island Expwy. (I-278), go south on Richmond Ave. to Travis Ave., where you turn right. Take Travis Ave. one block to park drive on left. Keep a sharp eye out, because the road leading into the refuge is somewhat obscured by foliage most of the year. Limited parking available. *By bus*: S112 to Travis Ave.

Open daily, year-round, during daylight hours. Free.

For Additional Information:

Staten Island Institute of Arts
and Sciences
75 Stuyvesant Pl.
Staten Island, NY 10301
212-727-1135

Urban Park Rangers—Staten
Island
Clove Lakes/Silver Lake Parks
1150 Clove Rd.
Staten Island, NY 10301
212-442-1304 or 212-442-7640

Great Kills Park

See listing under Gateway National Recreation Area, Staten Island Unit, page 9.

High Rock Park Conservation Center

Staten Island is noted as the hilliest of New York City boroughs, and High Rock Park, rising to 225 feet above sea level, is an impressive segment of that hilly terrain. This 94-acre tract of hardwood forest is less than an hour from Times Square, yet it's a world apart, for it's a serene and rustic land. Wild azaleas bloom during the spring and early summer, and the only sounds you may hear are those of the wood thrush or a bullfrog boasting loudly in one of the small marshes. In autumn, myriads of grackles swoop down over the treetops in undulating black waves.

The U.S. Department of the Interior has designated High Rock a National Environmental Education Landmark because of its outstanding environment and programs. The visitor's center houses a delightful Discovery Room containing environmental exhibits and displays. Near the center of the parkland, a feel-touch-smell garden for the blind has been established. In the Stone House is an environmental education reference library housing some 2,000 volumes and providing a large variety of free informational materials. During the year, special programs such as free outdoor concerts (in the summer) and workshops on a variety of subjects are held.

High Rock Park Conservation Center, a branch of the Staten Island Institute of Arts and Sciences, which co-administers this area with the New York City parks department, will be able to offer visitors even more varied experiences in the near future. Plans call for the staff to take over the management of two other city-owned natural areas on Staten Island. One of them, Blue Heron Park, is described elsewhere. The second is the Reeds Basket Willow Swamp, which recently was designated a State Freshwater Wetland of unusual local significance. It occupies 30 acres of the east slope of Todt Hill, which at a height of 410 feet above sea level is the highest point along the entire eastern seaboard south of Maine. Naturalist-guided tours will be offered to the public.

Hiking

Five woodland trails lead the hiker past a loosestrife swamp, water lily pond, and many rock outcroppings and boulders, physical evidence that this was the southernmost limit of the last great glacier. Along the Haiku Trail are markers with verses translated from the Japanese. Trail maps and printed guides are available at the visitor's center, or at the Stone House. On weekends, free tours are available to family groups or organizations.

How to Get There: Located in central Staten Island. From the Richmond Rd. exit on Staten Island Expwy. (I-278), head south on Richmond Rd. to Rockland Ave., where you turn right. Continue on Rockland Ave. for about 2½ blocks to Nevada Ave. Turn right and continue to parking lot for center at end of Nevada. *By bus*: S111 to Rockland and Nevada Aves.

Open daily, 9:00 A.M.–5:00 P.M., year-round. Sometimes closed Christmas Day. Free.

For Additional Information:

High Rock Park Conservation
Center
200 Nevada Ave.
Staten Island, NY 10306
212-987-6233

Staten Island Institute of Arts
and Sciences
75 Stuyvesant Pl.
Staten Island, NY 10301
212-727-1135

Urban Park Rangers—Staten
Island
Clove Lakes/Silver Lake Park
1150 Clove Rd.
Staten Island, NY 10301
212-442-1304 or 212-442-7640

LaTourette Park

Along the serpentine backbone of Staten Island, bordering
Richmond Creek, is a linear green space called LaTourette
Park. It is marked by a chain of hills and contains both
woodland and marsh. Bird-watchers find it a rewarding spot,
with more than 150 species sighted. Along the watercourse are
marsh hawks, red-shouldered hawks, long-billed marsh wrens,
ducks, gulls, and several types of herons.

Buck's Hollow, a valley located at the northeastern end of
the park, encompasses about 125 acres of natural beech and
oak woodland. The grapevines seen here are the remnants of
an old vineyard. Each fall, a grove of about eighty-five persim-
mon trees bears fruit. Many species of birds winter in this
protected area, and in the spring, the yellow-breasted chat
performs his gyrations.

Hiking and Horseback Riding

Paths are found throughout the park, but in Buck's Hollow
both bridle trails (no rentals) and hiking trails lead through the
area for more than 5 miles.

Winter Sports

Skiers and sledders enjoy the snowy slopes of the park's golf
course.

How to Get There: Located in central Staten Island. From Richmond Rd. exit on Staten Island Expwy. (I-278), go south on Richmond Rd. Head to junction of Richmond Rd., Arthur Kill Rd., and
Richmond Hill Rd. near St. Andrew's Church. Turn right on Richmond Hill Rd. through park, or turn left off Richmond Hill Rd. onto
Old Mill Rd., which also leads through park. To reach Buck's Hollow,
proceed on Richmond Hill Rd. to Forest Hill Rd. along park's western
boundary and turn right; at Rockland Ave. turn right again. Rockland
Ave. forms the park's northern boundary; Buck's Hollow borders
Rockland Ave. on right side between Forest Hill Rd. and Meisner Ave.
By bus: S113 to Richmondtown.

Park open at all times. Free.

For Additional Information:
Urban Park Rangers—Staten Island
1150 Clove Rd.
Clove Lakes/Silver Lake Parks
Staten Island, NY 10301
212-442-1304 or 212-442-7640

Moravian Cemetery

Cemeteries are often overlooked as places of interest to nature lovers, when in fact they can provide a good habitat for birds as well as other wildlife. The Moravian Cemetery on Staten Island, among the most beautiful cemeteries in the nation, is one such place. Located on the south slope of Todt Hill, highest point on the eastern seaboard south of Maine, it is not just a lovely place to see, but also provides an essential link in the Staten Island Greenbelt (described elsewhere).

Near the back of the cemetery is a stretch of mixed hardwood forest where several ponds provide habitat for wood duck, muskrat, turtle, and frog. The ponds are adorned with water lilies and bordered by white lance-leaved violets.

Birds gather in great numbers in the cemetery to feed off the berries that grow there. Vegetation includes the Asiatic Hercules' club, Russian olive, Amor cork tree, blue spruce, white and red pine, and a hemlock grove. In the blooming season, the rhododendron and azalea are laden with flowers, some reflected in the ponds.

The showplace of the cemetery is the elaborate mausoleum of Commodore Cornelius Vanderbilt and his family and descendants. It sits in isolated splendor in a grove of magnificent old trees.

How to Get There: Located in central Staten Island. From Richmond Rd. exit on Staten Island Expwy. (I-278), go south on Richmond Rd. to cemetery entrance on right side of road in community of New Dorp, just south of Todt Hill Rd. *By bus:* S113 to Richmond Rd. near Altamont St.

Open daily, year-round, during daylight hours. Free.

For Additional Information:
Moravian Cemetery
Richmond Rd.
New Dorp
Staten Island, NY 10304
212-351-0136

SALT Adventures

When most of us consider a raft trip, we think of such wild rivers as the Colorado winding through Grand Canyon, or the

Salmon in Idaho. But an unusual rafting adventure can be enjoyed along the New York–New Jersey shoreline.

Operating under the name of SALT and using inflatable, motorized rafts 33 feet long, outfitter Mike Notarfrancesco may take you into Long Island Sound, southward down portions of the Intracoastal Waterway, into the open Atlantic, or up the Hudson River. All waters navigated are either tidal brackish or salt, and you'll travel 20 to 30 miles a day.

Each trip is limited to six persons, plus two crew members (a licensed skipper and a cook). Meals consist in part of fish caught along the way, and the food is excellent. The itinerary is flexible and open to the desires of the group, but it generally includes fishing in the ocean and bay, clamming, crabbing, bird-watching, swimming, exploring coastal wetlands and beaches, and photography. All trips are nature-oriented.

Participants should be experienced campers, as you'll sleep in tents in all kinds of weather and at primitive sites.

Special charters can be arranged for specific interests.

For Additional Information:
Mike Notarfrancesco
SALT
Box 294
Staten Island, NY 10302
212-981-1017

Staten Island Greenbelt

In the very heart of Staten Island lies a great, green, U-shaped corridor of land known as the Staten Island Greenbelt. It forms a chain of open space that includes Todt Hill, the Moravian Cemetery, High Rock Park Conservation Center, LaTourette Park, and, on the western arm of the U, the Davis Wildlife Refuge and a swath of undeveloped parkland known as Fresh Kills Park (all but Todt Hill and Fresh Kills Park are described elsewhere).

Rising 409.8 feet above sea level, Todt Hill is the highest point on the entire eastern seaboard between Mount Desert, Me., and Key West, Fla. It is about 14 miles long and 8 miles wide and provides sweeping views of this most rural of all New York City boroughs. At the top of it is a never-dry kettle-hole pond. Todt Hill lies roughly east of the intersection of Ocean Terrace and Todt Hill Road.

Containing 808 totally undeveloped acres, Fresh Kills Park is the largest city park on Staten Island and the sixth largest in the entire city. It is primarily a park of waters, protecting most of the watersheds of Richmond and Main Creeks, which merge within park boundaries to form the stream known as Fresh

Kills. A linear park, it extends from Travis Avenue on the north to Arthur Kill Road on the south.

The entire eastern arm of the greenbelt offers an experience unique within the metropolitan area, the only network of cleared and marked trails within New York City. A demonstration project for urban trails, the Olmsted Network of Trails was laid out by volunteers from a nonprofit organization called Conservation & The Outdoors. For a nominal fee, you may obtain a trail map from them (address follows).

Hiking

Five cleared and color-designated trails total approximately 35 miles. Only one, the Richmondtown Circular, begins and ends at the same place. It is also the longest trail, a little over 13 miles. Others range from about 5 miles to about 7 miles. You may also combine portions of different trails, but this is not recommended until you are familiar with the area. Be prepared for some steep terrain.

How to Get There: The eastern arm of the greenbelt begins near Staten Island Expwy. (I-278), extends southward through LaTourette Park to Arthur Kill Rd., then turns northward again and becomes the western arm through the length of Fresh Kills Park and William T. Davis Wildlife Refuge, ending just north of Travis Ave. The greenbelt is bordered by Victory Blvd. on the west and Richmond Rd. on the east. When most residents discuss the greenbelt, they are referring to the eastern arm, and it is this arm that contains the Olmsted Network of Trails.

From the Richmond Rd. exit on Staten Island Expwy. (I-278), go south on Richmond Rd. to Richmond Hill Rd. and turn right. Richmond Hill Rd. cuts through the eastern arm of the greenbelt near its center. Park on area streets. *By bus:* S107, S111, or S113 take you to different trail heads. The trail map sold by Conservation & The Outdoors provides more details (at this writing, it costs a dollar plus a stamped self-addressed envelope).

For Additional Information:

Director
Conservation & The Outdoors
P.O. Box 284
New York, NY 10031
212-721-8156

Urban Park Rangers—Staten Island
Clove Lakes/Silver Lake Park
1150 Clove Rd.
Staten Island, NY 10301
212-442-1304 or 212-442-7640

Staten Island Zoo

The Staten Island Zoo's philosophy is that big isn't necessarily good. It has earned a reputation as one of the best small zoos in the country, and its collection of reptiles (snakes, turtles, and alligators) is famous around the world, surpassing even the Bronx Zoo's. It is noted particularly for the variety of rattlesnakes it displays. Exhibits of tropical fish, birds, invertebrates, and such exotic mammals as tigers, chimps, and baboons round out the zoo. Established in 1936, it was the first zoo in the country to be built with educational as well as exhibition facilities; its classrooms, library, and biology laboratory share the spotlight with its animal exhibits.

A popular attraction with families, particularly those with small children, is the miniature working farm. Children are encouraged to pet and feed the animals, sometimes right from their hands.

Tiny Barrett Park, which surrounds the zoo, was once a tree nursery. Its remnant trees, now monarchs, are well worth seeing.

How to Get There: Located in north central Staten Island. From Slosson Ave. exit on Staten Island Expwy. (I-278), go north on Slosson Ave. until it ends at Martling Ave. Turn right onto Martling and continue to its end at Clove Rd. The Clove Rd. entrance to the zoo will be directly in front of you, with free parking to your right. *By bus:* S107 to Broadway and Forest Ave.

Open daily, year-round, 10:00 A.M.–4:45 P.M. (children's zoo open May through September); closed Thanksgiving, December 25, and January 1. Free on Wednesday; nominal admission rest of time.

For Additional Information:
Staten Island Zoological Society, Inc.
Staten Island Zoo
614 Broadway
Staten Island, NY 10310
212-442-3100

Von Briesen Park

A spectacular look at The Narrows is just one of the delights awaiting you at tiny Von Briesen Park. Small, well landscaped, and undoubtedly one of the cleanest parks in New York City, it is seldom crowded. Because of the many unusual trees planted here, the park is also a veritable arboretum.

Von Briesen is the site of an old estate donated to the New York City Parks Department in 1949 by members of the Von Briesen family, who had long collected all kinds of plants, shrubs, and trees for planting here. Today, you may see the fruits of their labor—bald cypress, English oak, European purple beech, European linden, an empress tree, Chinese scholar tree, tamarack, sugar maple, mulberry, hackberry, and Hercules'-club or devil's walking stick.

Birds by the hundreds converge upon the park, which occupies little more than a couple of city blocks. At the rear of the park, the gentle slope of the land rises to its highest point for a panoramic view of The Narrows, the bridge that spans it, sailboats on the river far below, and, on a clear day, lower Manhattan.

On the north side of the park, resembling a Monet painting come to life, is a small, exquisite lily pond that seems to emphasize the serenity of this park.

Von Briesen is adjacent to Fort Wadsworth, a military installation that recently became part of Gateway National Recreation Area (described elsewhere).

How to Get There: Located along northeast shore of Staten Island, just north of Fort Wadsworth. From School Rd. exit on Staten Island Expwy. (I-278), go northeast on School Rd. to Bay St., where you'll see the parking lot for Von Briesen Park just across the street. *By bus*: S2.

Open at all times. Free.

For Additional Information:
Urban Park Rangers—Staten Island
Clove Lakes/Silver Lake Parks
1150 Clove Rd.
Staten Island, NY 10301
212-442-1304 or 212-442-7640

Ward's Point Park

Arcing around the southernmost tip of Staten Island, jutting into Raritan Bay, is a verdant rural park known as Ward's Point. Focal point of the park is the Conference (or Billop) House, erected in 1680. On September 11, 1776, it was the site of the only peace conference between the Americans and the British held during the Revolutionary War. The conference failed, but the house stands a monument to those proceedings. Around it, vast green lawns shaded by huge old trees slope gently down to meet the waters of the bay. A stretch of pebbly sand beach here is a major gathering place for all kinds of shorebirds, gulls, and sometimes great wading birds. During the early summer, horseshoe crabs come into the shallow waters to lay their eggs and often are washed ashore, where they perish. There is a multitude of shells as well, including the rare little wentletrap. An outcropping of fossil shells may be seen near the pavilion.

On the upper reaches of the shore grow such plants as Russian thistle, high-tide weed, sea rocket, and seaside goldenrod. And in the fall, asters and goldenrod adorn the fields.

How to Get There: From the Hylan Blvd. exit on Staten Island Expwy. (I-278), go south on Hylan Blvd. Park lies at end of Hylan. This park is also known as Conference House Park. *By rail*: SIRT to Tottenville station. *By bus*: S103 to Craig Ave.

Park open at all times. Free. Conference House open Tuesday through Sunday, 1:00–5:00 P.M., April through September; Tuesday through Sunday, 1:00–4:00 P.M., rest of year. Closed Monday. Free Tuesday and Thursday, nominal fee other days.

For Additional Information:

Conference House
South End of Hylan Blvd.
Staten Island, NY 10307
212-984-2086

Urban Park Rangers—Staten Island
Clove Lakes/Silver Lake Parks
1150 Clove Rd.
Staten Island, NY 10301
212-442-1304 or 212-442-7640

Wolfe's Pond Park

Along Staten Island's Atlantic coastline, on the southernmost part of the island, is Wolfe's Pond Park, part of which still exists in a natural state. Its 224 acres of ocean beach, fresh-water pond and lake, bog, woodland, and meadow are considered excellent for bird-watching. Many birds, including migrating waterfowl, spend the winter here.

The beach has been developed as a public swimming area, but the northern half of the park, across Hylan Boulevard, is untouched natural woodland, encompassing a pond favored by naturalists. In the summertime, the pond is fringed with rose mallow and pickerel weed, and there's a frenzy of wildlife activity. Damselflies, dragonflies, and purple martins dart back and forth across the pond's surface, feeding on mosquitoes. Great blue and black-crowned night herons are often found in the park.

The woodland area is composed mostly of oak, hickory, and sweet gum, with an understory of spicebush. Trout lilies and Canada mayflowers grow in profusion in the spring.

A short distance southwest of Wolfe's Pond Park, Lemon Creek flows into Prince's Bay. A group of nesting houses here are home to the only colony of purple martins in New York City. Some acreage along the creek and around its mouth has been purchased and left undeveloped by the New York City Parks Department; it is known as Lemon Creek Park.

Hiking

Trails lead through many sections of the park, but there are tangles of briers and poison ivy in places. Beach walking is pleasant, particularly on weekdays during early morning and late afternoon, and also after the swimming season is over. It's also possible to hike along the shore to Lemon Creek Park, a short distance to the southwest.

Fishing and Boating

Rowboats may be rented for use on the lake, and there's a marina near Lemon Creek Park. Fishing is permitted on the park's lake and pond, and also in the surf.

How to Get There: From Hylan Blvd. exit on Staten Island Expwy. (I-278), go south on Hylan Blvd. to park entrance on left side of road. Although park lands are found on both sides of Hylan, the parking area is near the beach. *By rail:* SIRT to Prince's Bay station. *By bus:* S103 to park.

Open at all times. Nominal parking fee charged during summer only.

For Additional Information:

Urban Park Rangers—Staten Island
Clove Lakes/Silver Lake Parks
1150 Clove Rd.
Staten Island, NY 10301
212-442-1304 or 212-442-7640

Part 5

Natural Attractions in
Long Island

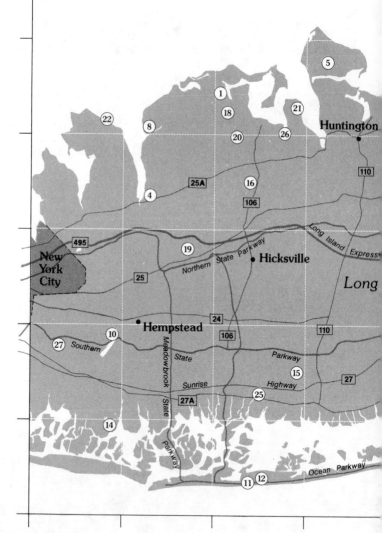

LONG ISLAND

1. Bailey Arboretum **C-2**
2. Bayard Cutting Arboretum **G-5**
3. Belmont Lake State Park **E-5**
4. Bryant Preserve **B-3**
5. Caumsett State Park **D-2**
6. Connetquot River State Park **G-4**
7. Fire Island National Seashore **H-6**
8. Garvies Point Museum & Preserve **B-2**
9. Heckscher State Park **F-5**
10. Hempstead Lake State Park **A-5**
11. Jones Beach State Park **C-6**
12. John F. Kennedy Memorial Wildlife Sanctuary **C-6**
13. Long Island Greenbelt Trail **F-4**
14. Marine Nature Study Area **A-6**

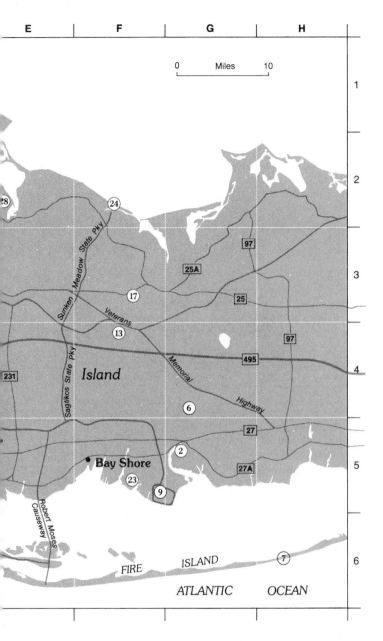

Bailey Arboretum

Located in Lattingtown, the Bailey Arboretum, the former home of Mr. and Mrs. Frank Bailey, is a 42-acre estate with lush landscaped grounds and gardens. The arboretum contains many unusual and rare trees from all over the world, some labeled. Among them are several that are the largest of their kind in New York State and a distinguished striped maple recognized as one of the largest of its species in the country.

In a small area adjacent to the pond grow giant tulip trees, oaks, and maples, many of them more than a century old. A huge black walnut tree, native to the area, grows near the Bailey home.

Collections of flowers include a rose garden, tree peonies, and a large iris border. There are also a collection of dwarf evergreens, a spring-flowering bulb garden, a shade-loving ground cover collection, and an impressive rock garden.

In the spring, the forest floor is a carpet of wildflowers—trout lilies, mayapples, jacks-in-the-pulpit, violets, and trilliums color the landscape. They may be seen along the arboretum's mile-long Interpretive Nature Trail, which circles through a bog area.

How to Get There: From Exit 39 of Long Island Expwy. (I-495), go north on Glen Cove Rd. to NY 25A and turn right. At Wolver Hollow Rd. turn left and go to Piping Rock Rd. Then turn left and go to Buckram Rd. At Buckram, turn right and head to Bayville Rd.; turn left and continue to arboretum at northeast corner of Bayville and Feeks Lane. Entrance is off Bayville Rd. *By rail:* LIRR to Oyster Bay.

Open 9:00 A.M.–5:00 P.M., Tuesday through Sunday, April through October; closed Mondays. Visitors limited to 200 at a time; children under 18 must be accompanied by an adult. Nominal entrance fee.

For Additional Information:

Bailey Arboretum
Bayville Rd. & Feeks Ln.
Lattingtown, NY 11560
516-292-4116

Nassau County Dept. of
Recreation & Parks
Eisenhower Park
East Meadow, NY 11554
516-542-4422

Bayard Cutting Arboretum

At Great River, not far from Great South Bay, is the 690-acre Bayard Cutting Arboretum. A part of the Long Island state park system, it features some of the prettiest and best nature walks on the island.

One area not to be missed is a pinetum that boasts the largest and finest specimens of conifers on Long Island. The arboretum grounds, located along the Connetquot River just before it empties into Great South Bay, are made up of tidewater meadows and marshes, streams, ponds, and native woodlands, as well as landscaped gardens.

Nature Trails

The longest of several nature trails is the Bird Watchers' Walk, which follows the river shoreline to a bird sanctuary. Along the Swamp Cypress Trail, you see a swamp cypress displaying thirty "knees" in its muddy setting. The Wildflower Walk is one of the finest of its kind on Long Island. Under a cover of winter snow, all walks take on a new dimension of beauty.

How to Get There: From Exit 45 on Southern State Pkwy., go east on NY 27A (Montauk Hwy.) to arboretum entrance on right side of road. *By rail:* LIRR stops at Great River station.

Open 10:00 A.M.–5:30 P.M. (to 4:30 P.M. when Eastern Standard Time is in effect), Wednesday through Sunday and holidays, year-round. Nominal fee charged; children under 12 free.

For Additional Information:

Bayard Cutting Arboretum
P.O. Box 66
Montauk Hwy., NY 27A
Oakdale, NY 11769
516-581-1002

Long Island State Park &
Recreation Commission
Belmont Lake State Park
Babylon, NY 11702
516-669-1000

Belmont Lake State Park

A long, narrow strip of green space, this 459-acre park offers a mix of natural attractions and recreation. Most of the activity centers around 40-acre Belmont Lake near the northern end of the park, where there are shaded picnic areas, playfields, and boat rentals. Extending southward toward Great South Bay, the park follows a brook for its entire length. At the southern end of the park is Southard's Pond; and just southwest of here, though not in the park itself, is Lake Argyle, a bird sanctuary where such rare species of duck as the European widgeon and ring-neck may be seen. The entire park harbors waterfowl in the winter. Sightings may include the shoveler, gadwall, green-winged teal, canvasback, ruddy duck, and hooded merganser.

The Long Island State Park & Recreation Commission has its headquarters in this park.

Hiking, Bicycling, and Horseback Riding

Trails lead through the woods in all directions. One completely encircles Belmont Lake, with a loop trail leading off to the north along the brook that runs the length of the park. The portion of the park south of Southern State Parkway is undeveloped except for a bridle path and parallel bike trail along the brook. Both trails may also be used by hikers. A livery stable just outside of the parking area has horses for hire (for information, phone Babylon Riding Academy, 516-587-7778).

Fishing and Boating

Fishing is permitted in Belmont Lake, and rental rowboats are available during summer months.

Winter Sports

Ice skating is permitted on Belmont Lake.

How to Get There: Located north of Babylon in southwestern Suffolk County. Exit 38 on Southern State Pkwy. is within park; proceed north from this exit to parking lot. *By rail:* LIRR stops at Babylon.

Park open daily, 8:00 A.M.–sunset, year-round. Nominal parking fee Memorial Day weekend through Labor Day weekend.

For Additional Information:

Superintendent
Belmont Lake State Park
Southern State Pkwy.
Babylon, NY 11702
516-667-5055

Long Island State Park &
Recreation Commission
Belmont Lake State Park
Babylon, NY 11702
516-669-1000

Bryant Preserve

A great sanctuary of meadows, manicured lawns and gardens, and dense woodland, this 175-acre preserve is named for William Cullen Bryant (1794–1878), who lived in the Roslyn area for some forty years. Bryant was instrumental in fostering a nationwide interest in conservation, and he, perhaps more than anyone else, was responsible for the creation of Central Park in Manhattan. The board-and-batten cottage he built when he owned 80 acres of Bryant Preserve still stands.

A large sprawling mansion on the preserve was once the home of naturalist-businessman Childs Frick, who preserved the grounds in the early twentieth century with the same environmental concern as had Bryant. He planted a pinetum here, sometimes spending as much as $50,000 to transplant a single grown tree. More than 190 species of conifers, some quite rare, thrive today, including a few sequoia trees believed to be the largest east of the Mississippi River.

The preserve is now the property of the Nassau County Department of Recreation & Parks, and the former Frick Mansion houses the Nassau County Museum for Fine Arts. Self-guided walking tours follow the many paths that lace the grounds.

How to Get There: From Exit 39 on Long Island Expwy. (I-495) go north on Glen Cove Rd. to Northern Blvd. (NY 25A) and turn left; continue to preserve entrance at Museum Dr. Look for sign marking entrance to Nassau County Museum for Fine Arts, and turn right onto Museum Dr. into preserve. *By rail*: LIRR to Roslyn.

Open daily, year-round, 9:30 A.M.–4:30 P.M., Monday through Friday, and 1:00 P.M.–5:00 P.M., Saturday and Sunday. Free.

For Additional Information:

William Cullen Bryant Preserve
Northern Blvd., P.O. Box D
Roslyn, NY 11576
516-484-9337

Nassau County Dept. of
Recreation & Parks
Eisenhower Park
East Meadow, NY 11554
516-542-4422

Caumsett State Park

On Lloyd's Neck jutting out into Long Island Sound is 1,500-acre Caumsett State Park, named after a Matinecock Indian word meaning "place by a sharp rock." Before becoming a state park, it was the country estate of Marshall Field III, grandson of the department store pioneer.

Since the estate was developed into a state park in 1961, it has been allowed to revert to a more natural setting, penetrated by hiking trails and equestrian paths. The woods have grown more mature, the setting more scenic. It's an excellent place for bird-watching; a 90-acre salt marsh is a haven for migrating duck and geese.

Hickory, oak, pine, black birch, black locust, yellow poplar, and white birch trees grow tall here. Along the shore are sand dunes where beach grasses, pussy willow, rose hips, and beach plum grow. Other vegetation includes the Christmas fern, fox grape, and a flat, horizontal fungus called artist's palette.

Hiking, Bicycling, and Horseback Riding

Several miles of hiking trails crisscross the park's wooded grounds. The gently rolling terrain makes for mostly easy walking. There are also bicycling and bridle trails in the park; a stable has horses for hire. Guided hikes and bike tours are conducted by a park naturalist.

Fishing

There is excellent fishing in Long Island Sound.

Winter Sports

A cross-country ski trail has been laid out.

How to Get There: Located in northwest corner of Suffolk County. From intersection of NY 110 and NY 25A in Huntington, go west on 25A to West Neck Rd. Turn right and go north on West Neck Rd. (later called Lloyd Harbor Rd.) to park on Lloyd's Neck.

Open daily, year-round, 8:00 A.M.–4:30 P.M. Nominal admission fee Memorial Day through Labor Day.

For Additional Information:

Superintendent
Caumsett State Park
West Neck Rd.
Lloyd's Neck, NY 11743
516-423-1770

Long Island State Park &
Recreation Commission
Belmont Lake State Park
Babylon, NY 11702
516-669-1000

Connetquot River State Park

If there's one thing Connetquot River State Park should be noted for, it's the great population of barn and tree swallows that congregate each spring to nest and raise young. Approximately fifty pairs of each species migrate to the area as soon as the weather becomes hot enough to produce lots of flying insects (the swallows catch all their food on the wing).

Most of the feeding is done above the Main Pond, as well as in the open meadow areas, and people come just to marvel at the swallows' acrobatics as they speed through the air in pursuit of insects. Many of the barn swallows nest in the maintenance garage at the south end of the park. Both species leave with their young for South America in August, and normally do not return again until May.

This 3,500-acre park was once the exclusive Southside Sportsmen's Club, established for the protection and propagation of game birds and fish. It has been beautifully preserved, with dense forests bordering much of the river. Native trees, shrubs, and wildflowers adorn a setting of tributary streams and freshwater ponds.

Hiking and Horseback Riding

A complex of hiking trails leads through the park. A guided 2-mile nature hike, featuring an old grist mill, fish hatchery, and some of the history and ecology of the park, is offered regularly. Horseback riding permitted on designated trails; daily or annual permit available. No rentals.

Fishing

There's a fish hatchery in the park, and trout are stocked in park streams.

Winter Sports

This is a fine area for cross-country skiing.

How to Get There: Located northeast of Bay Shore in Suffolk County. Park entrance road runs north from Sunrise Hwy. (NY 27), just east of Exit 44 on Southern State Pkwy. *By rail:* LIRR to Islip station.

Open daily, during daylight hours, except Monday unless Monday is a holiday. Nominal entrance fee Memorial Day weekend through Labor Day. Entry is available only to those who apply in advance by writing for a permit.

For Additional Information:

Connetquot River State Park
Sunrise Highway
Box 505
Oakdale, NY 11769
516-581-1005

Long Island State Park &
Recreation Commission
Belmont Lake State Park
Babylon, NY 11702
516-669-1000

Fire Island National Seashore

Fire Island, a long, narrow strip of land lying parallel to Long Island's southern shoreline, is the wildest beach and dune area of greater New York City. It has long been one of the area's most popular summer playgrounds, but many nature lovers come in the off-season when crowds have dwindled. This windswept barrier island harbors many seaside plant communities and varied wildlife of the salt marsh. Administered by the National Park Service, it has been preserved to give future generations the chance to see a remnant of an unspoiled seashore little changed from that seen by early settlers.

This pencillike island, which extends some 30 miles in an east-west direction, varies in width from about 550 feet to about 1,700 feet. It is separated from Long Island by shallow Great South Bay and Moriches Bay, at a few places by no more than 500 feet of water. Although some of the foredunes reach a height of about 40 feet, most of the island is only a few feet above sea level.

Many sections of the island have good vegetative cover— sea oats, marsh grass, wild salt rose, and even poison ivy— which deters the eroding forces of wind and water. Near the center of the national seashore is a sunken marine forest of pristine pines—one of the most outstanding natural phenomena on Fire Island—that further aids the island's preservation and stabilization.

The forest, located in the Sailors Haven area, rises no higher than the surge line of wind and salt spray above the surrounding dunes. Thus it presents the appearance of a sunken forest, with dunes rising higher than the treetops. The tops of the trees are continuously pruned by the elements. Upon entering, one experiences a new dimension, totally different from the dunes or beach and ocean environment. Here all is quiet and cool, even on the hottest summer day, and the sun only occasionally penetrates the umbrella canopy. Stout hollies with glossy leaves and trunks 2 feet in diameter; oak trees perhaps a century or more old, but only 35 feet tall; pine, black gum, maple, sassafras—all crowd together in a virgin stand, laying down a spongy carpet of leaf mold on the sand. Vines rooting there have curtained over the woods—grape, poison ivy, catbrier all spun into a lattice binding together the elements of the Sunken Forest.

Blueberries, shadbush, Canada mayflowers, and ferns grow in the forest where enough sunlight filters through the canopy to nourish them. Occasionally, one finds a cattail marsh opening where tricolored blackbirds nest in spring, and towhees and catbirds sing.

Along the bay shore are pure stands of reed grass as tall as one's head, cord grass, rushes gradually giving away to sea lettuce, widgeon grass, and eelgrass. The forest environment affords protection and cover for a good variety of wild creatures, including red fox, raccoon, cottontail rabbit, several types of field mice, and white-tailed deer. Crabs, clams, oysters, mussels, snails, and marine worms are found close to shore, along with bluefish, winter flounder, and blowfish in the shallow bay waters. On the ocean side of the island are kingfish, blues, mackerel, fluke, and striped bass. Small populations of wild ducks and Canada geese live and breed in the bay; and during spring and autumn migrations, the quiet waters hold huge rafts of migrating ducks and hundreds of Canada geese. In late September and early October, the hawk migration is at its peak and provides one of the island's most outstanding natural spectacles.

Between Watch Hill and Smith Point County Park to the east lie some 1,300 acres of totally wild and primitive land. Known as the Eight-Mile Zone, it was designated a Federal Wilderness Area in late 1980. Even on summer weekends, the deer outnumber the people.

Hiking

No hiking trails exist on the island, but you may find excellent walking on the hard-packed sand beach the entire length of the island. Most rewarding for wildlife is the wilderness area between Watch Hill and Smith Point County Park at the island's east end; extending nearly 8 miles, it's primitive and isolated. There are several nature trails, including one through the Sunken Forest. Under no circumstances, though, should you walk on the dunes; their vegetative cover is much too fragile to survive the traffic.

Swimming

Atlantic beaches with lifeguards are available at Watch Hill and Sailors Haven.

Camping

A popular 35-unit tent campground is available at Watch Hill; reservations required (best to make them well in advance). Free. Regular season May 1 through October 15; limited facilities in winter.

How to Get There: There are no roads within Fire Island National Seashore. Ferries serve visitors in many locations. From NY 27A

(Montauk Hwy.) in Bay Shore, Sayville, or Patchogue, follow signs to ferries. From Bay Shore, ferries go to three day-use recreation areas. A Sayville ferry goes to Sailors Haven Visitor Center within the National Seashore; a Patchogue ferry goes to the Watch Hill area, where the National Park Service has another Visitor Center. Or you may charter a boat to Fire Island. Farther east on NY 27A, you may turn south on William Floyd Pkwy. at Shirley, which leads via a toll bridge to Smith Point County Park, a Suffolk County facility on the eastern end of Fire Island within the National Seashore; a small National Park Service Visitor Center is located here also. *By rail*: LIRR to Bay Shore, Sayville, or Patchogue; taxi or minibus from train station to ferry.

Open daily, year-round, during daylight hours. Free admission; fee for ferry.

For Additional Information:

Superintendent
Fire Island National Seashore
120 Laurel St.
Patchogue, NY 11772
516-289-4810
516-597-6633 (Camping Reservations)

Garvies Point Museum & Preserve

The 72-acre Garvies Point Preserve, in Glen Cove in Nassau County, consists of meadows, woodlands, cliffs, beaches, and a freshwater pond. With such diverse habitat, it's a natural place for a variety of wildlife and birds. More than 140 species of birds have been sighted here. Among them are the ring-necked pheasant, yellow-shafted flicker, brown thrasher, Philadelphia vireo, evening grosbeak, blackpoll warbler, scarlet tanager, and migrating waterfowl.

Forty-four species of trees, representing twenty-nine genera and twenty-three families, are found here. High cliffs along the shoreline of Hempstead Harbor exhibit erosional features, some rather dramatic alluvial fans, talus slopes, and slumping as a result of ancient multicolored clays oozing from the beach.

The Nassau County Museum of Natural History at the preserve specializes in regional geology and archaeology. Geology exhibits illustrate the evolution of Long Island's landscape. Several workshops and special exhibits are offered periodically throughout the year.

Both the preserve and museum are owned and operated by Nassau County.

Hiking

Some 5 miles of interlacing trails pass through varied wooded areas.

How to Get There: From Exit 39 on Long Island Expwy. (I-495), take Glen Cove Rd. north to Glen Cove bypass. Continue on bypass (keep left at fork) to last traffic light at Glen Cove Fire House. Follow signs to museum. (Museum is on Barry Dr., not Garvies Point Rd.) *By rail*: LIRR to Glen Cove.

Preserve open daily, year-round, 8:00 A.M. to "As Posted." Free. Very nominal admission charge to museum, which is open daily, 9:00 A.M.–5:00 P.M., except holidays.

For Additional Information:

Garvies Point Preserve
Barry Drive
Glen Cove, NY 11542
516-671-0300

Nassau County Dept. of
Recreation & Parks
Eisenhower Park
East Meadow, NY 11554
516-542-4422

Heckscher State Park

This is a fine park, just 50 miles from New York City near East Islip, in which to spend a weekend or a vacation; people come to camp, picnic, swim, hike, ride horses and bicycles, study nature, fish, and go boating.

Sprawling over more than 1,700 acres that jut out into Great South Bay, Heckscher State Park consists of marshes, open fields, woodlands, and waterfront. The great horned owl nests here, along an east-west canal in a quiet corner of the park. Many species of land birds stop here during the fall migration, while the rough-legged hawk and various types of waterfowl are wintertime visitors.

A large, marshy island, rich in flora and fauna, lies in the southwest corner of the park. Although inaccessible by foot, it may be viewed from the northern bank of the east-west canal or from a boat.

A scenic loop road leads through woods, past marshes, and along the beach. Often, at dusk, you can see the park's resident herd of deer emerging from the wooded areas to feed.

Hiking, Bicycling, and Horseback Riding

To the west of the park road are woods and marshes worth exploring on foot. An east-west canal cuts through this area and creates a large, marshy island, inaccessible by foot, but visible from the north bank of the canal. There are more woods to roam east of the park road, and both woods and marsh within the loop road. Nearly 2½ miles of beach fronts on Great South and Nicoll Bays; although generally crowded with bathers in the summer, it is a marvelous place to walk from fall through spring. The southern terminus of the Long Island Greenbelt Trail (described elsewhere) is here.

A paved bicycle path bisects the park from north to south, then turns east along the beach. Horseback riders will find a loop trail through the woods in the northeast corner of the park; no rentals.

Camping

Nearly seventy tent and trailer sites, with platforms for tents. No hookups, no showers. Open May 1 through November 30.

Swimming

You may choose between saltwater swimming in Great South Bay and a freshwater swimming pool with an ocean view. Lifeguards on duty June 21 through Labor Day. Bathhouse with lockers; bathing suits, beach chairs, and umbrellas may be rented.

Fishing and Boating

There is saltwater fishing in Great South Bay; boat launching ramp, but no rentals.

Winter Sports

When weather conditions are right, cross-country skiing is good here.

How to Get There: The eastern terminus of Southern State Pkwy. is within Heckscher State Park. *By rail:* LIRR stops at Islip and Great River.

Open daily, year-round, 8:00 A.M.–sunset. Nominal admission fee Memorial Day weekend through Labor Day.

For Additional Information:

Superintendent
Heckscher State Park
Heckscher State Pkwy.
East Islip, NY 11730
516-581-2100

Long Island State Park &
Recreation Commission
Belmont Lake State Park
Babylon, NY 11702
516-669-1000

Hempstead Lake State Park

A narrow, 3-mile-long strip running north and south, Hempstead Lake State Park near Rockville Centre has long been a favorite of bird-watchers. Its 867 acres, which include woodland, stream, open fields, a swamp, several ponds, and Hempstead Reservoir, attract many species of birds. In the northernmost reaches of the park, including the marshy end of the reservoir, look for wintering ducks. From autumn to spring, except when frozen over, the open part of the reservoir in the park's midsection may host mallards, black ducks, greater and lesser scaups, green-winged teal, and several other species of ducks. Just below the dam at the southern end of the reservoir is a wooded area that has been designated a bird sanctuary. Pied-billed grebes and wood ducks are often seen here, as well as spring warblers. Smith Pond is noted for the variety of its waterfowl, including the ring-necked duck and the hooded merganser. Occasionally, waterfowl and a few shorebirds may be seen on South Pond. Another wooded strip in the southern part of the park is especially good for spring migrants.

Developed areas around the reservoir have picnic tables, tennis courts, an archery range, a free children's carousel, and various game fields. This popular park lies only 21 miles east of Manhattan.

Hiking, Bicycling, and Horseback Riding

A hiking trail encircles the lake and leads off through cool woodlands and a maple swamp in the southern portion of the park. You may also wander through Tanglewood Preserve, an undeveloped 10-acre tract of woodland located just southwest of the park at the corner of Ocean Avenue and Peninsula Boulevard. Bikers and horseback riders may follow shaded paths around the lake, a distance of about 5 miles.

How to Get There: From Exit 18 on Southern State Pkwy., turn south on Lake Dr., which skirts the reservoir within the park. *By rail:* LIRR stops at Rockville Centre.

Jones Beach is the most popular beach in the New York area.

Open daily, year-round, 8:00 A.M.–sunset. Nominal parking fee Memorial Day weekend through Labor Day.

For Additional Information:

Superintendent
Hempstead Lake State Park
Southern State Pkwy.
Rockville Centre, NY 11572
516-766-1029

Long Island State Park &
Recreation Commission
Belmont Lake State Park
Babylon, NY 11702
516-669-1000

Jones Beach State Park

Jones Beach is perhaps the most renowned beach of the greater New York City region, luring more than 12 million visitors each year. Most come to sunbathe, swim, or walk along the ocean's edge. The parking lots alone cover almost 125 acres, and a marine theater seats nearly 10,000 people at a

New York Convention & Visitors Bureau

time. It is, in essence, a city in itself. And yet, there are still natural areas worth mentioning.

The park contains 2,413 acres, with 6 miles of white sand beach and ½ mile of bay frontage for still-water bathing. The beach is man-made, as are the few sand dunes. But the marshes of the park are not; they once covered the entire area.

Canada geese and ducks come in great numbers, for few people visit the beach in October, November, and December when the Hudson and Atlantic flyways have the heaviest bird traffic.

Other birds, too—gulls, terns, skimmers, egrets, and some mallard and canvasback ducks—build their nests and intermingle with people year-round. Raccoon, rabbit, and opossum flourish in greater numbers than they did before the area became a state park.

A large nesting colony of common terns is located at West End Beach 2, with about 2,000 pairs nesting adjacent to a large parking lot there. Since the nests are virtually invisible except to a trained eye and are easily destroyed by anyone walking into the area, you should stay on the pavement and watch the terns from the roadway or parking lot.

Hiking

If you like hiking along the beach, this is a fine place to walk for miles. Best times are very early morning during warm-weather months, as well as any time before Memorial Day and after Labor Day. One of the best winter birding walks in the East is in this park. From Parking Field 4, head north around the Fishing Station and east along the northern shore of Zachs Bay.

Fishing and Boating

Four fishing piers are open year-round, and there are locations for surf fishing (by permit). Rowboats may be rented at Parking Field 10.

Swimming

Eight separate areas on the Atlantic Ocean, one on Zachs Bay, and swimming and diving pools at the East and West Bath Houses provide a choice between freshwater and saltwater bathing.

How to Get There: From Exit 22 on Southern State Pkwy., take Meadowbrook State Pkwy. south to park. *By rail:* LIRR to Freeport or Wantagh, then take Jones Beach buses from railroad stations to park (buses run regularly during warm-weather months). *By bus:* Take Jones Beach bus from Port Authority Bus Terminal in Manhattan to park during warm-weather months.

Open daily, year-round, during daylight hours and at night for special events. Nominal parking fee daily from late May through Labor Day.

For Additional Information:

Superintendent
Jones Beach State Park
Ocean Dr.
Wantagh, NY 11793
516-785-1600

Long Island State Park &
Recreation Commission
Belmont Lake State Park
Babylon, NY 11702
516-669-1000

John F. Kennedy Memorial Wildlife Sanctuary

A 500-acre stretch of salt marsh and sand dunes with intermittent patches of bayberry and catbrier, the John F. Kennedy Wildlife Sanctuary is a quiet, lovely place. Thousands of ducks and geese stop here regularly during their autumn migration along the Atlantic flyway, lured by a shallow brackish pond in the midst of the sanctuary and pollution-free wetlands.

Among the birds found here regularly are the green-winged teal, red-breasted merganser, baldpate, gadwall, rail, and European widgeon, scaup, snowy egret, common snipe, coot, bufflehead, piping plover, least tern, laughing gull, red-throated loon, horned grebe, osprey, short-eared owl, marbled godwit, and belted kingfisher. The undisturbed habitat also attracts fox, weasel, skunk, opossum, cottontail rabbit, and white-tailed deer, and in the surrounding waters are some sixty species of fish. When masses of monarch butterflies stop by during their annual fall migration, they create for a brief time a fantasy world of black and orange. The sanctuary is owned by the town of Oyster Bay and managed by the New York Department of Environmental Conservation under a joint agreement. Since a permit is required for entry, the sanctuary is never crowded.

Hiking

Some 4½ miles of foot trails lead through portions of the various ecosystems of the sanctuary. Along the way, you'll find blinds and a 36-foot observation tower.

How to Get There: From Exit 22 on Southern State Pkwy., take Meadowbrook State Pkwy. south to Ocean Pkwy. in Jones Beach State Park. Turn left and continue to Tobay Beach parking lot, just east of parking area #9 in Jones Beach State Park, on left side of road. Drive into preserve from west end of parking lot and use parking space provided in preserve.

Open daily, year-round; dawn to dusk during bathing season at Tobay Beach; dawn to 4:00 P.M. from Labor Day to Memorial Day. All visitors must acquire a permit in advance from the Superintendent of Beaches in Oyster Bay; permits are free, but are not honored during hunting season.

For Additional Information:
Superintendent
Department of Beaches
Town Hall
Oyster Bay, NY 11771
516-922-5800 (Extension 578)

Long Island Greenbelt Trail

Officially opened in 1978, Long Island's Greenbelt Trail stretches for 34 miles from Heckscher State Park on Great South Bay to Sunken Meadow State Park on Long Island Sound. The trail is unparalleled as an educational resource for exploring the geology, history, and ecology of Long Island. Hikers follow the beautiful valleys of the Connetquot and Nissequogue Rivers through pine barrens and wetlands, over moraines (where glaciers pushed up small hills), and through deciduous forests.

Deer, turtles, rabbits, chipmunks, and hundreds of species of birds are common sights along the pathway, and it's not unusual to spot great blue herons, ospreys and red foxes. Many of Long Island's magnificent trees may be seen along the way—larches, pitch pines, oaks, maples, and a grove of white pines. Wildflowers include marsh marigold, swamp rose mallow, day lily, wild rose, and the rare pink lady's slipper.

The trail originated in 1976, when Nancy Manfredonia (current director of the Greenbelt Trail Conference, which maintains the hiking path) and several volunteers set out on a "trail-finders'" hike from the South Shore to the North Shore. They followed old Native American trails, abandoned wagon trails, and deer paths; and, incredible as it may seem, they were able to mark a meandering trail the entire distance. Except at points where the path necessarily had to cross some east-west highways, virtually the entire route passed through parks and natural areas. Today, it preserves one of the last remaining strips of wilderness on Long Island.

The trail conference has prepared an excellent free booklet that depicts the route of the trail in eight sectional maps and lists all regulations governing its use. To obtain a copy, send a self-addressed stamped envelope to the address that follows this listing. Hikers may follow part of the trail as a day hike, or walk the entire route, camping along the way at one of two designated Long Island Greenbelt campsites; both are free. The trail is mostly flat.

How to Get There: Heckscher State Park lies at eastern terminus of Southern State Pkwy. Sunken Meadow State Pkwy. leads north from Exit 53 of Long Island Expwy. (I-495) to Sunken Meadow State Park. The Greenbelt Trail is accessible at each park, as well as at several points between the two. *By rail*: The trail is within walking or taxi distance of five LIRR stations—Great River, Central Islip, Ronkonkoma, Smithtown, and Kings Park.

Open daily, year-round; the portions of the trail through Connetquot and Nissequogue River State Parks are closed on Mondays. A nominal parking fee is charged in some areas. Reservations to hike are required, since the number of people using the trail at the same time is limited. Children under 18 must be with an adult.

For Additional Information:

Director
Greenbelt Trail Conference, Inc.
23 Deer Path Rd.
Central Islip, NY 11722
516-234-3112

Marine Nature Study Area

Near Oceanside, along Long Island's south shore, the Town of Hempstead is preserving a fabulous 17,000-acre tract of wetland. The Marine Nature Study Area, which encompasses 52 acres of this estuary, was opened to the public in 1970. It attempts to explain the functions of the salt marsh ecosystem and the role it plays in maintaining the balance of nature. Sand dunes, beach, ponds, and marsh are included in this oasis of serenity bordered by water on three sides.

There are seven designated observation and study sites, along with a rustic shelter adjacent to the pond for bird study and photography. Botanists have counted more than 150 native plants, in addition to some 15 species introduced to attract wildlife. More than 170 species of birds have been sighted here.

An interpretive center has live tanks, nature mountings, exhibits of salt marsh flora and fauna, and reading material.

Hiking

A network of trails traverses the 52-acre area, leading to seven study sites, each of which presents a different aspect of marsh life. To preserve delicate communities, some elevated boardwalks have been constructed. It's possible to quickly walk through the entire area in an hour, but allow more time to immerse yourself in this wetlands environment.

How to Get There: From Sunrise Hwy. (NY 27) east of Rockville Centre, take Oceanside Rd. south to Waukena Ave. and turn left. At Park Ave. turn right, and then at Golf Dr. turn left. Head to Slice Dr. and turn right. Study area is at end of Slice Dr. *By rail*: LIRR to Oceanside.

Open 9:00 A.M.–5:00 P.M. April 1 through October 31; Tuesday through Saturday in April, July, and August; Tuesday through Sunday in May, June, September, and October. Free.

For Additional Information:
Marine Nature Study Area
Town of Hempstead
Slice Dr.
Oceanside, NY 11572
516-766-1580

Massapequa State Park

A narrow strip of open space running approximately 2½ miles in a north-south direction, Massapequa Park's 596 acres of undeveloped land nestle in the midst of superhighways and dense population. There are no facilities here, no crowds, very little noise ... this is a place for walking beneath a shaded canopy, for breathing in the fragrance of wildflowers, for watching a family of black ducks float through the reeds.

In August the air is permeated with the scent of the sweet pepperbush. The deep pink petals and bright yellow centers of the rose mallow, interspersed with the glowing orange jewel-weed, add Chagallian color to the landscape.

Massapequa Park was established primarily to preserve the watershed of the stream that flows through it. It has one of the most diversified wildlife and plant populations in Nassau County. Two ponds attract an abundance of waterfowl, particularly during migration.

Hiking

Enter the park through a fence along Clark Boulevard, walk north for 1½ miles along the east bank of the stream and back again. Along the way, paths branch off into the woods and around ponds. This is the quietest part of the park.

How to Get There: From Exit 30 on Southern State Pkwy., go south on Broadway to Clark Blvd. and turn left. Preserve runs both north and south off Clark Blvd. Park on Lake Shore Dr., which borders preserve on the east, or on Parkside Blvd. along the western border. *By rail:* LIRR stops at Massapequa Park station, a short walk from preserve.

Open daily, year-round, during daylight hours. Free.

For Additional Information:
Superintendent, Massapequa State Park
Long Island State Park & Recreation Commission
Belmont Lake State Park
Babylon, NY 11702
516-669-1000

Mill Neck Sanctuary

See listing under North Shore Bird & Game Sanctuary, page 214.

Muttontown Nature Preserve

At Muttontown Nature Preserve on the north shore of Long Island, you may take a quiet walk along twisting paths that wend their way across open fields, through moist woodland and marsh areas, and past kettle ponds. The lush woodlands are filled with ferns, spicebush, arrowwood, and sweet pepperbush. A stand of eastern white pine and European larch, a cool retreat on the hottest summer day, dates back to the turn of the century. There are hardwoods, too—oak, black birch, hickory, red maple, and sassafras—and in the shrub layer of the forest, American chestnut sprouts grow.

The rolling hills and kettle ponds of Muttontown Preserve were formed more than 15,000 years ago. A kame, or dome-shaped hill of sand and gravel, stands on the northeast corner of the property; it's made up of glacial stream deposits that spilled from the melting ice.

The diversity of habitats, sprawling over more than 500 acres, attracts white-tailed deer, raccoon, rabbit, pheasant, quail, woodcock, various amphibians and reptiles, opossum, skunk, and woodchuck. Among the hundreds of species of birds sighted here is the locally rare red-bellied woodpecker. During the autumn migration, ducks and geese settle down on the ponds for short rests.

Muttontown Preserve is owned by the Nassau County Department of Parks and Recreation.

Hiking and Horseback Riding

Several miles of hiking and bridle trails (no rentals) weave through the preserve, touching upon all the various types of terrain. This is a good place to look for animal tracks during winter snows; the office displays sketches of tracks and provides trail maps.

How to Get There: From Exit 41 on Long Island Expwy. (I-495), go north on NY 106 to NY 25A (here called North Hempstead Turnpike) and turn left. At Muttontown Ln. turn left and head into preserve. *By rail*: LIRR to Oyster Bay.

Open daily, year-round, 9:30 A.M.–4:30 P.M. Free.

For Additional Information:

Muttontown Preserve
Muttontown Lane
East Norwich, NY 11732
516-922-3123

Nassau County Dept. of
Recreation & Parks
Eisenhower Park
East Meadow, NY 11554
516-542-4422

Nassau County Parks

Although some of the most heavily used facilities (such as swimming pools) may be used by county residents only, Nassau County parks are as a rule open to the general public. There are too many properties to list in this book, but readers will find the following described elsewhere: Bailey Arboretum, Garvies Point Museum & Preserve, Muttontown Preserve, Sands Point Park & Preserve, and Tackapausha Preserve. These represent some of the prime natural areas in the system, but the parks department also owns several passive preserves, open green spaces with no facilities that are used primarily for walking and nature study. Among them are Mill Neck Preserve, north of Locust Valley on Mill Neck Bay; Roosevelt South Preserve, southeast of the town of Roosevelt and directly south of Roosevelt Park (a county facility with developed recreation areas); and Tanglewood Preserve, just west of Rockville Centre near Hempstead Lake State Park (described elsewhere). There are nature walks also at Baxter's Pond, Hall's Pond, Loft Pond, Christopher Morley, and Silver Lake Parks. In Cow Meadow Park, there's a marshland preserve; and tiny Cammann Pond and Mill Pond Parks are sanctuaries for birds and ducks.

These and many other areas are administered by the Nassau County Department of Recreation and Parks. Park grounds open daily year-round; hours vary.

For Additional Information:
Public Information Officer
Nassau County Dept. of Recreation & Parks
Eisenhower Park
East Meadow, NY 11554
516-542-4422

The Nature Conservancy, Long Island Chapter

The Nature Conservancy is a national conservation organization committed to preserving unique natural areas. Its Long Island Chapter, with offices in Cold Spring Harbor, manages nearly forty preserves in Nassau and Suffolk Counties, and more are being established all the time. Ranging in size from 1 acre to about 100 acres, these preserves include some of the finest natural lands remaining on Long Island. All are open to the public, but several have suffered from overuse in the past. So that The Nature Conservancy may exercise some control over the number of visitors, the Long Island Chapter requests that anyone interested in seeing a preserve first contact its office by letter or phone. Exact directions will be given then.

A few Long Island preserves deserving special mention are: Davenport Sanctuary in Syosset, 8 acres of woods and fields with a kettle-hole pond on one of the highest glacial moraines on Long Island; Fox Hollow Preserve, in the Village of Laurel Hollow, 27 acres of hilly upland climax woods, with a fifty-year-old grove of white pines; Mill Cove Waterfowl Sanctuary, in the Village of Lloyd Harbor, 17 acres including a dammed brackish pond, a freshwater marsh, and a multitude of ducks and geese during migration; St. John's Pond Preserve, 14 acres in Cold Spring Harbor, with a pond, swamp, many wildflowers, some rare mute swans, and wood ducks; Smoky Hollow Bog on Fire Island, a 1-acre acid bog in an interdunal depression supporting cranberry and sphagnum moss, plus many species of wild orchids; Thorne Sanctuary, 87 acres in Bay Shore with a spartina and phragmites marsh, a peat bog, and a great blue heron rookery; and David Weld Sanctuary in St. James, approximately 100 acres of woods, wetlands, dunes, and beach, with rare flora, including a pure white variety of moccasin flower, and a breathtaking view of Long Island Sound.

Self-guided trail leaflets for many of these wild areas may be obtained from the chapter's office. The chapter also publishes a directory that gives brief descriptions of each of its preserves.

For Additional Information:
Executive Director
The Nature Conservancy
Long Island Chapter
Lawrence Hill Rd.
Box 72
Cold Spring Harbor, NY 11724
516-367-3225

Nissequogue River State Park

At Smithtown is beautiful Nissequogue River State Park, some 500 acres that have been maintained in their natural state for more than 100 years—until 1962, as a private hunting club. Today, it's a pristine environmental preserve with guided nature walks, interpretative tours, some fishing, and environmental education activities.

Part of the park is covered by a mixed hardwood forest, and the meadows are slowly being reclaimed by native maples, tulips, and cedars. The river and two ponds within the park attract large numbers of wildlife, including a multitude of birds, raccoons, white-tailed deer, opossums, and rabbits. In the fall, the ducks come—hooded mergansers, ruddy ducks, redheads, gadwalls, and ring-necked ducks. Rainbow, brook and brown trout fill the river.

The Nissequogue River Museum in the park, opened in 1979, has exhibits on the natural and social history of the river.

Hiking

A system of hiking trails on mostly flat terrain leads through dense woodlands, along the river, and around ponds.

Fishing

Fishing is permitted by fee permit only, April through November. Use a fly rod for brook, brown, and rainbow trout in the river. Youngsters may fish for free, but must register at the park office.

Canoeing

The Nissequogue River, running north about 7 miles from NY 25/25A junction at the park's northern border to Long Island Sound, is an excellent place for a canoe trip on a tidal stream. The mouth of the river edges the easternmost portion of Sunken Meadow State Park. You will pass through an unspoiled world, weaving among small marshy islands where snowy egrets pause to rest and turtles swim and sunbathe. Wild irises adorn the landscape in season. Rental canoes available in Nesconset (516-724-5433). Be sure to check tide tables when planning your trip.

Winter Sports

A cross-country ski trail has been laid out in the northern half of the park.

How to Get There: From Exit 44 on Northern State Pkwy., go north on Sunken Meadow State Pkwy. to NY 25 (Jericho Turnpike) and turn east. Park extends both north and south of NY 25. *By rail*: LIRR to Smithtown.

Open daily, during daylight hours, except Monday. Open on Monday only if it's a holiday. Nominal entrance fee Memorial Day weekend through Labor Day. Entry is available only to those who write in advance for a permit.

For Additional Information:

Superintendent
Nissequogue River State Park
Jericho Turnpike
Smithtown, NY 11787
516-265-1054

Long Island State Park &
Recreation Commission
Belmont Lake State Park
Babylon, NY 11702
516-669-1000

North Shore Bird & Game Sanctuary

This small ravine on the North Shore is a wonderland of forest, marshes, brackish and freshwater ponds, and a meandering stream teeming with wildlife. But its special glory is a magnificent stand of ancient tulip trees. Although tulip trees are scattered throughout Long Island, none rivals this concentration of trees more than 150 years old. Growing tall and straight, without branches for the first 50 feet or so, perfectly symmetrical, some exceeding 4 feet in diameter, they tower more than 100 feet above the earth.

Yellow-bellied sapsuckers, common flickers, black-throated green warblers, hermit thrushes, and many more birds flit from branch to branch. Canada geese and wood ducks nest in the sanctuary; and it is visited by mute and whistling swans, snowy egrets, and yellow-crowned night herons.

Also known as Mill Neck Sanctuary, Shu Swamp, and the Charles T. Church Wildlife Refuge, this 33-acre sanctuary is protected by a fence that completely encircles it. Just north of here is Beaver Lake, a fine bird-watching area.

Formerly a preserve of The Nature Conservancy and managed by its Long Island Chapter, the sanctuary was conveyed several years ago to the North Shore Bird & Game Sanctuary, Inc.

How to Get There: From intersection of NY 106 and Main St. in Village of Oyster Bay, go west on Main St. to West Shore Rd. and turn right. At The Cleft Rd. turn left. Just before you reach Beaver Dam and Lake, turn left on Frost Mill Rd. and continue to Mill Neck Railroad Station. Sanctuary is just south of railroad tracks and west of Frost Mill Rd. The only parking available is inside sanctuary (no parking along any roads in Village of Mill Neck at any time). Since the gate may sometimes be locked, it's best to write ahead to the North Shore Bird & Game Sanctuary, Inc., and let them know when you plan to come. *By rail*: LIRR to Mill Neck Station.

Sanctuary open daily except Friday, 7:00 A.M.–7:00 P.M., April through September; 7:00 A.M.–5:00 P.M., the rest of the year. Free.

For Additional Information:

North Shore Bird & Game
Sanctuary, Inc.
P.O. Box 214
Mill Neck, NY 11765
516-671-0283

Executive Director
The Nature Conservancy
Long Island Chapter
Lawrence Hill Rd.
Box 72
Cold Spring Harbor, NY 11724
516-367-3225

Old Westbury Gardens

Once this was the elaborate estate of the late John S. Phipps, sportsman and financier. Now it is one of the most exquisite gardens in the greater New York area. Opened to the public in 1959 as a nonprofit museum and botanical garden, these 100 acres of natural beauty are a haven from the urban world. Around the stately Georgian mansion are five gardens, planned for continuous floral display in all seasons except winter. Among thousands of trees is the largest alternate-leaf dogwood in the United States. Other fine old specimens include a crack willow, red and silver maples, white and Korean pines, a blue Atlas cedar, and a cucumber magnolia.

In the Boxwood Garden are huge plants well over a century old. The Cottage Garden, surrounding a child's tiny thatched cottage, presents a fairyland of pink and white flowering shrubs, dogwood, hawthorn, and azaleas. A staff of twenty gardeners is necessary to maintain the Italian Garden, more than 2 acres of herbaceous plants, ornamental pools, and fountains.

Wildflowers brighten a woodland walk, and there are displays of such perennials as delphiniums, roses, Canterbury bells, and irises. Also on the grounds are a pinetum, a lily pond, and a demonstration vegetable garden.

Wild Canada geese nest at a spacious lake in front of the mansion. During the spring and early summer, you can watch them closely, for they are accustomed to people.

This beautiful estate was the setting for part of the movie *Love Story*. Its many splendors may be explored via miles of interesting paths.

How to Get There: From Exit 39 on Long Island Expwy. (I-495), go east on service road 1.2 miles to Old Westbury Rd. Turn right and continue to gardens on left side of road.

Open Wednesday through Sunday, 10:00 A.M.–5:00 P.M., early May through late October, and on Veterans Day. Nominal fee; special rates for children and groups. The stately Georgian mansion, on the National Register of Historic Places, may be toured for an additional fee.

For Additional Information:
Old Westbury Gardens
P.O. Box 430
Old Westbury, NY 11568
516-333-0048

Planting Fields Arboretum

Although Planting Fields Arboretum near Oyster Bay is interesting at any time of the year, it's most spectacular in April and May. Then it becomes a fairyland, as one burst of blossoms after another heralds the arrival of spring. Rhododendrons, dogwoods, Japanese cherries, magnolias, crabapples, and azaleas are among the scores of flowering trees and shrubs.

Of Planting Fields' roughly 400 acres, 160 are developed as an arboretum, with the remaining fields and woods preserved in their natural state. The extraordinary collection of trees here, labeled and well maintained, include some New York State champions and nearly thirty that are the largest of their species on Long Island.

Other not-to-be missed displays are the collections of azalea, rhododendron, holly, and some camellias growing under glass that normally bloom in February and March.

In the bird sanctuary, you may see woodpeckers, thrushes, warblers, and finches.

Children love to play here—to jump off rocks, run on the vast lawns, and roll down the gently sloping hills.

The Arboretum is part of the New York State park system.

How to Get There: From Exit 39 on Long Island Expwy. (I-495), go north on Glen Cove Rd. to NY 25A (North Hempstead Turnpike). Turn right and go to Wolver Hollow Rd., then left and continue to Chicken Valley Rd. Turn right and head to Planting Fields Rd.; turn right again and proceed to arboretum entrance on right.

Open daily, 10:00 A.M.–5:00 P.M., year-round. Greenhouses open daily 10:00 A.M.–4:00 P.M. Nominal admission charged on Saturday, Sunday, and holidays only.

For Additional Information:

Planting Fields Arboretum	Long Island State Park &
Box 58	Recreation Commission
Oyster Bay, NY 11771	Belmont Lake State Park
516-922-9200	Babylon, NY 11702
	516-669-1000

Sagamore Hill National Historic Site

On a high bluff on Cove Neck, along Long Island's north shore, the home of Theodore Roosevelt stands amid 83 acres of rolling hills and dense woodlands. The woods and well-landscaped grounds immediately surrounding the mansion are now maintained by the National Park Service as a National Historic Site. It was this land that gave birth to Roosevelt's lifelong love affair with the outdoors and the creatures that inhabit it.

From the third floor of the twenty-two-room house, you have an excellent view of Oyster Bay. Much of the house is shaded by huge old trees; the giant European copper beech near the front entrance is particularly impressive.

Beyond the lawn are the deep woods that Roosevelt loved to roam with his children during the middle years of his life. An avid bird-watcher, he found many species near Sagamore Hill. More than 150 kinds have been sighted here.

Sagamore Hill remained Roosevelt's permanent home until his death in 1919, and he chose to be buried near here (see Theodore Roosevelt Sanctuary).

On summer weekends, park rangers conduct guided nature

tours within a National Environmental Study Area of 25 wooded acres on Sagamore Hill's grounds, as well as a guided history tour that includes farm structures, landscaped lawns, and a flower garden. A self-guided nature trail is also available.

You may also visit the Old Orchard Museum, where furnishings and exhibits illustrate Roosevelt's interest in his family, natural history, and conservation.

How to Get There: From intersection of NY 106 and Main St. in Village of Oyster Bay, go east on E. Main St. to Cove Neck Rd.; turn left and head to Sagamore Hill. Watch for signs.

Grounds open daily, year-round, during daylight hours. Free. Home and museum open daily, year-round: 9:30 A.M.–6:00 P.M., June through August; 9:30 A.M.–5:00 P.M., March through late May and September through November; 9:30 A.M.–4:30 P.M., December through February; closed January 1, Thanksgiving, December 25. Very nominal admission charge; under 16 and over 62 free.

For Additional Information:

Superintendent
Sagamore Hill National Historic Site
Cove Neck Rd., Box 304
Oyster Bay, NY 11771
516-922-4447

Sands Point Park & Preserve

On a lovely 209-acre tract bordering Long Island Sound stands an opulent estate built in the early 1900s by Howard Gould, son of financier and railroad tycoon Jay Gould. In 1971, following a succession of several owners, the huge, castlelike home called Falaise, and most of the original grounds were turned over to the Nassau County park system for environmental and recreational use.

Away from the mansion and the landscaped terrain surrounding it, the land gives the impression that little has been changed, except by nature, since white settlers first came to the area. Glacial boulders and sandy cliffs along Long Island Sound are remnants of the last Ice Age. The woods include such native species as white and chestnut oak, tulip, maple, pitch pine, and rhododendron, and in the summer there are massive glens of ferns. Introduced trees, such as Norway maple and mazzard cherry, have naturalized and now grow wild in the forest.

Wild ducks live on a 1½-acre pond and during autumn, migrating warblers dart about. White-tailed deer, skunk, raccoon, opossum, and eastern cottontail rabbit inhabit the woods and meadows. Thick sumac and bramble patches provide food and cover for all kinds of wildlife. Wildflowers grow in abundance here—goldenrod, heath aster, multiflora rose, trumpet creeper, Canada mayflower, Solomon's seal, garlic mustard, and wild geranium.

Along the pebble beach, nearly a mile in length, you might see horseshoe crabs, moon snails, razor clams, and whelk egg cases. Saltwort, sea-rocket, and beach clotbur are found in the intertidal zone. A colony of bank swallows nests in the cliff faces.

Nature Trails

There are five distinct nature trails; two of them have labeled trees and shrubs with numbered stations that correlate to printed trail guides. Trails are well marked and easy to follow.

How to Get There: Located north of Port Washington. From Exit 36 on Long Island Expwy. (I-495), go north on NY 101 (called first Searingtown Rd., then Port Washington Blvd., and then Middleneck Rd.) to preserve entrance. Park is on right side of Middleneck Rd.

Open Saturday through Wednesday, 10:00 A.M.–5:00 P.M., May through October. Nominal admission fee; additional fee for guided tours. Falaise may be visited only by escorted tour.

For Additional Information:

Sands Point Park & Preserve
Middleneck Rd.
Port Washington, NY 11050
516-883-1612

Nassau County Dept. of
Recreation & Parks
Eisenhower Park
East Meadow, NY 11554
516-542-4422

South Shore Nature Center

The new South Shore Nature Center, a 206-acre wildlife preserve administered by the Town of Islip, is a mosaic of several different environments. With eight distinct habitats—upland forest, field, open meadow, succession forest, freshwater marsh, saltwater marsh, bottomlands, and transition areas—this preserve boasts the greatest diversity of ecosystems in the greater New York City area.

Here, in this quiet, undisturbed corner, both people and wildlife are assured of a serene retreat. Only certain sections of the preserve lands are open at this writing, but a surprising array of programs and workshops is scheduled throughout the year. You may learn marine ecology, join an evening walk for a look at nature's nightlife, learn how to make natural dyes and teas from local plants, and leave the beaten path to practice orienteering skills.

Hiking

Two trails, the upland and freshwater environment loops, begin at the center and can be taken individually or together. A saltwater environment trail system begins and ends south of the freshwater area. Stations are numbered and described in a trail booklet available from the center. A resident naturalist is on hand to answer any questions.

How to Get There: From Exit 43 on Southern State Pkwy., go south on NY 111 (Islip Ave.) to NY 27A (Montauk Hwy.). Turn left and continue to Bay View Ave., then right and proceed to nature center. Although the center has properties on both the east and west sides of Bay View Ave., only those on the west are open to the public at this time.

Open year-round. From April 1 through October 31, 9:00 A.M.–4:30 P.M., Thursday–Monday; appointments necessary on weekdays; closed Tuesday and Wednesday. From November 1 through March 31, 9:00 A.M.–4:30 P.M., Monday–Friday by appointment only; closed Saturday and Sunday. Very nominal admission charge. Guided tours available.

For Additional Information:

Resident Naturalist
South Shore Nature Center
Department of Parks,
Recreation & Cultural Affairs
Islip, NY 11751
516-224-5436

Sunken Meadow State Park

This 1,266-acre park, extending along Long Island's north shore for about 2½ miles, takes its name from the low meadowland that separates the narrow sandy beach from the uplands. The bluffs that hover above the beach in places afford dramatic views of Long Island Sound with the Connecticut shoreline in the distance. Dense forest is interspersed with marsh, open field, and a meandering creek. The park also has breeding rails, and in winter, hawks, horned larks, snow buntings, and many types of waterfowl make it their home. Near the park's eastern boundary is the mouth of the Nissequogue River, a good vantage point for observing waterbirds. The entire park is an excellent area in which to study the ecology of the north shore of Long Island.

Hiking and Bicycling

A mile-long boardwalk follows the beach, and you may also wander over the sand along most of the waterfront. At the eastern end of the park are some woods with shaded walks. The Long Island Greenbelt Trail (described elsewhere) reaches its northern terminus near the beach. A paved bike path runs parallel to part of the entrance road, then turns east to follow the creek.

Swimming

The beach here is one of the safest and most attractive on Long Island Sound. Lifeguards are on duty late May through early September. Modern bathhouse; beach chair and umbrella rental.

Fishing

Surf fishing is permitted. Free permits for after-sunset parking for night fishing are available from the Long Island State Park & Recreation Commission.

Canoeing

The Nissequogue River east of the park provides an excellent opportunity for a canoe trip on a tidal stream (see description under Nissequogue River State Park).

Winter Sports

A cross-country ski trail follows the beach part of the way, then turns through the woods.

How to Get There: From Exit 44 on Northern State Pkwy., go north on Sunken Meadow Pkwy., which ends in the park.

Open daily, year-round, 8:00 A.M.–sunset. Nominal parking fee Memorial Day weekend through Labor Day.

For Additional Information:

Superintendent
Sunken Meadow State Park
Sunken Meadow State Pkwy.
Kings Park, NY 11754
516-269-4333

Long Island State Park &
Recreation Commission
Belmont Lake State Park
Babylon, NY 11702
516-669-1000

Tackapausha Preserve

When Nassau County acquired this 80-acre tract near Seaford, the name Tackapausha was adopted in memory of the *sachem* "chief" of the Massapequa Indians who once lived here. It became the county's first nature preserve. Seaford Creek, edged by freshwater marshes, swamps, and moist, deciduous woods, lazily snakes its way southward through this wild sanctuary. A small, well-drained grassy area is reminiscent of the now-vanished Hempstead Plains, and a stand of Atlantic white cedar is one of the last remaining on Long Island.

More than 40 species of birds breed here, and more than 200 have been sighted. Green herons, mallards, and other water birds visit a small pond near the center of the preserve. Small mammals, primarily nocturnal, share residence here with about 10 species of reptiles and amphibians.

In a small but excellent museum, a branch of the Long Island Museum of Natural History, are absorbing displays related to the life sciences. Outdoors behind the museum building is a menagerie of live animals of the region.

Nature Trails

Self-guided trails, all easy to walk, extend throughout the long, narrow preserve; entrance to the northern wooded section is by special permit only.

How to Get There: Located in southeast Nassau County. From Sunrise Hwy. (NY 27), go south on Seaford-Oyster Bay Expwy. to Merrick Rd., and turn left (east). Head to Washington Ave., and turn left again. Preserve entrance is on right side of Washington Ave.

Preserve open daily, year-round, during daylight hours. Museum open daily, year-round, 10:00 A.M.–5:00 P.M.; closed holidays. Very nominal admission fee includes both preserve and museum. Children under 5 free.

For Additional Information:

Tackapausha Preserve
Washington Ave.
Seaford, NY 11783
516-292-4266

Nassau County Dept. of
Recreation & Parks
Eisenhower Park
East Meadow, NY 11554
516-542-4422

Theodore Roosevelt Sanctuary

Located along a peaceful, tree-lined street in Oyster Bay, the Theodore Roosevelt Sanctuary was the first National Audubon Sanctuary in the country. This 12-acre songbird and botanical preserve was given to the National Audubon Society by a cousin of the former president. Footpaths lead through the dense growth of trees, shrubs, and vines planted to attract wildlife; visitors will find some forty types of trees and about sixty species of shrubs. More than seventy-five species of birds call the sanctuary home, including scarlet tanagers, yellow-bellied sapsuckers, Carolina wrens, and the great horned owl.

A trailside museum, which houses exhibits of Long Island flora and fauna, is nestled among the trees. It offers one of the most outstanding outdoor education programs in the country, especially for children. Bird-banding is done here, and the U.S. Fish & Wildlife Service has designated the preserve as a rescue center for the care of waterfowl caught in oil spills.

Marvelously quiet and well-tended, this sanctuary is a fitting memorial to a noted conservationist. When Roosevelt lived at nearby Sagamore Hill (described elsewhere), he often walked and rode horseback on this very land. In Young's Memorial Cemetery, a small graveyard filled with trees and birdsong that abuts the sanctuary on the west, you may visit Roosevelt's hillside grave.

The children's monument at the
Theodore Roosevelt Sanctuary *Bill Thomas*

How to Get There: From intersection of NY 106 and Main St. in Village of Oyster Bay, go east on E. Main St.; follow signs about 1¾ miles to Roosevelt's grave and the bird sanctuary on right side of street. A sign identifies the spot, and there's a small gravel pull-off area near the cemetery for parking. Walk east along the sidewalk a few yards, past cemetery and caretaker's house, to sanctuary entrance.

Grounds open daily, year-round, usually 9:00 A.M.–sunset. Museum open 9:00 A.M.–2:00 P.M., Monday through Thursday and some weekends. Groups should phone two weeks in advance; group size limited to thirty. Guided tours available.

For Additional Information:

Director
Theodore Roosevelt Sanctuary
P.O. Box 5
Oyster Bay, NY 11771
516-922-3200

National Audubon Society
Sanctuary Director
Miles Wildlife Sanctuary
West Cornwall Road
Sharon, CT 06069
203-364-0048

Valley Stream State Park

Like most Long Island state parks, Valley Stream is more interesting to visit during the off-season. Then the human population diminishes, and the duck population reigns supreme. In the summer, the woods at the northern end of this 97-acre park are filled with songbirds. Two forks of the stream that enters the park at its northern boundary merge here, flowing on with combined strength to their eventual destination in Jamaica Bay. It was to protect this stream and the lake it feeds near the park's southern boundary that this land was originally turned into parkland in the 1920s. Today, it is the Long Island state park nearest to New York City. Located just 18 miles east of Manhattan in southwest Nassau County, it attracts many visitors who want to spend a day away from the city and perhaps enjoy a picnic lunch in the shade of tall trees.

Hiking and Bicycling
A hiking/biking path loops among the trees throughout the park.

How to Get There: From Exit 14 on Southern State Pkwy., head south to park entrance road. The park lies south and east of this exit.

Open daily, year-round, 8:00 A.M.–sunset. Nominal parking fee Memorial Day weekend through Labor Day.

For Additional Information:

Superintendent
Valley Stream State Park
Southern State Pkwy.
Valley Stream, NY 11580
516-825-4128

Long Island State Park &
Recreation Commission
Belmont Lake State Park
Babylon, NY 11702
516-669-1000

Vanderbilt Museum and Planetarium

In a 24-room mansion and nearby two-story house, more than 17,000 varieties of marine life and wildlife, as well as works of art and personal memorabilia, are on display. They were gathered from around the world by the late William K. Vanderbilt II between 1928 and 1944.

The planetarium here is one of the dozen largest and one of the three best equipped in the country, noted for its special effects. One projector accurately locates more than 11,000 stars on an artificial sky. A simulated thunderstorm climaxes with the startling special effect of rain falling on the audience. Following evening shows, visitors may use a research-grade telescope to observe the real heavens.

Surrounding the house and courtyard are mosaic walks inspired by the pebble walks of Madeira. Some 180 linden trees from Germany shade the landscape. From its beautiful garden setting on the crest of a hill, the museum overlooks picturesque Northport Harbor along Long Island's north shore. Vanderbilt called his estate—and appropriately so—Eagle's Nest.

How to Get There: Located in northwest corner of Suffolk County. From intersection of NY 110 and NY 25A in Huntington, go east on NY 25A to Little Neck Rd. in Centerport and turn left. Continue to museum.

Museum open Tuesday through Saturday, 10:00 A.M.–4:00 P.M.; Sunday and holidays, noon–5:00 P.M.; May through October. Nominal admission charge. Planetarium open for special shows on Saturday, Sunday, and holidays, year-round; additional shows in July and August. Schedules vary, and reservations are recommended. Nominal admission charge. Both museum and planetarium offer special rates for senior citizens and children under 12.

For Additional Information:

Vanderbilt Museum and Planetarium
Vanderbilt Museum Commission
180 Little Neck Rd.
Centerport, NY 11721
516-261-5656 (Museum)
516-757-7500 (Planetarium)

Part 6

Natural Attractions in
New York State

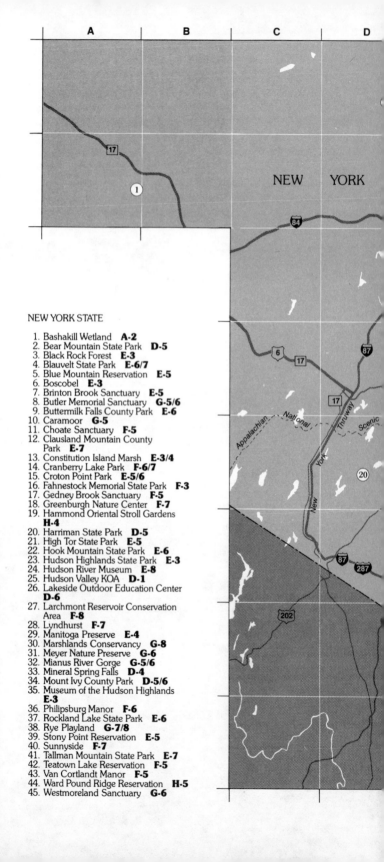

NEW YORK

YORK

NEW YORK STATE

1. Bashakill Wetland **A-2**
2. Bear Mountain State Park **D-5**
3. Black Rock Forest **E-3**
4. Blauvelt State Park **E-6/7**
5. Blue Mountain Reservation **E-5**
6. Boscobel **E-3**
7. Brinton Brook Sanctuary **E-5**
8. Butler Memorial Sanctuary **G-5/6**
9. Buttermilk Falls County Park **E-6**
10. Caramoor **G-5**
11. Choate Sanctuary **F-5**
12. Clausland Mountain County Park **E-7**
13. Constitution Island Marsh **E-3/4**
14. Cranberry Lake Park **F-6/7**
15. Croton Point Park **E-5/6**
16. Fahnestock Memorial State Park **F-3**
17. Gedney Brook Sanctuary **F-5**
18. Greenburgh Nature Center **F-7**
19. Hammond Oriental Stroll Gardens **H-4**
20. Harriman State Park **D-5**
21. High Tor State Park **E-5**
22. Hook Mountain State Park **E-6**
23. Hudson Highlands State Park **E-3**
24. Hudson River Museum **E-8**
25. Hudson Valley KOA **D-1**
26. Lakeside Outdoor Education Center **D-6**
27. Larchmont Reservoir Conservation Area **F-8**
28. Lyndhurst **F-7**
29. Manitoga Preserve **E-4**
30. Marshlands Conservancy **G-8**
31. Meyer Nature Preserve **G-6**
32. Mianus River Gorge **G-5/6**
33. Mineral Spring Falls **D-4**
34. Mount Ivy County Park **D-5/6**
35. Museum of the Hudson Highlands **E-3**
36. Philipsburg Manor **F-6**
37. Rockland Lake State Park **E-6**
38. Rye Playland **G-7/8**
39. Stony Point Reservation **E-5**
40. Sunnyside **F-7**
41. Tallman Mountain State Park **E-7**
42. Teatown Lake Reservation **F-5**
43. Van Cortlandt Manor **F-5**
44. Ward Pound Ridge Reservation **H-5**
45. Westmoreland Sanctuary **G-6**

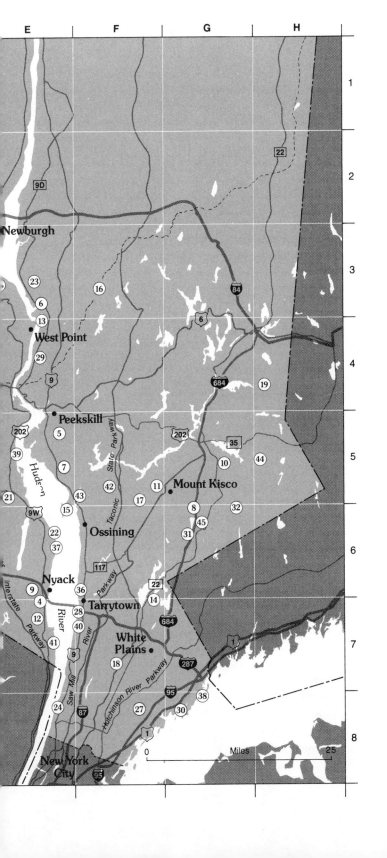

Bashakill Wetland

In Sullivan County, not far north of the New Jersey–New York border, is an outstandingly beautiful freshwater marsh called Bashakill, a 2,000-acre aquatic garden. Thousands of species of plants, insects, and wildlife thrive here, some of them rare or endangered. Bashakill Creek has been a favorite local fishing hole for years, and the entire wetland teems with life. Although somewhat beyond the 50-mile radius prescribed for this book, it is such a special place that it has been included here. Environmentalists have called it one of the state's greatest natural treasures.

Purchased in 1979 by the New York State Department of Environmental Conservation, the Bashakill, which extends for 5 miles along its namesake creek, is being preserved as a wildlife sanctuary. Birding is a prime activity, with more than 217 different species sighted. Among them are the osprey (an endangered species in New York), peregrine falcon, and numerous hawks and owls. The rare bald eagle is a regular springtime visitor. During migration periods, Canada geese and an array of wild ducks stop here. The eastern bluebird is frequently seen, along with occasional great blue herons, wood ducks, hooded mergansers, and numerous songbirds.

White-tailed deer, raccoon, eastern cottontail, mink, muskrat, beaver, river otter, fox, wild turkey, and porcupine are residents of the marsh and surrounding woodland. Along the edge of the marsh are limestone outcroppings that have contributed to the formation of extensive underground caves, ideal habitat for several species of bats. Some experts claim they are the most magnificent caverns in New York.

In spring the marsh becomes an aquatic flower garden. Lilies, arrowhead, pickerel weed, and many other species of wildflowers burst into bloom.

At this writing, plans are still being formulated for management of this area, which has been designated a State Wildlife Management Area.

Hiking

Haven and South Roads, which run through and alongside the marsh, are little traveled, scenic, and good for hiking. Vistors may walk along the Delaware & Hudson Canal roadway and an abandoned railroad bed to see flora and fauna close up. More trails are being developed.

Fishing and Boating

Fishermen have made some good catches of pickerel, catfish, and largemouth bass here. Fish from the bridge on Haven Road, or launch a cartop boat into the waterway. Canoeing is an ideal way to experience the marsh. Only electric motors are permitted on power boats. Launch points are being established at several locations.

Winter Sports

This is a fine area for cross-country skiing and snowshoeing.

How to Get There: Located south of Wurtsboro. Wetland extends southeast from intersection of US 209 and NY 17. To drive through it, go south from intersection on US 209 about 3 miles to Haven Rd. and turn left into marsh. Haven Rd. ends at South Rd., which extends both north and south through the marsh.

Currently open at all times. May be closed in future from March through mid-June because of nesting waterfowl. Free.

For Additional Information:
Wildlife Manager, Region 3
Department of Environmental Conservation
New York State
21 South Putt Corners Rd.
New Paltz, NY 12561
914-255-5453

Bear Mountain State Park

See listing under Palisades Interstate Park, page 12.

Bedford Audubon Society Sanctuaries

The Bedford Audubon Society maintains four sanctuaries in Westchester County that are open to the public. The smallest, 25-acre Palmer Lewis Sanctuary near Bedford, has a spectacular rock formation, a nesting program for Eastern bluebirds and, in the springtime, groves of flowering dogwoods. Two others, the Franklin and Fels Sanctuaries, adjoin each other. Located near North Salem, they offer 202 acres of woodlands penetrated by trails. Songbirds are attracted by the berry-producing shrubs, and there are extensive areas of ferns and wildflowers. A fourth preserve, the Ramsey Hunt Wildlife Sanctuary, consists of 173 acres of hills, woods, swamp marsh, and spring-fed streams.

All of the preceding sanctuaries are actually owned by the National Audubon Society, with the Bedford Audubon Society assuming managerial responsibilities. Guided nature walks are occasionally scheduled.

How to Get There: The society prefers that you contact them for directions before visiting a sanctuary. For further details, contact one of the addresses below. All sanctuaries are open daily, year-round, during daylight hours; and all are free.

For Additional Information:

Naturalist
Bedford Audubon Society
R.D. 2, Rt. 100
Katonah, NY 10536
914-232-8349

National Audubon Society
Sanctuary Director
Miles Wildlife Sanctuary
West Cornwall Road
Sharon, CT 06069
203-364-0048

Managing Director of Regional
Activities
National Audubon Society
950 Third Ave.
New York, NY 10022
212-832-3200

Black Rock Forest

Hikers will be delighted with Black Rock Forest. Its 3,600 acres in the awesome highlands west of the Hudson River probably resemble, more than any other area in today's Hudson Valley, the woodlands originally seen by the Dutch explorers of the early seventeenth century.

Sprawled atop a high granite plateau, the forest boasts a dozen summits more than 1,400 feet above sea level and scenic views of distant horizons in every direction. You'll also see freshwater springs, granite rock outcroppings, swamps and bogs, and many picturesque streams, as well as a few man-made structures that attest to past uses of the area. And when you feel like resting a bit, seek out one of many secluded glens. On a hot summer day, they're always shaded and cool.

Nearly all ponds and waterways supply water for the nearby municipalities of Cornwall and Highland Falls and are therefore closed to swimming and fishing, but they enhance the beauty of the area and are attractive to wildlife. Though deer are fairly plentiful, it is still a thrill to suddenly come upon one of these creatures with liquid eyes and velvet bodies.

Now owned by Harvard University and used primarily for research, the forest is open to the public for walking and nature study only. The result is a serene wilderness retreat, little known and never crowded.

Hiking

Explore the forest via 15 miles of marked trails or 16 miles of gravel roads. Along the way, you'll see several signs bearing narrative descriptions about the history and ecology of the area. Some portions of the trails are steep and rugged, with a cover of loose rock, so exercise some caution.

How to Get There: Located northwest of West Point Military Reservation in Orange County. From Continental Rd. exit on US 9W near Cornwall, go south on Continental Rd. to forest. There are several roads leading to forest boundaries, so it's best to obtain a map before going there. The maps are free, but enclose a self-addressed stamped envelope with your request; write to address below.

Open daily, year-round, during daylight hours. Free.

For Additional Information:
Harvard Black Rock Forest
P.O. Box 483
Cornwall, NY 12518
914-534-4517

Blauvelt State Park

See listing under Palisades Interstate Park, page 14.

Blue Mountain Reservation

A Civilian Conservation Corps camp during Franklin D. Roosevelt's administration, the Blue Mountain Reservation in Westchester County contains some 1,586 acres of rolling glaciated woodland. In some places the boulders dropped by the great glacier are numerous, creating intriguing geological features. Blue Mountain, for which the reservation is named, reaches an elevation of 665 feet. When weather conditions are right, the mountain provides a good vantage point from which to watch the fall hawk migration.

The mixed hardwood forest is basically oak, hickory, tulip, sassafras, and dogwood, with some sugar maple, birch, and beech. White-tailed deer, bobcat, rabbit, opossum, skunk, squirrel, and numerous birds reside here.

On the reservation are two ponds, created originally as part of a family-owned ice business before the advent of refrigeration. Huge chunks of ice were cut from the lake during the winter, then stored in sawdust and sold in the summer months.

Hiking and Horseback Riding
Some 16 miles of hiking and bridle trails loop through the park. One hiking trail leads to the peak of Blue Mountain. No horse rentals in park, but there's a stable in Peekskill (Circle P Riding Academy, Inc.).

Swimming
Five-acre Lounsbury Pond has a 150-yard swimming beach along its western shore; open daily 10:00 to 8:00 during summer. Nominal admission charge.

How to Get There: From Peekskill, go south on US 9 to park entrance road (Welcher Ave.) and turn left. Watch for signs.

Open daily, year-round, during daylight hours. Nominal entrance fee during summer months only.

For Additional Information:
County Naturalist
Westchester County
Dept. of Parks, Recreation & Conservation
148 Martine Ave.
White Plains, NY 10601
914-682-2637

Boscobel

On a bluff high above the Hudson River near Garrison, across the river from West Point, stands beautiful Boscobel Mansion. From the front lawn, visitors may enjoy a spectacular panoramic view of the river valley. Surrounding the lovely nineteenth-century house are 16 acres of orchards, gardens, and magnificent trees that alone make a visit worthwhile, especially in the fall. White pines border the parking area, while huge tubs of oleander line the walk leading to the carriage house near the entrance.

At the center of a formal rose garden stands a fountain encircled in late summer by the purple and white blooms of petunia. An orangerie, where citrus trees and other tender plants are kept in winter, stands adjacent to a period herb garden. Visitors will also find a wildflower garden, a small pond, an apple orchard, splendid fig trees loaded with fruit in season, and old-fashioned beehives called skeps.

The historic mansion, authentically restored and open for tours, is an outstanding example of New York Federal domestic architecture.

How to Get There: Located north of Garrison in Putnam County. From Garrison, go north on NY 9D to Boscobel on left side of road.

Open 10:00 A.M.–4:30 P.M., Wednesday through Monday, April through October; November, December, and March, 10:00 A.M.–3:30 P.M.; closed Tuesday, Thanksgiving, December 25, months of January and February. Admission charged; half-price under 21. Only two children per adult admitted in mansion at one time. Group rates by advance reservation.

For Additional Information:
Executive Director
Boscobel Restoration, Inc.
Rt. 9D
Garrison-on-Hudson, NY 10524
914-265-3638 or 212-562-7444

Brinton Brook Sanctuary

Not far from the banks of the Hudson River, near Croton-on-Hudson, 129 acres of land owned by the National Audubon Society include a mix of upland hardwoods, rocky outcroppings, a pond, an orchard, and a small ravine. Many species of birds, including herons, ducks, American woodcocks, ruffed grouse, woodpeckers, and warblers, are attracted by the varied habitats. In season, the sanctuary teems with flowering plants—trillium, violets, fringed gentians, dogwood, mountain laurel. Rock ledges with glacial grooves and a boulder balanced atop smaller rocks attract students of geology.

A trail map is available at the entrance. The property is managed by the Saw Mill River Audubon Society.

How to Get There: Take NY 9A north from Croton-on-Hudson. You'll soon pass a "Sky View Haven" sign on the left side of the road. From there, clock three-tenths of a mile to the Brinton Brook sign on the left side of the road. Turn right, going uphill about 300 yards to sanctuary sign indicating parking on right. Entrance road starts out paved, soon becomes dirt.

Open daily, year-round, during daylight hours. Free. Groups larger than families should call ahead to avoid conflict with other groups. Guided tours may be arranged.

For Additional Information:

Naturalist & Sanctuary Coordinator
Saw Mill River Audubon Society, Inc.
2660 Quaker Church Rd.
Yorktown Heights, NY 10598
914-962-9330

National Audubon Society
Sanctuary Director
Miles Wildlife Sanctuary
West Cornwall Rd.
Sharon, CT 06069
203-364-0048

Butler Memorial Sanctuary

A prime place for viewing the annual hawk migration down the Hudson Valley is from the top of a ridge in the 357-acre Butler Memorial Sanctuary near Bedford. Thousands of hawks of all types have been recorded during the course of a single fall weekend here. Along with the hawks, bald and golden eagles are sometimes spotted.

While an upland deciduous forest dominates this preserve, there's a good mixture of ecosystems, including a freshwater marsh, a 30-acre red maple swamp, several smaller swamps, open fields and meadows, as well as white pine and Norway spruce plantations. Several small streams flow through the sanctuary much of the year.

It's an interesting place for geological study, too. You'll find steep rock faces and other outcroppings along the two ridges that traverse the preserve.

This land was purchased from Native Americans as part of the "New Purchase" in 1700, but it was so hilly and rocky that little farming was done. It was grazed, however; thus the remnants of stone fences you see today.

The Lower Hudson Chapter of The Nature Conservancy has its headquarters at Butler Memorial Sanctuary. There's also a resident naturalist.

Hiking and Horseback Riding

A well-marked, color-coded trail system of some 10 miles, including a self-guided geology trail, laces the sanctuary. Trail maps may be obtained at the small shelter near the sanctuary's main entrance. Visitors are asked to register. Guided nature walks are frequently offered by the resident naturalist. One trail is provided for horseback riders (no rentals). Interconnecting trails lead to the nearby Meyer Sanctuary (described elsewhere).

Winter Sports

Cross-country skiers and snowshoers may use the trails during winter snows.

How to Get There: From I-684 near Mt. Kisco, take NY 172 (Bedford Rd.) west to Chestnut Ridge Rd. and turn left. Go across an overpass above I-684 to preserve on right side of road.

Open daily, year-round, during daylight hours. Free.

For Additional Information:
Executive Director
Lower Hudson Chapter
The Nature Conservancy
RFD 2, Chestnut Ridge Rd.
Mount Kisco, NY 10549
914-666-5365

Buttermilk Falls County Park

Steep, wooded hills surround a cascading waterfall at Buttermilk Falls, an undeveloped Rockland County park near Central Nyack. At present, the park contains 50 acres, but plans call for it to be enlarged to 163 or more acres. Geologically, the land is a segment of the Palisades ridge.

Although the park was acquired in 1976–1977, the falls, steep gorge, and ravines have been a natural attraction for decades. The park is therefore a great place for nature interpretation and geologic study.

Hiking

The principal trail now in use runs from the parking lot to the falls area. The Long Path Hiking Trail (see Palisades Interstate

Park) crosses land that has been proposed for acquisition in the near future.

How to Get There: From Nyack, go west on NY 59 to Greenbush Rd. and turn left; go past Rockland Center for the Arts to park on left side of road. Parking on property.

Open daily, year-round, during daylight hours. Free.

For Additional Information:

Rockland County Park
Commission
380 Phillips Hill Rd.
New City, NY 10956
914-425-5100

Rockland County Planning Board
18 New Hempstead Rd.
New City, NY 10956
914-425-5480

Caramoor

Located amid the gentle hills of Katonah, Caramoor is a former country home now used as a center for music and the arts. The magnificent setting includes 117 acres of lush wild woodlands and more than 20 acres of well-tended lawns and informal gardens. Late spring and early summer are blooming times, with lilies and day lilies appearing in several varieties and colors, as well as roses, summer dahlias, peonies, phlox, and many unusual annuals. A Cedar Walk is bordered by rhododendron, while the walk to the picturesque grape arbor nestles between two massive sculptured spruce hedges, and a cypress-lined walkway leads to sunken gardens. Also on the grounds is an unusual pagoda bird feeder.

When visitors have completed their tour of the landscaped grounds, they may want to wander off into the woods and listen to the songbirds. In this quiet, lovely spot, no highway sounds can be heard even faintly, and few planes fly overhead.

The Mediterranean-style house, which is the focal point of the estate, was opened to the public as a museum in 1970. It includes entire rooms imported from European palaces and houses, period furniture that dates from the Middle Ages to the eighteenth century, and art objects from several Chinese dynasties.

A summer music festival is held here each year from late June to mid-August. All performances are out-of-doors, and the programming is top-notch.

How to Get There: From I-684 near Katonah, go east on NY 35 to NY 22 and turn right. Proceed to junction of NY 22, NY 137, and Maple Ave. Go east on 137 for half a mile to Caramoor's gates on right side of road.

Open 10:00 A.M.–4:00 P.M., Wednesday through Saturday, and 1:00–4:00 P.M. Sunday, April through November. Admission fee; special rates for children under 12 and groups of senior citizens.

For Additional Information:
Director of Development
Caramoor
P.O. Box R
Katonah, NY 10536
914-232-3246

Choate Sanctuary

A mix of open fields and woodland, this small sanctuary near Mt. Kisco is the property of the Saw Mill River Audubon Society. Although there's no way to escape the noise of traffic from a nearby highway, hikers will find a variety of plants and wildlife to study. The fruits of the barberry and honeysuckle bushes attract many birds. Bluebirds have been seen here in the winter, and winter wrens forage along a brook that runs through the 25-acre property. Among the trees here are black birch, oak, and hickory, as well as a grove of sugar maples. There also are many dead and dying gray birches; those already dead host many pretty shelf fungi and provide food and nesting sites for woodpeckers. Other vegetation includes the maple-leaf viburnum, spicebush, witch hazel, many wild-flowers, a great variety of ferns, and four different lycopodiums (evergreen ground covers) that are protected under New York State laws.

The only open areas of the sanctuary are a small meadow near the brook and a marsh near the eastern boundary that supports a large stand of sweet flags.

Exposed surfaces of Fordham gneiss, one of the principal underlying rocks of Westchester County, may be seen on the faces of the rock cliffs in this area. The high, rocky hills and low damp areas create a varied terrain attractive to such animals as deer, squirrel, raccoon, skunk, fox, mice, and shrew.

Running through the woods are stone walls that once served as fences for farm pastures. The age of these walls is evident in the growth of lichens on the stones.

A figure-eight trail approximately three-quarters of a mile in length winds through the property. All trails are marked with white dots. The hill terrain peaks at 400 feet.

How to Get There: From Mt. Kisco, go west on NY 133 (Main St.), past Saw Mill River Pkwy., to Crow Hill Rd., which is on right opposite a Presbyterian church. Park on shoulder of NY 133 just west of Crow Hill Rd., and walk 100 feet north along Crow Hill Rd. to sanctuary sign on left side.

Open daily, year-round, during daylight hours. Free. Groups larger than families are requested to let Audubon's office know when they will be visiting to avoid possible conflicts with other groups. Guided tours may be arranged.

For Additional Information:
Naturalist & Sanctuary Coordinator
Saw Mill River Audubon Society, Inc.
2660 Quaker Church Rd.
Yorktown Heights, NY 10598
914-962-9330

Clausland Mountain County Park

Clausland Mountain Park, along the Palisades Ridge in Rockland County, is a tract of 500 densely wooded acres that are
home to white-tailed deer and raccoon, and northern finches
during winter. The land has been kept in its natural state with
sweeping scenic views and outstanding geological formations.
Established in 1969, it adjoins Tackamack Town Park.

Hiking
The Long Path Hiking Trail (see Palisades Interstate Park)
passes through both Clausland Mountain County Park and
Tackamack Town Park, providing access from one to the
other.

How to Get There: From Exit 11 on I-87 (NY Thruway), go south
on Highland Ave. Highland Ave. becomes Clausland Mountain Rd.
and curves to west. Continue to Tackamack Town Park on left side of
Clausland Mountain Rd. Enter county park along town park's southern border.
   Open daily, year-round, during daylight hours. Free.

For Additional Information:
Rockland County Park
Commission
380 Phillips Hill Rd.
New City, NY 10956
914-425-5100

Rockland County Planning Board
18 New Hempstead Rd.
New City, NY 10956
914-425-5480

Constitution Island Marsh

Along the east bank of the Hudson River, just north of Garrison, are 267 acres of tidal marsh, the largest and healthiest
such marsh in the Hudson estuary. Bounded on the west by
historic Constitution Island, part of the West Point Military
Reservation on the opposite bank of the river, the marsh
extends north and south for about one mile. It serves as an
important nursery area for such aquatic life as striped bass,
shad, and herring and as habitat for more than 100 species of
birds. Red-tailed hawks, kestrel, osprey, shorebirds, waterfowl,
a wide variety of warblers, and, occasionally in the winter,
eagles have been observed here.
   Although New York State owns this property, the marsh is

managed as a National Audubon Sanctuary. An Audubon warden/biologist is on duty full-time.

Canoeing and Boating

The marsh may be visited at any time by people coming in off the river. However, no motor-driven boats are permitted on the sanctuary. Canoes, kayaks, and rowboats are most suitable.

How to Get There: Located north of Garrison. Since land access to the marsh is over private land, it is necessary to make arrangements through the resident Audubon manager before visiting; more explicit directions will be given at that time.

For Additional Information:
Warden/Biologist
National Audubon Society
Constitution Island Marsh Sanctuary
RFD 2, Route 9D
Garrison, NY 10524
914-265-3119

Cranberry Lake Park

In this 142-acre park in Westchester County, the emphasis is on nature study. The 10-acre lake from which the park derives its name is the focal point of the area. Its shoreline merges into adjacent wetlands and bogs adorned with cranberry plants. The remaining terrain is generally rugged, featuring some interesting rock formations and heavily wooded hills. An over-look along one of the trails permits a bird's-eye view of the area.

The park, preserved in a natural unspoiled state, is part of Westchester County's permanent open space system. A care-taker resides near the entrance.

Hiking

A 1½-mile Lake Trail loops around the lake, passing the cranberry bogs and wetlands. A second trail, ½-mile long, leads to a dike and quarry created during the construction of nearby Kensico Dam at the turn of the century. Trail maps and a billboard outlining the area are posted at the entrance.

How to Get There: Located just east of Kensico Reservoir. From Exit 27 on Bronx River Pkwy., go north on NY 22 to Old Orchard St., the first right after passing Kensico Dam, and turn right. Proceed about 200 feet to park entrance on right side of road.

Open daily, year-round, usually from 10:00 A.M. to dusk. Free. Gate may be closed during winter months, but hikers may park outside and walk in. Open to residents of Westchester County every day; open to nonresidents on Wednesday, Friday, and Sunday.

For Additional Information:
County Naturalist
Westchester County
Dept. of Parks, Recreation & Conservation
148 Martine Ave.
White Plains, NY 10601
914-682-2637

Croton Point Park

Along the east bank of the Hudson, on a promontory jutting out into the river, lies Croton Point Park, one of the most beautiful parks in Westchester County. Unfortunately, you must pass the Croton dump in order to get there, but don't let that discourage you from visiting.

Although primarily a recreation area, often crowded on summer weekends, the park is fringed with marsh at its southernmost point. From an overlook above the marsh, you have an excellent view along the Hudson River to the south, overlooking cattails and marsh grass.

Croton Park once had a reputation as the best lookout in the region for bald eagles during the winter, and occasionally today one is spotted. You may also see red-necked grebes, "white-winged" gulls, hawks, and rafts of waterfowl. Owls are attracted to a pine grove on the southern slope of the point. This is also a fine place to observe birds during migration seasons.

Swimming

A good-sized beach with lifeguard is located near the entrance; it's open 10:00 to 8:00, mid-June through Labor Day. Very nominal fee for swimming and bathhouse.

Fishing

Bank fishing is popular here, with catches of white perch, striped bass, eels, shad, blues, snappers, and even an occasional sturgeon being hooked.

How to Get There: Located northwest of Ossining. From Ossining, go north on NY 9D to Croton Ave. and turn left; continue to park.

Open daily, year-round, 8:00 A.M.–8:00 P.M. Nominal parking fee charged in summer.

For Additional Information:
County Naturalist
Westchester County Dept. of Parks, Recreation & Conservation
148 Martine Ave.
White Plains, NY 10601
914-682-2637 (County Office)
914-271-3293 (Croton Point Park)

Fahnestock Memorial State Park

Covering more than 6,000 acres adjacent to the Taconic State Parkway in Putnam County, Fahnestock State Park is devoted primarily to passive recreation in a hilly woodland setting. In the southwest portion of the park, Canopus Creek flows through a rugged ravine. Much of the rolling terrain in the rest of the park is covered with a few old hemlock groves and second-growth hardwood forests. Although many portions of the park are not particularly rugged, they nevertheless are difficult to penetrate because of swampy areas and dense undergrowth of laurel.

Beaver activity is often evident in many of the swamps, and numerous deer inhabit the forests. In addition to several types of songbirds, hawks may often be seen riding the updrafts at the face of Candlewood Hill, and partridges are found here in abundance.

This is a popular year-round park, but even when it's most crowded, you can always find a quiet corner.

Hiking and Horseback Riding

There are three main trails in the park, including a stretch of the Appalachian Trail (described elsewhere). Lengths vary from 5 to 7 miles. Some bridle paths have been established; no rentals.

Camping

More than eighty tent and trailer campsites are available near Pelton Pond, but there are no hookups. Trailers up to 30 feet; campground open all year.

Swimming

Although not permitted in this park, there are excellent swimming facilities at two nearby state parks that are primarily recreation areas. Mohansic State Park is 15 miles to the south, and James Baird State Park is 15 miles to the north, both via Taconic State Parkway. Fahnestock campers may present their permits at the gate of either park and gain free entrance.

Fishing and Boating

The lakes and ponds of Fahnestock are well known throughout the area for the productive fishing they offer. Stillwater Lake is managed for trout and Canopus Lake for bass. In addition, there are four small ponds open to anglers. Ice fishing is permitted.

Boats may be rented here and launched on park ramps.

Winter Sports

Fahnestock Park is much colder than many neighboring districts, and the snow often remains deep until the end of March.

Ice skating, snowshoeing, cross-country skiing, and sledding are popular.

How to Get There: Park extends in all directions from intersection of Taconic State Pkwy. and NY 301 in northern Putnam Co., although the major portion of it lies west of Taconic State Pkwy. To reach Canopus Lake parking area, go west on NY 301 from intersection.

Open daily, year-round, during daylight hours. Nominal parking fee from Memorial Day weekend through Labor Day.

For Additional Information:

Superintendent
Clarence Fahnestock Memorial
State Park
RD 2
Carmel, NY 10512
914-225-7207

Superintendent
Taconic State Park Commission
Staatsburg, NY 12580
914-889-4100

Fels Sanctuary

See listing under Bedford Audubon Society Sanctuaries, page 231.

Franklin Sanctuary

See listing under Bedford Audubon Society Sanctuaries, page 231.

Gedney Brook Sanctuary

This Audubon sanctuary of 50-plus acres near Mt. Kisco may be explored via several trails. Visitors will find varied habitats here, including woodlands, an old orchard, a pond, and a swamp. The orchard is a brushy area that attracts catbirds, towhees, and thrashers.

Locust, birch, and beech trees grow on a hillside topped with grapevines and honeysuckle. Some very old stumps, covered with moss and lichen, are the remains of American chestnut.

In another area, stands of large oaks, many of them chestnut oaks with their heavily ridged bark, are dominant. Erosion of nearby rock outcroppings has resulted in some intriguing formations.

Dead trees remain where they fall so that woodpeckers, raccoons, and squirrels may den in them. On the floor of the moist valley, lush growths of ferns and many wildflowers adorn the landscape. A labeled collection in the parking area helps you identify ferns. Other vegetation includes lowbush blueberry, wild roses, azaleas, viburnum, and dogwood trees.

Numerous species of resident and migratory birds share the sanctuary with opossum, skunk, fox, frog, toad and turtle.

Hiking

A color-coded trail system, totaling about 1½ miles, leads up steep hills and into a moist valley. Top elevation is 500 feet. The pond may be reached by a boardwalk through the swamp (trails on the other side of the pond are on private land, so please respect owner's privacy and stay on clearly marked Audubon trail). *Caution:* Do not attempt to walk on the dike at the pond; it is dangerous. A map of the area is posted on a billboard at the parking area.

How to Get There: From Mt. Kisco, go west on NY 133 (Main St.) approximately 3½ miles, past Choate Sanctuary (described elsewhere) and past Seven Bridges Rd. intersection, to Woodmill Rd. Turn left on Woodmill. Sanctuary is off stub road at right, near end of Woodmill.

Open daily, year-round, during daylight hours. Free. Groups larger than families are requested to call ahead to avoid conflicts with other groups. Guided tours may be arranged.

For Additional Information:
Naturalist & Sanctuary Coordinator
Saw Mill River Audubon Society, Inc.
2660 Quaker Church Rd.
Yorktown Heights, NY 10598
914-962-9330

Greenburgh Nature Center

The Greenburgh Nature Center in Scarsdale contains 33 acres of near-climax woodland, a pond, an apple orchard, and some 5 acres of lawns and cultivated gardens. Centered around a twenty-one room manor house, the property contains a live animal museum, a clinic for injured and orphaned wildlife, a solar energy resource center, and a nature arts exhibit room. Staffed by professionals, the center is one of the finest small facilities in Westchester County. Within the 25-acre woodland is the pond, a brook, outcrops of Fordham gneiss rock, and several scattered glacial boulders. More than 30 species of trees are found here, along with 12 species of ferns and more than 40 species of native flowering plants. A small area in the forest is richly carpeted with club moss. More than 100 species of birds and numerous reptiles and amphibians make up part of the wildlife population.

Nature Trails

The center has some excellent short nature trails. Trail maps for those who wish to take self-guided walks are available for a very nominal fee.

How to Get There: From Exit 11 on Bronx River Pkwy., go west on Ardsley Rd. to NY 100 (Central Park Ave.) and turn right. Head to Dromore Rd. and turn right again. Nature center is at end of road.

Grounds open daily, year-round, during daylight hours. Manor house open 10:00 A.M.–5:00 P.M. daily, year-round, except Friday. No set fee, but contributions are recommended. Closed some holidays.

For Additional Information:
Greenburgh Nature Center
Dromore Road
Scarsdale, NY 10583
914-723-3470

Hammond Oriental Stroll Gardens

The Hammond Gardens adorn the grounds of a peaceful 20-acre estate in Westchester County. Situated atop a lofty hill, the land affords a 360-degree view of the surrounding country-side.

Inspired by a seventeenth-century Japanese form, the garden area is made up of fourteen small, interconnected gardens, each one different. You will pass alongside a reflecting pool, an enclosure designed for Zen meditation, and several water-falls, as well as collections of unusual trees and flowers.

The museum, which houses a fine collection of Oriental art, may also be toured.

How to Get There: Located in northeast Westchester County. From I-684 just east of Somers, take NY 116 east to NY 124. Turn left and continue for about one-quarter mile to Deveau Rd. Turn right and follow signs; gardens are on Deveau Rd.

Gardens open mid-May to late October, 11:00 A.M.–5:00 P.M., Wednesday through Sunday. Not recommended for children under 10. Museum open mid-May to mid-December, 11:00 A.M.–5:00 P.M., Wednesday through Sunday. Separate nominal admission charge for each.

For Additional Information:
Hammond Museum, Inc.
Deveau Road
North Salem, NY 10560
914-669-5135

Harriman State Park

See listing under Palisades Interstate Park, page 16.

Harvard Black Rock Forest

See listing under Black Rock Forest, page 232.

High Tor State Park

See listing under Palisades Interstate Park, page 17.

Hommocks Conservation Area

See listing under Larchmont Reservoir Conservation Area, page 249.

Hook Mountain State Park

See listing under Palisades Interstate Park, page 17.

Hudson Highlands State Park

In the northwest corner of Putnam County, reaching northward into Dutchess County, lies one of the most beautiful state parks in the New York City region. A wilderness area of approximately 3,700 acres, it runs eastward from the Hudson River into a rugged, mountainous terrain. The granites and gneisses of the hills, of interest geologically, include limestones, slates, and quartzites. A striking feature of the topography is the bold escarpment that rises abruptly from sea level along the Hudson to an altitude of 1,600 feet in places. Undeveloped except for a few trails, the park offers incomparable views of the Hudson River Gorge, which extends approximately from Bear Mountain Bridge north to Cornwall-on-Hudson. Within the forested areas are large groves of mature hemlocks.

Formally established in 1970, the park is administered by the Taconic State Park Commission.

Hiking

This is and will remain in the foreseeable future primarily a hiker's park. There are several blazed trails, ranging from 2 to 8 miles in length, and more are being planned for areas now inaccessible. Additional trail information may be obtained at nearby Fahnestock State Park (described elsewhere).

Winter Sports

If you like your wilderness blanketed with snow, this is an excellent cross-country skiing area.

How to Get There: Located in northwest Putnam County and southwest Dutchess County. This tract of parkland abuts both sides of NY 9D between Cold Spring and Beacon. Boaters may come to shore along the Hudson River, which forms this tract's western boundary. A second tract may be reached by traveling south on NY 9D from Cold Spring to NY 403. This part of the park extends southeast from intersection of NY 9D and NY 403.

Open daily, year-round, during daylight hours. Free.

For Additional Information:

Superintendent
Taconic State Park Commission
Staatsburg, NY 12580
914-889-4100

Superintendent
Clarence Fahnestock Memorial
State Park
RD 2
Carmel, NY 10512
914-225-7207

Hudson River Museum

This handsome, sophisticated museum offers changing exhibits depicting the history of the Hudson River. The Andrus Space Transit Planetarium is a special attraction. One of only eleven computer-driven planetariums in the entire world, Andrus can simulate actual spaceflight. Special effects let the audience experience the pitch of a spacecraft and see the stars as they might appear from the surface of any planet.

From the museum, a three-level award-winning building set into a hillside overlooking the Hudson River, visitors enjoy superb views of the Palisades along the New Jersey shoreline.

A thirty-five room Victorian mansion called Glenview, built in 1875, adjoins the museum and may be toured. It and the museum occupy a tract of land known as Trevor Park. When Glenview was originally landscaped, new trees were placed artfully among those already growing there to create a parklike effect. Along a half-mile nature trail that winds through the woods grow weeping cherry, river birch, larch, and several varieties of maple. Printed trail guides are available at the museum sales desk. The steep hillside sloping down to the Hudson is dotted with copper beech and red oak trees. An open sculpture court links the modern concrete museum building to the Glenview mansion.

How to Get There: From Exit 5 on Saw Mill River Pkwy., go west on Yonkers Ave. to Nepperhan Ave. Turn right and head to Ashburton Ave. Then turn left and continue to Warburton Ave.; turn right to museum in Trevor Park, located on left side of road.

Park open daily, year-round, during daylight hours. Museum open year-round, 10:00 A.M.–5:00 P.M., Wednesday through Saturday; 1:00–5:00 P.M., Sunday and some holidays. Free. Nominal charge for planetarium shows; special rates for children under 12. Museum hours occasionally vary, so it's best to check before going there. Also check schedule for planetarium shows.

For Additional Information:

Hudson River Museum
511 Warburton Ave.
Yonkers, NY 10701
914-963-4550

Hudson Valley KOA

Only a handful of campgrounds in the metropolitan area provide first-class accommodations and yet preserve the natural qualities of the land. One that deserves mention is the Hudson Valley KOA at Newburgh. Although slightly beyond our 50-mile radius, it is worth including, as it provides excellent facilities for nature-loving campers. The campground is a fine destination point for area residents who want a quiet spot in which to spend a weekend or vacation.

Outstanding bird-watching and wildlife observations are possible on these 65 densely wooded acres. A pond near the entrance road is a home for turtles and frogs and a watering hole for other types of wildlife, including white-tailed deer. Skunk, opossum, fox, squirrel, raccoon, and woodchuck live in the area and sometimes come into the campground or close by.

The campground has more than 100 wooded sites, many with full hookups; some are quite secluded.

Nature Trail

A half-mile-long nature trail leads through a primeval woodland; the only reminder of man's intrusion is an ancient stone fence dating back to a time before the turn of this century when the area was farmed.

Swimming

Two large swimming pools supervised by a lifeguard are available for KOA guests, and there are free swimming instructions on weekday mornings in the summer.

How to Get There: From Exit 17 on I-87 near Newburgh, pick up Union Ave. north. Union Ave. becomes Union Ave. Extension, then NY 32. Stay on NY 32 to Freetown Hwy. and turn right to KOA. Follow signs along way.

Open April through October. Reservations suggested. Private fee campground.

For Additional Information:
Hudson Valley KOA
P.O. Box B134
Plattekill, NY 12568
914-564-2836

Lakeside Outdoor Education Center

Forests, streams, ponds, meadows, swamps, cultivated fields, an orchard, and a tree farm make up the 150-acre setting of this outdoor learning facility near Spring Valley. Part of the land is preserved as a plant and wildlife sanctuary and may be explored via a system of nature trails.

Occupying another part of the grounds is a working farm that offers year-round demonstrations of organic agricultural techniques. The center is working to make this demonstration farm energy self-sufficient by the use of such devices as windmills, water mills, solar collectors, and alcohol fuels.

Such skills as orienteering, tapping maple trees, caring for farm animals, and creating natural dyes are taught through a variety of programs and workshops. An interpretive building houses a reference library, small museum, and menagerie.

In season, Lakeside Center sells Christmas trees. Visitors may cut or dig their own evergreens at the center's tree plantation.

The Edwin Gould Foundation also owns and administers two other facilities just north of Brewster, the Hillside Outdoor Education and Green Chimneys Farm centers. Although slightly beyond the 50-mile radius prescribed for this book, they offer a variety of programs and workshops similar to those at Lakeside. More information may be obtained from the Lakeside staff.

How to Get There: Located in south central Rockland County. From Spring Valley, go south on NY 45 about 2 miles to entrance to Lakeside property on right side of road.

Open 9:00 A.M.–5:00 P.M., Monday through Friday, year-round; open Saturday by previous appointment. Both guided and self-guided tours available. Grounds free; fees charged for special programs and workshops. Excellent full-time staff.

For Additional Information:

Director
Lakeside Outdoor Education Center
South Main St.
Spring Valley, NY 10977
914-356-7032
212-562-7729 (extension 244)

Larchmont Reservoir Conservation Area

Between the Towns of Mamaroneck and New Rochelle is an excellent bird-watching area, the 13-acre Larchmont Reservoir Conservation Area. Heavily wooded with Norway spruce, flowering dogwoods, white ash, sassafras, American elm, sugar maple, oak, beech, and black cherry, it also contains lower wetland areas where marsh grasses, skunk cabbage, and swamp oak grow. Sycamores border the stream. Occasional rock outcroppings dot the gently rolling terrain.

The diversity of habitat attracts a wide variety of birds. And because it is very close to Long Island Sound, you may see great numbers of Canada geese and rafts of ducks during fall months.

The Town of Mamaroneck has two more conservation areas deserving mention: Hommocks, a 5-acre mix of meadows, woodland, and marsh; and Sheldrake River Trails, covering 24 densely wooded acres.

All three tracts of land have been handsomely preserved and are well worth a visit. For a very nominal fee, you can purchase guides to the trail system of each. The trails are short (one-fifth-mile to one-mile long) and easy to walk.

How to Get There: From Exit 10S on I-95, take Fenimore Rd. northwest to Cornell St. and turn left. Continue to Weaver St., then turn left again. At Lakewood Ln. turn right to conservation area along shores of Larchmont Reservoir (Sheldrake Lake).

Open daily, during daylight hours, year-round. Free.

For Additional Information:
Conservation Advisory Committee
Town of Mamaroneck
740 W. Boston Post Rd.
Mamaroneck, NY 10543
914-698-4929

Lyndhurst

In a magnificent wooded setting on a hilltop along the banks of the Hudson River, Lyndhurst brings to life a gilded age from the past. Focal point of the estate, located just south of Tarrytown, is a richly furnished Gothic Revival castle once owned by railroad magnate Jay Gould. Built in 1838, it's owned by the National Trust for Historic Preservation and may be toured.

Many of the trees that grace the 67 acres of lawns were planted during the last century and have grown into magnificent specimens. The cut-leaf Japanese maples are among the largest in the United States, and there's a particularly handsome ginkgo. Among the other old trees found here are copper beech, weeping beech, star magnolia, larch, linden, and horse chestnut.

Roses still bloom at Lyndhurst in an old-fashioned garden surrounding a gazebo, and most of the 500 or so plants are labeled.

Each summer, from early July through mid-August, outdoor musical concerts are held on a great sweep of lawn behind the castle that reaches down toward the river. Scheduled once a week on Saturday evenings, the offerings range from Beethoven to bluegrass. From the lawn, your view extends across the widest, most majestic part of the Hudson. When the sun sets behind the wooded hills on the opposite shore, the lights on the Tappan Zee Bridge just to the north brighten up the night.

How to Get There: From Exit 9 on I-87 (NY Thruway), go south on

US 9 for about a quarter mile to Lyndhurst on right side of road.

Open daily, year-round, except December 25 and January 1; 10:00 A.M.–5:00 P.M., May through October; 10:00 A.M.–4:00 P.M., November through April. Admission fee; special rates for students and senior citizens; children under 6 free.

For Additional Information:

Administrator	The National Trust for Historic
Lyndhurst	Preservation
635 S. Broadway	740-748 Jackson Place, N.W.
Tarrytown, NY 10591	Washington, DC 20006
914-631-0313	*202-638-5200*

Manitoga Preserve

Eight-acre Manitoga Preserve serves as both a natural sanctuary and a center for the arts. The land was acquired by the late industrial designer Russel Wright in 1941. He immediately began covering the scars left by an extensive quarrying business that was once carried on here and, over the next thirty-four years, transformed the property into an exceedingly beautiful area. In 1975, he donated Manitoga to The Nature Conservancy, and it was first opened to the public in 1976.

Dragon Rock, the house Wright built, is cut into the side of an old quarry and surrounded by fern glens. From nearby comes the lyrical sound of a waterfall. Although the house is not open, it can be glimpsed from one of the trails.

Dense stands of hemlock, laurel thickets, upland deciduous forests, and fern glens partially constitute the plant life of this remarkable place. Openings in the forest afford occasional views of the Hudson River to the west. Deer wander through the woods, as do porcupine, raccoon, rabbit, squirrel, and many other small creatures.

During the summer, special events such as concerts and dance performances are held.

Nature Trails

Naturalist-led walks are offered frequently. In addition, there's a self-guided trail that may be used by visitors; a trail guide may be obtained at the building near the parking lot. The trail system totals about 4 miles and is extremely scenic. There is a nominal charge for using trails.

Winter Sports

The trail system is opened to cross-country skiers and snowshoers when weather conditions are right.

How to Get There: Located in southwest Putnam County. Preserve lies on east side of NY 9D about 2½ miles north of Bear Mountain Bridge and about 2 miles south of Garrison.

Open to the public 10:30 A.M.–5:00 P.M., on weekends only, April 15 through November, and during the week for groups by appointment. Nominal fee for use of the trails.

For Additional Information:

Executive Director
Lower Hudson Chapter
The Nature Conservancy
RFD 2, Chestnut Ridge Rd.
Mount Kisco, NY 10549
914-666-5365

Marshlands Conservancy

Woodland, salt marsh, meadow, and seashore all are part of the Marshlands Conservancy in Rye. It is one of the most complete wildlife sanctuaries and nature education centers in the greater New York area.

The 120-acre park includes overlooks and a visitor's center that houses exhibits pertaining to the natural history of the area. More than 250 species of birds have been sighted, and there's an abundance of wildlife, including raccoon, opossum, skunk, and such great wading birds as the snowy egret. Other birds sighted include Canada geese, American bittern, Virginia rail, least tern, various swallows, warblers, and sparrows. Rafts of ducks sometimes stop here during the autumn migration.

A seashore trail leads to Melton Harbor, where you may study marine life and exposed bedrock. In the fields of Marshlands grows the orange butterfly weed, endangered in this area.

Nature Trails

Excellent short hiking trails lead through Marshlands, and there's a special trail for the blind. Guided tours are offered by appointment.

How to Get There: From Exit 11 on I-95, take Playland Pkwy. southeast ½ mile to US 1 (Boston Post Rd.) and turn right. Continue about 1½ miles to Marshlands on left side of road.

Grounds open daily, year-round, during daylight hours. Center open 9:00 A.M.–5:00 P.M., Wednesday through Sunday, year-round. Free.

For Additional Information:

Curator
Marshlands Conservancy
U.S. 1, Boston Post Rd.
Rye, NY 10580
914-835-4466

County Naturalist
Westchester County Dept. of
Parks, Recreation &
Conservation
148 Martine Ave.
White Plains, NY 10601
914-682-2637

Meyer Nature Preserve

Ephemeral woodland pools and a steep hemlock ravine distinguish this Nature Conservancy preserve in Westchester County. Heavily wooded with a mixed hardwood forest, the sanctuary also includes an extensive swamp and large areas of high, open meadows where white-tailed deer may sometimes be seen grazing in early mornings and late afternoons during warm weather months. Rock outcrops of banded and granite gneiss may be seen, along with such other minerals as quartz, muscovite, garnet, feldspar, and tourmaline.

The atmosphere here is one of wild and rugged beauty, with few reminders of man's influence upon the land, and you can always find an uncrowded corner within its 246 acres.

Hiking

Approximately 6½ miles of color-coded trails lace the sanctuary, including a self-guided geology trail. The Cliff Trail overlooks Byram Lake, offering the hiker scenic views to the east of the preserve. Interconnecting trails lead to The Nature Conservancy's Butler Sanctuary nearby (described elsewhere). Guided nature hikes are conducted periodically by the resident naturalist at Butler Sanctuary.

How to Get There: Located southeast of Mt. Kisco. From I-684, go west on NY 172 to Sarles St. (fourth left) and turn left. At Oregon Rd., turn left again and look for preserve entrance on left side of road.

Open daily, year-round, during daylight hours. Free.

For Additional Information:
Executive Director
Lower Hudson Chapter
The Nature Conservancy
RFD 2, Chestnut Ridge Rd.
Mount Kisco, NY 10549
914-666-5365

Mianus River Gorge

Little more than a whisper from Manhattan is the Mianus River Gorge, an exquisite place where one can forget that a world other than this exists. The hiker here enters a forest primeval, accompanied only by birdsong and the lyrical sound of white water tumbling through a spectacular hemlock gorge. Along the way, the ancient trees are reflected in intermittent tranquil pools.

Located in Westchester County near the Connecticut border, this was the first preserve created by that remarkable organization, The Nature Conservancy, which has since been responsible for purchasing and setting aside lands of outstanding natural qualities coast to coast. This 389-acre site was established in 1953, and you need to walk only a few paces on the well-marked trail leading along the river to realize the reason this area is being preserved.

Rock outcroppings of Bedford gneiss, mica, and white and pink quartz form the geological backdrop.

The climax forest of eastern hemlock, including some trees that are well over 300 years old, was produced in part by the cool, moist microclimate of the gorge. Beech, yellow birch, and oaks form other component parts of the woodland.

While its steep terrain protected the gorge itself from being timbered, other parts of the land were cleared during the early part of this century by man or by natural fire and display good examples of various stages of succession—the act of nature reclaiming itself. More than 800 species of trees, shrubs and vines, wildflowers, lichens, and ferns are found here. The primitive terrain attracts many wild creatures.

In 1964, the unique natural qualities of the gorge were recognized when it was designated a National Natural Landmark by the U.S. Department of the Interior. A book, *Flora and Fauna of the Mianus River Gorge Wildlife Refuge and Botanical Preserve,* may be purchased from the preserve's warden/naturalist or through the Mianus River Gorge Conservation Committee.

Hiking

You must hike to see this area, and the trails are occasionally rugged. A half-day hike will allow you to see the most scenic parts, but to do the preserve justice, you should plan a full day. The trails are well marked, and many of the plants are labeled. Hikers should register at the trail shelter beside the parking lot. The Brink of the Gorge Trail leads to the southern end of the preserve, and the Fringe of the Forest Trail returns along a different route, completing a 5-mile loop. Two other trail intersections allow shorter loops to be made. A short Bank of the River Trail offers the best view of the Mianus River, which is small here (it widens as it moves downstream to flow eventually into Long Island Sound).

How to Get There: Located southeast of Bedford Village and east of Mt. Kisco. From I-684 near Mt. Kisco, go east on NY 172 (Bedford Rd.) to US 22. Turn left and head to Bedford Village; bear right at the triangular green here onto Pound Ridge Rd., and proceed one mile to Stamford Rd. Turn right and continue for seven-tenths mile to Miller's Mill Rd.; turn right again and go one-tenth mile over bridge. At Mianus River Rd. turn left. Entrance sign and small parking lot are six-tenths mile down road on left.

Open daily, 9:30 A.M.–5:30 P.M., from about April through November (this may vary somewhat according to weather conditions). War-

A trail of solitude at Mianus River Gorge   *Bill Thomas*

den/naturalists are on duty on weekends and holidays during open season. Guided tours for groups should be arranged at least two weeks in advance. Free, but contributions are gratefully accepted.

For Additional Information:

The Mianus River Gorge
Conservation Committee
Office at Bartlett Arboretum
151 Brookdale Rd.
Stamford, CT 06903
203-322-9148

Executive Director
Lower Hudson Chapter
The Nature Conservancy
RFD 2, Chestnut Ridge Rd.
Mount Kisco, NY 10549
914-666-5365

Mineral Spring Falls

A spectacular 100-foot waterfall, created by the cascading waters of Mineral Spring Brook, makes this Nature Conservancy preserve in Orange County one of the most scenic in the greater New York area. The preserve is also a haven for rare and endangered plants, including nineteen plant species on the New York State list of protected native plants. From atop Fifth of July Rock, visitors enjoy a scenic view of Schenemuck Mountain and Woodbury Valley.

Although the preserve includes little more than 119 acres, it is part of a vast complex of protected lands. Bordering it on the east is the 3,600-acre Black Rock Forest (described elsewhere), maintained by Harvard University for scientific and educational purposes. To the south and east of the preserve are restricted woodlands belonging to West Point Military Academy.

Hiking

The main trail, marked with white blazes, is a portion of the New York–New Jersey Conference Scenic Trail. It enters the preserve via an old wagon road, leads to the base of the falls, and then runs north out of the sanctuary. An orange-blazed trail leads from the main trail to above the falls and follows old logging roads to the border of the West Point Military Academy lands. Another side trail leads to Fifth of July Rock.

Winter Sports

All trails are open for cross-country skiing and snowshoeing when snow depth is sufficient (about 6 inches).

How to Get There: Located in Orange County. From Angola Rd. Exit on US 9W just south of Cornwall, go west on Angola Rd. When road forks, head left on Mineral Spring Rd. and look for preserve on left side of road. Entrance is via a dirt road. No parking on dirt road, but you can legally park on shoulder of Mineral Spring Rd. in a 50-foot stretch south of the dirt road.

Open daily, dawn to dusk, year-round. Free.

For Additional Information:
Executive Director
Lower Hudson Chapter
The Nature Conservancy
RFD 2, Chestnut Ridge Rd.
Mount Kisco, NY 10549
914-666-5365

Mount Ivy County Park

Most of Mount Ivy, an undeveloped Rockland County park, is natural marsh. It's an excellent place to study a freshwater marsh habitat, as well as the wildlife and plant life associated with it. The marsh, accessible by means of a few short footpaths, is home to muskrat, raccoon, and such birds as the rail, egret, and various herons.

This is also an excellent, little-known place just to get away from it all. You'll find 203 acres to roam.

How to Get There: Located in central Rockland County. From Spring Valley, go north about 4½ miles on NY 45 to Pomona Rd. Turn left and head to Fireman's Memorial Dr. Turn right and continue to park, where road ends. Parking available on unpaved area.

Open daily, during daylight hours, year-round. Free.

For Additional Information:

Rockland County Park
Commission
380 Phillips Hill Rd.
New City, NY 10956
914-425-5100

Rockland County Planning Board
18 New Hempstead Rd.
New City, NY 10956
914-425-5480

Museum of the Hudson Highlands

Perched on the side of a mountain, surrounded by some 70 acres of woodland, this museum preserves and records the natural history of the Highlands that border both sides of the Hudson River for approximately 10 miles. It is located near Cornwall-on-Hudson just north of Storm King Mountain, which along with Breakneck Ridge on the east side of the river forms the northern gateway of the lovely Highlands region. From this point to the southern boundary of the Highlands near Bear Mountain Bridge, the Hudson River is a winding, narrow stream flanked on either side by hills of 1,000 feet or more. Within this gorge, near Constitution Island opposite West Point, the river reaches its greatest depth—202 feet.

The museum focuses on the indigenous plant and animal life, as well as the geologic and human history, of this region. Exhibits are developed and maintained by junior and senior high school students, who also collect and care for the live animals and plants and serve as guides. Displays are housed in a small building that has won architectural awards.

Visitors may explore the wooded grounds via several short nature trails.

How to Get There: Located south of Newburgh in Orange County. From Cornwall-on-Hudson, go south on NY 218, past Cornwall Inn to Mountain Rd. Turn right. At The Boulevard turn right again to the museum. Follow signs.

Open year-round; 11:00 A.M.–5:00 P.M., Monday through Thursday and Saturday; 2:00–5:00 P.M., Sunday, June 21 through September 21. Open 2:00–5:00 P.M., Monday through Thursday and Sunday; 11:00 A.M.–5:00 P.M., Saturday, rest of year. Closed Friday, January 1, July 4, Thanksgiving, December 25. Free.

For Additional Information:

Curator
Museum of the Hudson Highlands
The Boulevard
Cornwall-on-Hudson, NY 12520
914-534-7781

The Nature Conservancy, Lower Hudson Chapter

The Nature Conservancy, one of the finest national conservation organizations in the country, is very active in the lower Hudson Valley. The local chapter maintains nearly thirty preserves in Orange, Putnam, Rockland, and Westchester Counties; and they include some of the most beautiful and secluded natural areas in the region. In addition, new preserves are being added all the time, and old preserves are being enlarged.

Several of these preserves (Butler Memorial Sanctuary, Manitoga Preserve, Meyer Nature Preserve, Mianus River Gorge, and Mineral Spring Falls) are described separately elsewhere, but space does not permit us to describe all of them. Each preserve, however, is significant ecologically, and each is open year-round free of charge for such passive recreational use as nature study, hiking, photography, and, where the terrain is suitable, cross-country skiing.

In the 81-acre Nichols Preserve near Armonk, you can see a healthy, 40-foot American chestnut tree (a species extremely rare in this country since the great chestnut blight earlier this century). Serious hikers will enjoy exploring the Indian Brook Assemblage near Katonah, a 144-acre composite of three preserves where scenic trails wander through a rugged terrain of meadows, swamps, and woods. The 10-acre Schwartz Preserve near South Salem, with its swamp and maze of waterways, is reminiscent of a southern lagoon. All of these preserves are located in Westchester County.

At this writing, the Lower Hudson Chapter is preparing a guidebook that includes descriptions of each of their properties and directions for getting there. The chapter will also be happy to provide information about any individual preserve of interest to you.

For Additional Information:
Executive Director
Lower Hudson Chapter
The Nature Conservancy
RFD 2, Chestnut Ridge Rd.
Mount Kisco, NY 10549
914-666-5365

Palmer Lewis Sanctuary

See listing under Bedford Audubon Society Sanctuaries, page 231.

Philipsburg Manor

See listing under Sleepy Hollow Restorations, page 261.

Ramsey Hunt Wildlife Sanctuary

See listing under Bedford Audubon Society Sanctuaries, page 231.

Rockland Lake State Park

See listing under Palisades Interstate Park, page 17.

Rye Playland

Though perhaps better known for its famous amusement park, this Westchester County facility also has much to offer nature lovers, particularly bird-watchers.

Manursing Island in the northernmost part of the park is set aside as a bird sanctuary. On the east, Manursing Island is bordered by Long Island Sound; on its west, by man-made 80-acre Playland Lake. The island and lake provide a combination of marsh, meadows, woods, tidal flats, and bays that teems with bird life.

In the spring and fall, the woodlands north and south of the lake host such migrating land birds as flycatchers, thrushes, and warblers. In early winter, the ducks arrive at the lake; on one October morning in recent years, 12,000 greater scaup were counted. Other ducks come here, too—black ducks, canvasbacks, three species of mergansers, and more. Flocks of Canada geese stop to rest. In the winter, great blue herons are found along the shores of the seven small islands in the lake. Breeding birds include the belted kingfisher, Traill's flycatcher, Carolina wren, and the white-eyed vireo. Red-tailed and marsh hawks winter here; and in the spring, osprey arrive.

Rye Town Park, a 25-acre woodland sanctuary that adjoins Playland Park on the south, has more birds; a biologist is in residence.

During the summer, when the bird population is lowest, the woods of Manursing Island still offer a cool retreat, and the beaches provide views of Long Island Sound and seabirds.

Swimming

Swimmers may choose between a quarter-mile-long beach along Long Island Sound or an Olympic-size pool. Bathing suit rentals available at bathhouse. The beach is usually quite crowded on weekends.

Fishing and Boating

Throughout the year, anglers may rent rowboats with or without motors for Long Island Sound fishing; or, from May to October, they may pay a nominal fee and do their casting from Playland Pier. A limited number of rods and reels are available for rent, and live bait is sold in the park. During summer months, visitors may rent rowboats and pedal boats to explore Playland Lake and its seven islands.

How to Get There: From Exit 11 on I-95, take Playland Pkwy. southeast to Playland entrance. To drive to Manursing Island, turn left on Forest Ave., near Playland entrance, to Manursing Way, and turn right. When Manursing Way ends near beach, turn right on Van Rensselaer Rd. to park (park does not occupy entire island).

Some areas are seasonal, but nature areas are open daily, year-round. Hours vary from month to month; best to call or check local paper for current hours before going. Nominal parking fee; higher on weekends and holidays.

For Additional Information:

County Naturalist
Westchester County Department of Parks,
Recreation & Conservation
148 Martine Ave.
White Plains, NY 10601
914-682-2637

Saw Mill River Audubon Sanctuaries

One of the most active Audubon societies in the Hudson River Valley, the Saw Mill River chapter manages nine sanctuaries in Westchester County. Some of the largest—Brinton Brook, Choate, and Gedney Brook—are described elsewhere.

Two others, both of which adjoin other public lands to form mini-greenbelts, are well worth a visit. Graff Sanctuary near Croton-on-Hudson adjoins a county park along the Hudson River and contains 33 acres of dense, primitive woodland including an exceptional stand of tulip trees. Pinecliff Sanctuary in Chappaqua has a pond with large populations of frogs, toads, salamanders, wood ducks, and little green herons; Audubon owns only 7 acres here, but the sanctuary adjoins two larger tracts of parkland owned by the Town of New Castle and the East Hudson Parkway Authority respectively.

How to Get There: A map showing the location of all sanctuaries owned or maintained by the Saw Mill River Audubon Society, along with directions for reaching each one, will be sent upon request.

All sanctuaries are free and are open daily, year-round, during daylight hours. Groups larger than families are requested to phone ahead to avoid conflicts with other groups. Guided tours can be arranged.

For Additional Information:
Naturalist & Sanctuary Coordinator
Saw Mill River Audubon Society, Inc.
2660 Quaker Church Rd.
Yorktown Heights, NY 10598
914-962-9330

Sheldrake River Trails Conservation Area

See listing under Larchmont Reservoir Conservation Area, page 249.

Sleepy Hollow Restorations

North of Manhattan, along the eastern bank of the Hudson River, are the Sleepy Hollow Restorations. There are three of them, and all possess lovely, tranquil atmospheres.

Sunnyside, Washington Irving's nineteenth-century home, lies closest to New York City. It's located in Tarrytown, about a mile south of the Tappan Zee Bridge. Irving's story "The Legend of Sleepy Hollow" inspired the name for this trilogy of restorations. One of the most picturesque homes in America, it's surrounded by gardens, orchards, and wooded paths planned by Irving himself. Swans glide gracefully across the pond Irving called "Little Mediterranean," and magnificent old trees—blue spruces, crabapples, dogwoods, poplars, sycamores, huge plane trees—are scattered about the 24-acre grounds.

Two miles north, in North Tarrytown, is Philipsburg Manor. The stone manor house and gristmill date from the early 1700s and were the headquarters of the Philipses, a Dutch family who backed the British during the American Revolution and subsequently lost their vast land holdings. The gristmill is operated daily, and early farm life is often demonstrated for visitors by men and women in period costumes. Flowers and vegetables in varieties grown 200 years ago have been planted on the 20-acre estate.

Third of the Sleepy Hollow Restorations is Van Cortlandt Manor, a few miles farther north at Croton-on-Hudson. It features a Dutch-style manor house, a restored tavern, eighteenth-century gardens, fruit orchards, and a 750-foot-long brick walk. Known as the Long Walk, it's bordered by flowers that bloom from early spring into September. Eighty percent of the manor's 175 acres are marsh and riverbed.

How to Get There: From Exit 9 on I-87 (NY Thruway), go south on US 9 to Sunnyside Ln. and turn right to Sunnyside. To reach Philipsburg Manor, return to US 9 and head north, through Tarrytown and North Tarrytown, to manor on left side of highway. To reach Van Cortlandt Manor, continue north on US 9, past Ossining, to Croton Point Ave.; turn right and go one block to Riverside Ave., turn right again and head ¼ mile to Van Cortlandt Manor.

Open daily, 10:00 A.M.–5:00 P.M., year-round, except January 1, Thanksgiving, and December 25. Nominal admission fee; special rates for senior citizens and children under 14.

For Additional Information:
Sleepy Hollow Restorations
Tarrytown, NY 10591
914-631-8200

Stony Point Reservation

See listing under Palisades Interstate Park, page 18.

Sunnyside

See listing under Sleepy Hollow Restorations, page 261.

Tallman Mountain State Park

See listing under Palisades Interstate Park, page 18.

Philipsburg Manor, one of the Sleepy Hollow Restorations
New York State Department of Commerce Photo by Donald Doremus

Teatown Lake Reservation

Established in 1963 as an outreach station of the Brooklyn Botanic Garden, Teatown Lake Reservation subsequently developed into a major 355-acre preserve including a 33-acre lake and a vast complex of hiking trails through extensive woodlands. Dominated by a deciduous forest, primarily second growth, the rolling terrain also includes evergreen woods, wetlands, and open meadows. Carpets of wildflowers decorate the grounds, particularly during spring and fall, and in midsummer a display of white water lilies may be seen near the boat house.

Most of the reservation's woodland is little changed from the days when—according to local legend—it was used as a black-market tea distribution point during Colonial times. Giant hemlock, tulip, oak, and maple trees adorn the land, providing cover for a variety of bird and animal life. All plants and wildlife, of course, are fully protected.

Hiking and Horseback Riding

Some 10 miles of trails extend throughout the reservation. Each of the seven basic trails has a distinct character all its own. The trail to Hidden Valley is decorated with blossoming mountain laurel in June, while the Marsh and Meadow Trail leads through a profusion of purple loosestrife in August. The rugged terrain of the upland trails offers the most challenging hikes during winter, while a summertime walk along the lake gives some insight into the plethora of activity engaged in by its tiny inhabitants.

One trail has been specifically designated for horseback riders; no rentals.

How to Get There: Located northeast of Ossining. From Taconic State Pkwy., go southwest on NY 134 to Spring Valley Rd. and turn right. Reservation is on right side of road.

Open year-round; 9:00 A.M.–5:00 P.M., Tuesday through Saturday, and 1:00–5:00 P.M., Sunday. Free to individuals and families; nominal fee and advance reservation required for large groups.

For Additional Information:

Teatown Lake Reservation
Spring Valley Road
Ossining, NY 10562
914-762-2912

Brooklyn Botanic Garden
1000 Washington Ave.
Brooklyn, NY 11225
212-622-4433

Trevor Park

See listing under Hudson River Museum, page 247.

Van Cortlandt Manor

See listing under Sleepy Hollow Restorations, page 261.

Ward Pound Ridge Reservation

Ward Pound Ridge Reservation, consisting of 4,500 acres of rugged, wooded hills and open meadows, was purchased in 1925 to be set aside as a sanctuary for wildlife, as well as for educational and recreational use. Today, it is still primarily a wild sanctuary, for only one-tenth of the land has been developed. Located in Westchester County, the reservation provides an ideal place of escape for those longing for a quiet retreat.

Ward Pound Ridge is virtually a world unto itself, the crown jewel of the Westchester County park system. To take advantage of all it has to offer, be sure to obtain a map at the entrance.

Of the 152 species of birds that make up the official bird list here, 52 are noted as rare. Bald eagles, herons, and vultures roost on the rock ledges and in tall trees, and the osprey is a migratory visitor. Along the stream banks, the playful river otters burrow. White-tailed deer browse here year-round, and bobcats occasionally prowl the highest ridges.

A trailside museum offers special programs at all times of the year. There are Eskimo snow games, Indian snake games, maple sugaring demonstrations, wildflower programs, haymaking parties, and studies of reptile and pond ecology. Clinics provide instructions on such nature-oriented activities as orienteering, cross-country skiing, hiking, dogsledding, and rock climbing. A one-acre wildflower garden, maintained near the museum, contains more than 100 varieties, while the 175-acre Meyer Arboretum includes plants native to Westchester County.

Hiking and Horseback Riding

A network of some 35 miles of trails provides challenging paths for hikers. The Fire Tower Trail takes you to an elevation of 938 feet, highest in the park; on a clear day, you can see the skyscrapers of Manhattan 40 miles away. If you're interested in rock formations, Spy Rock Trail is best. The River Trail is one of the most scenic. Trail maps are available at the entrance. Several marked bridle trails are also shown on the map; no rentals.

Camping

Limited camping is available only in twenty-six shelters, with each rustic stone-and-timber shelter sleeping up to eight people. No advance reservations; open all year. Shelters may be rented for overnight (4:00 P.M. to 9:00 A.M.) use, or for daylight use only. Each includes a fireplace and picnic table.

Fishing

Fishing is permitted in the Waccabuc River for largemouth bass, sunfish, and perch.

Winter Sports

Skiing is permitted both on established ski trails (2 to 6 miles long) and on open slopes. Tobogganing is also permitted on open slopes.

How to Get There: From I-684 near Katonah, go east on NY 35 to NY 121 and turn right. At Reservation Rd. turn left and head into park.

Open daily, year-round, 9:00 A.M.–sundown. Nominal parking fee. Trailside Museum open 9:00 A.M.–5:00 P.M., Wednesday through Sunday, year-round.

For Additional Information:

Superintendent
Ward Pound Ridge Reservation
Cross River, NY 10518
914-763-3493

County Naturalist
Westchester County
Department of Parks,
Recreation & Conservation
148 Martine Ave.
White Plains, NY 10601
914-682-2637

Westchester County Parks

Several Westchester County parks—Blue Mountain Reservation, Cranberry Lake Park, Croton Point Park, Marshlands Conservancy, Ward Pound Ridge Reservation—have been described elsewhere, but there are numerous other facilities within this county's park system that offer open spaces to roam and trails to hike.

Among them are Croton Gorge, Cortlandt; George's Island, Montrose; Graham Hills, Mt. Pleasant; Lasdon Bird and Nature Sanctuary, Somers; Muscoot Park, Somers; Oscawana, Cortlandt; Silver Lake, Harrison; and Wampus Pond, North Castle. All have trails the public is welcome to use for hiking and nature study.

Although all parks listed above are open to nonresidents, others are for county residents only. As a general rule, only parks in the congested southern part of the county are restricted to resident use exclusively.

Nearly all parks charge a nominal parking fee from late spring through early fall. For a list of parks and their facilities, contact the following address.

For Additional Information:
County Naturalist
Westchester County Department of Parks,
Recreation & Conservation
148 Martine Ave.
White Plains, NY 10601
914-682-2637

Westmoreland Sanctuary

A 200-year-old church, now reconstructed to serve as a museum and nature center, provides the nucleus of this natural sanctuary in Mt. Kisco. The former Presbyterian Church of Bedford Village, built in 1783, was taken down piece by piece and rebuilt in the sanctuary to save it from demolition crews. Today, it serves as an auditorium/classroom complex with exhibits around the boundary, including a live colony of honeybees and an aquarium of native fish. The eighteenth-century balcony around the four sides of the main room contains additional natural history displays.

On the grounds of this 330-acre sanctuary is a deciduous and coniferous forest, liberally sprinkled with ponds, streams, and marsh. An additional 113-acre wilderness tract along the Mianus River is open by appointment only for supervised group activities and scientific nature studies.

The hilly terrain ranges in altitude from 390 feet to 730 feet. Many birds live here, including the downy woodpecker, wood thrush, American woodcock, black-capped chickadee, and a variety of warblers, and there's also a nesting colony of wood ducks.

Two full-time naturalists are on the staff at the center. Some outstanding weekend programs are offered here on a variety of nature-oriented subjects, including the observation of the courtship dance of the male woodcock, bird-banding, maple sugaring, orienteering, and a cross-country ski clinic.

Hiking
Ten miles of easy to moderate hiking trails lace the sanctuary.

Winter Sports
Trails are open to cross-country skiers and snowshoers.

How to Get There: From I-684 near Mt. Kisco, go west on NY 172 (Bedford Rd.) to Chestnut Ridge Rd. and turn left. Sanctuary is on left side of road.

Grounds open daily, year-round, during daylight hours. Museum open 9:00 A.M.–5:00 P.M., Wednesday through Sunday, year-round. Admissions and all programs are free.

For Additional Information:

Director/Naturalist
Westmoreland Sanctuary
Chestnut Ridge Rd.
Mt. Kisco, NY 10549
914-666-8448

Index